APOSTLES TODAY

Apostles Today

*Making Sense of Contemporary Charismatic Apostolates:
A Historical and Theological Appraisal*

BENJAMIN G. MCNAIR SCOTT

PICKWICK *Publications* · Eugene, Oregon

APOSTLES TODAY
Making Sense of Contemporary Charismatic Apostolates:
A Historical and Theological Appraisal

Copyright © 2014 Benjamin G. McNair Scott. All rights reserved. Except for brief quotations in critical publications or reviews, no part of this book may be reproduced in any manner without prior written permission from the publisher. Write: Permissions, Wipf and Stock Publishers, 199 W. 8th Ave., Suite 3, Eugene, OR 97401.

Pickwick Publications
An Imprint of Wipf and Stock Publishers
199 W. 8th Ave., Suite 3
Eugene, OR 97401

www.wipfandstock.com

ISBN 13: 978-1-62564-118-2

Cataloguing-in-Publication data:

McNair Scott, Benjamin G.

Apostles today : making sense of contemporary charismatic apostolates: a historical and theological appraisal / Benjamin G. McNair Scott, with a foreword by William K. Kay.

xviii + 254 pp. ; 23 cm. Includes bibliographical references and indexes.

ISBN 13: 978-1-62564-118-2

1. Pentecostal churches. 2. Church renewal. 3. Christian leadership. I. Kay, William K., 1945–. II. Title.

BR1644.5 M151 2014

Manufactured in the U.S.A.

Contents

Foreword by William K. Kay vii
Acknowledgments ix
Introduction xi

Part One: Where We Are

1 Apostles Today: USA 3

2 Apostles Today: Britain 32

3 Popular Charismatic Teachers on Apostles 57

Part Two: How We Got Here

4 Post-biblical History of Charismatic Apostles 91

5 Shifting Perspectives: How a Minority Viewpoint Became Widespread 130

Part Three: What We Should Make of It

6 Biblical Counter-arguments and Legitimations for an Ongoing Charismatic Apostolate 147

7 Theological/Ecclesiological Critique of Popular Evangelical Conceptions of the Charismatic Apostolate 173

Part Four: Where it Might Go

Summary and Conclusion 213

Glossary 221
Bibliography 223
Index of Names 241
Index of Churches and Church Networks 249
Index of Scripture 253

Foreword

I TAKE THIS TO be an important book because it brings together ideas that, if they reach their final fruition, will alter the shape and state of the worldwide church in the twenty-first century. I cannot, of course, be sure of this, and none of us can with any certainty predict what adventures and adversities, what plateaux of calm prosperity, and what maelstroms of destruction, will reveal themselves. No one standing on a pinnacle in 1913 could have foreseen the carnage of the two world wars, the horrors of Auschwitz, the mushroom cloud of the Cold War, or the sudden global hyper-connectivity of the internet. Nor could they have predicted the rapid advance of Pentecostalism or neo-Pentecostalism or the charismatic movement (whatever nomenclature you choose) to every continent, to north and south, and even to the heartlands of Catholicism and the edges of the Islamosphere.

In around 1970, talk of the emergence of charismatic apostles began to circulate the Pentecostal/charismatic movement. There had been earlier trumpet sounds announcing that apostles were back: Edward Irving in the nineteenth century had said something similar; the Welsh Apostolic Church in 1910 had made bold claims of this kind; the Latter Rain Movement in Canada in the period after 1948 was similarly outspoken—but none of these quite managed to be heard with such clarity and over so wide a constituency as happened after the 1970s. This book is not a history of the idea of apostleship. It does not trace the spread of ideas but instead picks these ideas up and examines and classifies them and then, once it has done this, looks back to church history and sideways to contemporary scholarship to test and weigh the theology of apostleship. In doing so, it demonstrates not only that apostolic activity continued well beyond the New Testament period but also that one can now discern at least three different concepts that carry the apostolic label. These concepts are carefully distinguished and attached to the teachers who formulated and developed them (e.g., Derek Prince, Terry Virgo, Peter Wagner, and others), and then put through the fire of cessationist argument (Grudem and Stott). The cessationist case is then itself weighed and found to be flawed (Ruthven). All this is done without personal animosity or polemic, and, for my money, is convincing in its range and rigor. The final sections of the book look at apostolicity and ask how it might be applied ecumenically within the ecclesiology of all the main Christian groupings, including the various branches of Protestantism, as well as Roman Catholicism itself and Orthodoxy.

All this explains why this book is important. If the theological examination to which apostolicity has been subjected by McNair Scott is fair, and if apostolicity is indeed valid, then the twenty-first-century church is going to incorporate a reality that will eventually have an impact on its normative functioning and effectiveness. And, in saying this, one draws attention to the reasons behind the diffusion of apostolic ideas at this point in time: the church is facing intellectual and social challenges designed to accelerate the dissolution of Christendom and the legal and attitudinal presumptions that have been cherished in the West for more than a thousand years.

Prediction, as we have noted, is a tricky business. One can do so, as Philip Jenkins did in *The Next Christendom* (2003), by using current demographic data to estimate the future size of various religious populations. One can make deductions from biblically-based eschatological schemes and map these onto world events. One can construct complex computer models with multifarious types of data and, as has been done by climate scientists, make projections about average temperatures and weather patterns.[1] This book does none of these things. Rather it notes the breadth of the work of the Holy Spirit and accepts that, when charismatic gifts are restored to the church, other gifts, including those shown by apostles, will inevitably follow. Its projections are based on a confidence in the Holy Spirit and a recognition of the numerous cultural and ecclesial contexts impacted by this divine Person.

William K. Kay
University of Chester, UK
University of Glyndŵr, UK

---

1. See W. K. Kay, "The Future of Global Pentecostalism: Evaluating Prediction." Paper given at the fortieth meeting of the Society for Pentecostal Studies, 2011.

Acknowledgments

THIS BOOK BEGAN LIFE as a doctoral thesis at King's College London, therefore I would like to thank my supervisors, Professor Andrew Walker and Professor Andrew Wright: Professor Walker for his belief that this study was important and for his advice and encouragement; Professor Wright for his willingness to take up supervision in light of Andrew's illness, and casting a very insightful eye over everything and giving indispensable pointers.

I would also like to thank all those who contributed to this study through phone calls, e-mails and face-to-face interviews. I am indebted to Father Peter Hocken whose writings on the Charismatic movement provided me with a framework to see the challenge of new "stream movements" to the older churches, and the respective challenge that the older churches might have to these movements.

Thank you to Professor William Kay and Professor Allan Anderson for their helpful critiques of the original doctorate, and to William for writing the foreword. I feel privileged that such eminent scholars in this field have both encouraged me and interacted with my work.

I would also like to thank my father who has generously sponsored this study from first to last; to my mother and Dr Terry J. Wright for proofreading the original doctorate, and for his work on this manuscript; to Dr Robin Parry and the team at Pickwick for enabling this book to come into being. Finally, thanks to my wife Cecilia who not only encouraged me to pursue this but has lived with the consequence of me doing so over a number of years, despite the arrivals of three of our children!

Introduction

Book Theme

> We've become increasingly convinced that what the church needs to find its way out of the situation it's in at the beginning of the twenty-first century is not more faddish theories about how to grow the church without fundamentally reforming its structures.[1]
> *Michael Frost and Alan Hirsch*

THERE IS NOTHING NEW with Frost and Hirsch's call for a reformation of church structures for the sake of the gospel. The Reformation, the Radical Reformation, and their offshoots are proof of that. It is a call that is presently reverberating around churches new and old. One answer that is being put forward in several different contexts is the need for churches to incorporate a charismatic apostolate. Charismatic apostles or the charismatic apostolate[2] are not the phrases necessarily used by popular writers who often refer to them simply as "apostles"; nevertheless, the assumption underlying all of the contemporary Charismatic/Evangelical accounts of modern apostles is that these are Spirit-empowered/reliant pioneering ministers whose vocation and ministry have their origin in God. This charismatic "gift"/"ministry"/"office" of apostle is not, in popular Evangelical/Charismatic conceptions, synonymous with ordained ministry. This calling and ministry *can* coincide with an official church position—such as bishop, priest, deacon, elder, superintendent, and so on—and many advocates would hope that it does—but it does not mean *de facto* that you are a charismatically gifted apostle. The evidence of what the person does indicates whether they are an apostle, not their title or position.

---

1. Frost and Hirsch, *Shaping*, 6.
2. This is in keeping with Andrew Walker's use of the phrase "charismatic apostolate" in "Pentecostalism," 428–34.

Introduction

Advocates of the charismatic apostolate believe that the apostle is a gift of Christ to his church for the sake of its maturity and mission; the Scripture undergirding this idea is Ephesians 4:11–13: "The gifts he gave were that some would be *apostles* [emphasis mine], some prophets, some evangelists, some pastors and teachers, to equip the saints for the work of ministry, for building up the body of Christ, until all of us come to the unity of the faith and of the knowledge of the Son of God, to maturity, to the measure of the full stature of Christ." (NRSV)

As I will show this belief is not new, but there are novel aspects being promoted amongst modern charismatic apostolate advocates, and in light of the Pentecostal and Charismatic Movement it is a belief that has gained an extensive and international hearing.

One of the most popular arguments for why this ministry has become prominent recently is a Restorationist one. This is particularly the case with Peter Wagner, who claims that "just as the 1980s was a decade initiating the renewal of the biblical gift and office of prophet, the 1990s is shaping up to be the decade in which God is renewing the gift and office of apostle."[3] These are intriguing claims coming from a man who is renowned for observing current trends in the Evangelical world,[4] and whose influence is widespread in that sector of the church. He, along with other Evangelical/Charismatic leaders, is convinced that God has been restoring[5] charismatic apostles to the church. The claim is often made that God is doing something substantially new in restoring this apostolic company, and that this is a move of the Spirit, a "new thing"[6] which the church must take note of—in essence this is the "new wine"[7] that is being given to the

---

3. From Wagner's foreword in Hamon, *Apostles*, xxii.

4. In their article on Wagner—"Wagner," 1181—McGee and Pavia refer to him as "an authority on worldwide church growth."

5. Although many of these leaders use the word "restore," they usually believe that there are identifiable Charismatic apostles throughout the Church's history. Therefore Wagner stipulates that "there has never been a time in Church history when the Church has been without apostles." Wagner, *Apostles and Prophets*, 19.

6. "New thing" language is prominent in Charismatic circles, frequently used in connection with what the Spirit is apparently doing amongst God's people. The idea is lifted from Isaiah 43:19: "See, I am doing a new thing." (NIV).

7. Talk of "new wine" and "new wineskins" is popular in Charismatic circles. The idea is taken from Luke 5:37–8: "no one puts new wine into old wineskins; otherwise the new wine will burst the skins and will be spilled, and the skins will be destroyed. But new wine must be put into fresh wineskins." It is taken out of context to refer to the need for the work of the Spirit (the "new wine") to be incorporated into church structures that can contain them (the "new wineskin"). It is usually used by Restorationist Christians who believe that God is restoring the church to its God-given pattern and

Introduction

church which in turn must become the "new wineskin" to contain what God is currently giving. Aside from both the Restorationist reading, which is theologically problematic, and the unpersuasive fixating on a particular date (1990),[8] is Wagner correct? Is there evidence for a shift in the Evangelical/Charismatic world that would justify such a statement? Is it really something "new"? If it is, what is new about it? What is not new about it? Is it a view consistent with Scripture and the traditions of the church? Is it something the wider church needs to incorporate—and if so what aspects can and should be embraced?

This idea that Christ is still giving apostles to his Body is a concept that has a checkered history within the church. It is a view that still meets formidable opposition within certain branches of the church due to theological and ecclesiological traditions related to both apostolic succession (the belief that the original apostles' authority has been conferred to their successors the bishops) and cessationism (the idea that with the closing of the canon miraculous gifts and ministries died out as they were no longer needed).

Prior to the twentieth century there were minority Christian groups, often rejected and deemed heretical, that have advocated a charismatic apostolate. With the worldwide impact of the Pentecostal Charismatic Movement, that has changed—a marginal viewpoint has not only been widely accepted by participants in that movement,[9] but even people from within other traditions have thought again on the topic and have been promoting similar beliefs and forms of ministry.[10]

My personal interest in this subject came out of a desire to make sense of my own encounter with claims about apostolicity being made by the Christian groups I had either been in or was involved with. As a Religious Studies teacher in a Catholic school I was encountering the view that for Roman Catholics apostolic succession was vital to the very being of the church, and the Anglican orders that I was contemplating taking were null and void. The conservative Evangelical circles I had been a part of were uninterested in apostolic succession and deemed an ongoing gift

---

power to highlight that the old denominations (the "old wineskins") cannot contain the new works of the Spirit (the "new wine").

8. All those involved in the British Restorationist House Church movement (e.g., Terry Virgo—still a prominent Charismatic leader in Britain; Bryn Jones—now deceased; and Dave Tomlinson—who has become a priest in the Church of England) claimed a similar thing but believed it was occurring far earlier than the 1990s.

9. See chap. 2 for evidence of this.

10. For a more detailed defense of this, see chap. 5.

xiii

Introduction

of apostle as unbiblical; whilst at various Charismatic conferences and churches I had attended, leaders were arguing that an ongoing charismatic apostolate was thoroughly biblical and God was evidently restoring this gift to the church. How was I to make sense of these conflicting accounts? This book is ultimately my answer to that question.

To comprehend the contemporary charismatic apostolate I decided I would have to work both as a historian and a theologian. As a historian my aim was threefold: first, to garner enough information to give a detailed snapshot of the contemporary scene with regards to the charismatic apostolate; secondly, to find and describe historical precedents of the phenomenon; and thirdly, to draw attention to historical factors that have led to the current situation—the thought being that in bringing these naturally intertwining areas together, it would be possible to locate, appraise, and make sense of the charismatic apostolate historically.

To theologically appraise the modern popular concepts of the charismatic apostolate I used the "adjudicators" that are appealed to within the traditions that have shaped me. As a result the theological lens worn was an Evangelical, catholic/ecumenical, Anglican perspective: Evangelical in that the Scriptures are given pride of place in determining the doctrines of the church, and therefore careful attention was given to biblical exegesis; catholic/ecumenical in that both the history and traditions (past and present) of the "whole" church and an ecumenical awareness were seen as important in interpreting Scripture and applying it within our present context. Historically, Anglicanism has looked to a third strand alongside Scripture and Tradition, that of reason. It is that which I have been using both in reviewing the other two strands of Scripture and tradition, but also in contemplating whether the contemporary charismatic apostolate is a genuine charism of the Spirit—for if it is, then it will inevitably be edifying to the Body of Christ (1 Cor 12:7).

An insight from Father Peter Hocken helped provide me with another lens through which to investigate this subject.[11] Using Paul's argument in Romans 11 on how Jews and Gentiles should relate to one another in light of Christ, he argued that the older churches were akin to the Jews, and the new "stream" movements were akin to the Gentiles. Therefore, just as Paul had charged the Jews to recognize what God was doing amongst the Gentiles, so older churches need to embrace what God is doing in the newer movements; at the same time, just as Paul had warned the Gentiles from become proud and dismissive toward the Jews, so those part of these

---

11. Hocken, *Strategy*.

Introduction

new "streams" need to refrain from becoming haughty and affirm where they have come from and not be dismissive of the treasures within the older churches. Simply put, both groups need each other. Applying this reasoning to this study: What theologies and practices occurring within charismatic groups concerning the charismatic apostolate could the older churches learn from and potentially embrace as a genuine charism of the Spirit? What could the traditions and history of apostolicity within the older churches teach these new movements, which could prevent them from embracing erroneous ideas that are detrimental to the health of the Body of Christ?

To help structure this exploration and appraisal[12] I have outlined this book using the following sections: 1) where we are in regard to the charismatic apostolate; 2) how we got here; 3) what we should make of it theologically/ecclesiologically; and 4) where the charismatic apostolate might go.

Book Outline

Part 1: Where We Are

In chapter 1 a general outline of the older churches' understanding of "apostolic ministry" is given, followed by a look at the present beliefs on the charismatic apostolate being endorsed by and found amongst churches/denominations in America that have been affected by the Pentecostal Charismatic Movement. This has involved looking not only at statements put forward by the denomination when available, but also what Renewal organizations are promoting in that denomination. I look in a systematic way at differing groups according to their primary influence—Pentecostal or Charismatic—and form of church—denominational or independent. This chapter demonstrates that the charismatic apostolate is a noticeable component of Charismatic churches in the USA.

In chapter 2 I follow a similar format in relation to the British church as well as look at general trends prominent in the British Charismatic "world" that have bearing on the charismatic apostolate. There is also an important, though brief, discussion concerning the similarities and differences between the American and British church's attitude to and

12. This is not a claim for an authoritative explanation; however, I do offer a provisional yet substantial, retroductive explanation of the charismatic apostolate in relation to the disciplines of history and theology.

xv

Introduction

fascination with the charismatic apostolate. This chapter shows that the charismatic apostolate is an explicit feature of many churches and has become prominent within the independent sector and amongst denominational Charismatics. The overarching aim of these two chapters is to give a broad picture of the current scene in regards to charismatic apostles. In chapter 3 I describe the theology and theory of modern apostles from the perspective of several renowned teachers in the Charismatic/Evangelical sector whose ministries are affecting churches internationally: Derek Prince, Kenneth Hagin, Terry Virgo, Mike Breen, and Peter Wagner. Background information on each of the teachers is provided, followed by a detailed unpacking of their understanding of the charismatic apostolate focusing in on what they see as the characteristics of this ministry and how the church both local and universal should relate to it. In this discussion the aspects which are common to each of these teachers are highlighted as well as ways in which they differ, and finally the types of charismatic apostolate being advocated are grouped into three sets. As a result this chapter provides an in-depth description of popular modern conceptions of the charismatic apostolate.

Part 2: How We Got Here

In chapter 4 the current scene of the charismatic apostolate is put into its historical context through tracing the charismatic apostolate over the course of the church's history up till circa 1990, highlighting (and debating—when appropriate) common beliefs being advocated concerning apostles in different eras and commenting on the success/failure of previous movements which have incorporated a charismatic apostolate. In chapter 5 I consider what is new and not new about the theologies and theories about modern charismatic apostles looked at in chapter 3 in comparison with the ideas and practices looked at in chapter 4. This is followed by a discussion of the possible stepping stones that have led to the widespread attraction of this new emphasis in the West, in particular Britain, making use of influential church leaders' testimonies[13] as to why they have embraced belief in an ongoing charismatic apostolate alongside other factors which from my research I deem as significant. This involves a reflection on the impact of the Pentecostal Charismatic Movement, gift courses, Charismatic ecclesiologies, openness to the "prophetic," technological

13. Rev Barry Kissell, Rev Bruce Collins, the Rt. Rev David Pytches, Colin Urquhart, Dr Michael Eaton, and Professor Peter Wagner.

Introduction

advances, cultural changes and theological shifts in regards to missiology and apostolicity. This chapter collates evidence together in such a way that a possible explanation is given to why a minority perspective has become so widespread, and what contributes to its ongoing acceptance.

Part 3: What We Should Make of It

In chapter 6 I critically discuss the debate amongst Evangelicals concerning the Scriptural legitimacy of a charismatic apostolate. I do this by evaluating the arguments put forward by influential voices within Evangelicalism against modern conceptions of the charismatic apostolate, and critiquing the case for them made by a significant Pentecostal scholar. This discussion highlights the exegetical points of tension, as well as the strengths and weaknesses of both traditional arguments against an ongoing charismatic apostolate, and one of the strongest cases for it in light of New Testament scholarship on the individual texts. This chapter sets out the essential exegetical/hermeneutical issues that are at stake with any biblical argument for or against an ongoing charismatic apostolate. In chapter 7 I comment from an ecumenical perspective on the three main types of charismatic apostolate identified in chapter 3 and judge what might be helpful, scripturally justifiable and ecclesiologically acceptable for the church's mission in Britain. It is within this context that the disputes with the charismatic apostolate based upon apostolic succession and cessationism are discussed in relation to scholarship and ecumenical considerations. This chapter therefore considers the wider ecclesiological issues that must be taken into account when evaluating the different types of charismatic apostolate.

Part 4: Where It Might Go

In chapter 8 there is a summation of my findings and an envisaging of the possible future of the charismatic apostolate in Britain which is done by positing the likely responses to the three types of charismatic apostolate across the denominational spectrum. The chapter concludes with a consideration of potential avenues for future research within this field, as well as a final word concerning the challenge that this historical and theological appraisal brings to the church.

Part One

Where We Are

1

Apostles Today

USA

INTRODUCTION

HOW WIDESPREAD IS THE idea of the charismatic apostolate? What is being said about it across the churches? This and the next chapter attempt to provide an overview of what is happening and what is being advocated amongst churches in America and Britain. It is important to recognize that this whole phenomenon does not occur within a vacuum, there are well established traditions that already exist within churches which this concept comes into contact with. Therefore, we need to briefly highlight some of those traditions that have bearing upon any talk of an ongoing charismatic apostolate and which are prevalent amongst churches that have a substantial history and a large membership—the Roman Catholic Church; the Orthodox Church; the Anglican Church; the Presbyterian Church; the Lutheran Church; the Baptist Church; the Methodist Church. It is important to note that none of these churches have an official doctrine on the charismatic apostolate; however, they all have advocated certain forms of ministry which they connect to apostolicity. Inevitably, all of these churches will have had prominent figures within them who have not agreed with their official line on certain aspects of theology or ecclesiology; furthermore, although their own historic formularies and norms still have a profound impact upon the fashioning of ministries within these churches, the ecumenical climate of the twentieth century has softened some edges to former intransient perspectives.

Part One—Where We Are

The Roman Catholic, Orthodox, and Anglican churches hold that the bishop is the historic successor of the apostles, being the sole ministry able to ordain others, and possessing an apostolic sacramental ministry which they share with their co-workers the priests.[1] Lutherans and Methodists hold to a form of apostolic succession but believe it can be validly passed on via the presbyterate. These churches clearly differentiate between those first apostles who were eyewitnesses of the resurrected Lord, instructed directly by Jesus, receiving revelation that was to be part of the deposit of faith entrusted to all the saints, and their successors. Although they are seen as the successors of the apostles they have not tended to be called "apostles" themselves, but it is not unheard of; according to J. D. Bales, in the first couple of centuries of the church, there was a practice of referring to those who were ordained by the apostles as apostles themselves.[2] Nevertheless, it is not a tradition that had much support, as is evident from early church sources (see chap. 4) and is not one that has been retained in the oldest churches. Even so, acceptable traditions have developed of posthumously naming certain pioneering/missionary leaders as apostles so "Dionysius of Corinth was called the Apostle of France; Xavier was called the Apostle of the Indies."[3] Within the Orthodox Church it is a common practice to recognize such figures as "equal to the apostles," a term that in some Orthodox circles is even today applied to missionaries.

More recently a trend has occurred amongst Christians of a more catholic persuasion, popularized by Vatican II, which speaks of all Christians (ordained and lay) as apostles, in that all Christians are sent to bear witness to Christ in the world.[4] The Anglican bishop Stephen Cottrell follows in this tradition and justifies the use of this term as it highlights that "they have a share in the apostolic vocation of the church."[5] This use does not make any claims regarding the spiritual authority of Christians and merely highlights their common vocation; nevertheless, it is an important developing tradition as it reflects a wider fashion to use the language of "apostle." Even though these traditions are present, apostolic succession

---

1. Other churches that hold to this view are the Oriental Orthodox, Assyrian, and Independent Catholic churches.

2. Bales, *Apostates*, 41.

3. Ibid., 42.

4. In Vatican II's "Decree on the Apostolate of Lay People," it asserts that all the lay have the "right and duty to be apostles." Quotation taken from Bosch, *Transforming*, 471.

5. Cottrell, *Abundance*, 41.

churches tend to be wary of talk about charismatic apostolic ministry apart from historical succession.

There has been an overt rejection of the idea that there is a continuation of the apostolic office in any form amongst non-historical succession, non-Pentecostal Protestant churches. For example, the Westminster Standard states, "The officers which Christ hath appointed for the edification of his church, and the perfecting of the saints, are, some extraordinary, as apostles, evangelists, and prophets, which are ceased."[6] Although this is the mainstream view within the Baptist Church, it is important to note that they did have an office of "Messenger," which was modeled on New Testament trans-local apostolic ministry. Despite abandoning this development the Baptist Church has been very involved in sending people out as missionaries, as have other cessationist, anti-apostolic succession Protestant churches. Nevertheless, these churches and Apostolic Succession churches have been affected by the Pentecostal Charismatic Movement and felt the challenge of the emphasis on Charismatic gifts and ministries.

Pentecostal/Charismatic Churches and "Apostleship" Today

In the last couple of decades within Charismatic circles there have been many "prophetic" promises concerning the restoration of a charismatic apostolate: "God will bring forth the full stature of the Apostle"[7] (K. Hagin). "Some time ago, God spoke to me very clearly that He was shortly going to manifest apostles . . . in the body of Christ."[8] These particular predictions appear to be coming to pass if we are to believe that the number of Christian ministers who are claiming to embody or have this "anointing"/"office"/"ministry"/"gift"[9] are justified in so doing. There has been a wealth of popular books and articles written by denominational and non-denominational Charismatics advocating the charismatic

---

6. Westminster Assembly, *Westminster Confession*.

7. A "word" given by Kenneth Hagin in 1964: Prince, *Rediscovering*, 235.

8. Ibid.

9. All these are popular terms used to describe it; some authors are very particular on which term is used. However, whichever term is used they all agree that an apostle is one who is empowered by God's Spirit to do certain works that only an apostle can do—there is no general consensus of what those works are though.

apostolate.[10] This is not a new belief,[11] but, there is evidence to conclude that it has not been so widely accepted until recently. Nigel Wright's prediction in 1986 that "within a few years, references to apostolic ministries within the church will seem as acceptable and as natural as references to elders"[12] has been fulfilled in large parts of the church. The fact that David Barrett and Todd Johnson refer to neo-apostolic churches as a category for churches within their reference works *World Christian Trends AD 30–AD 2200: Interpreting the Annual Christian Megacensus*[13] and *World Christian Encyclopedia*[14] highlights how commonplace "apostolic" language now is, particularly in the USA where they are based. Wagner draws attention to the fact that according to Barrett's research, the neo-apostolics are now the second biggest group after the Roman Catholic Church and constitute the fastest growing churches.[15]

To explore how widespread this idea is I have undertaken a review of some prominent Pentecostal/Charismatic churches, networks, and Renewal organizations in the USA—the country which "has become . . . the center of global radiation, religiously, culturally, and economically"[16]—(this chapter) and Britain (next chapter). I will categorize them in the following fashion and look at the beliefs held by them:

Historic Pentecostal. These are those churches that arose within the first half of the twentieth century in connection to the Pentecostal movement that began with Charles Fox Parham, and then subsequently in Azusa under William Seymour, which believe in an experiential empowering of the Spirit post-conversion known as the baptism in the Spirit. Usually the gift of tongues is seen as the sign for many of the older Pentecostal denominations as proof of being baptized in the Spirit.

---

10. E.g., Breen (Anglican), *Notebook*; Pytches (Anglican), *Leadership*, chap. 1; C. Dye (Elim), "Apostolic"; and from the newer Churches: Urquhart (Kingdom Faith Church), *True Church*, chap. 2; Ekman, *Apostolic*. Also see Arsenal Books, "Books—Apostolic," for a list which includes numerous recent publications on the gift of the apostle.

11. For example Edward Irving and the Catholic Apostolic Church believed apostles were still being given to the church. For a good overview of the history of this Church see Walker, *Restoring*, chap. 11; for other examples see chap. 4 of this study.

12. Wright, *Radical Kingdom*, 76.

13. Barrett and Johnson, *Trends*.

14. Barrett et al., *Encyclopedia*.

15. Wagner, "Lecture AP825."

16. Martin, *Pentecostalism*, 34.

Historic Denominational Charismatic. This refers to Charismatics within older denominations, e.g., Catholic Charismatics, Anglican Charismatics, Baptist Charismatics, and so on, having their roots post-1959. These Charismatic groups initially imbibed a Pentecostal doctrine of Spirit Baptism, but have usually adapted Pentecostal doctrine to fit with Sacramental or Evangelical theology in accordance with their churchmanship—nevertheless, they would all advocate numerous "fillings" of the Spirit with the expectation of spiritual gifts.

Independent Charismatic and Modern Independent Pentecostal. These are churches that have been started post-1950, embracing Pentecostal gifts and ministries. The ICs do not necessarily advocate speaking in tongues as the sign of being baptized in the Spirit, nor necessarily hold that event as subsequent to conversion, unlike the MIPs.

Within all these different groups are "apostolic networks"—these are networks of people/groups/churches usually centered on an "apostolic" individual or ministry; they are particularly prominent in the Independent Charismatic sector. Despite many differences between these groups there is obviously overlap in terms of doctrine and practice as all of them are characterized by an expectation and belief that God is still empowering his church with the gifts of the Spirit mentioned in 1 Corinthians 12.

Historic Pentecostal Denominations: USA

With the advent of the Pentecostal "revival" that occurred in the USA, first at Charles Parham's Bible School, and then on a far broader scale at Azusa Street, a renewed interest in the empowering and enabling work of the Spirit came to the fore.[17] The Pentecostal movement was characterized by spiritual manifestations, particularly glossolalia, and those caught up in it saw themselves in a similar way to some of the Catholic Apostolics,[18] as recipients of the latter rain of the Spirit. With the emergence of tongues and demonstrations of other spiritual manifestations which were equated with the list Paul outlined in 1 Corinthians 12, there was a conviction amongst the Pentecostals that God was restoring the charismatic dimension to the

---

17. For helpful descriptions of these events see Hollenweger, *Pentecostals*, 22ff.

18. The Catholic Apostolic Church apostle, Rev N. Armstrong stated in a sermon, "The time of the latter rain is now come; the harvest is near at hand": "Exposition and Sermon; delivered at Salem Chapel, Deverell Street, Dover Road, Sunday Evening, November 11, 1832, by Rev N. Armstrong, A. B. Text is Zechariah 10.1," in *Tracts*, 2.

Part One—Where We Are

Christian life. Not only were the gifts of the Spirit being released amongst God's people but also the charismatic ministries. Donald Gee, in a book recounting the history of the Pentecostal movement in Britain, stated that, "The Pentecostal movement as a whole believes that Divine grace has distributed the gifts of Ephesians iv. 11 freely throughout the whole Body of Christ . . ."[19]

Pentecostalism developed in numerous directions within the USA, and had more vociferous doctrinal disputes leading to more divisions than it did in the United Kingdom; separations occurred due to divisions over sanctification teaching and the doctrine of the Trinity.[20] Despite the fact that all of the Pentecostal churches that emerged affirmed all five of the Ephesians ministries, the church structures that resulted in the major USA Pentecostal denominations did not really differ from older church forms and therefore did not include a church office of Apostle. Nevertheless, "apostles" are on the agenda for many of these churches, the largest ones being "the Church of God in Christ (COGIC, originally formed in 1885) and the Assemblies of God (AOG, founded in 1914), followed by the Church of God (Cleveland) (CGC, 1886), the International Church of the Foursquare Gospel (ICFG, 1927), the International Pentecostal Holiness Church (IPHC, 1895), the United Pentecostal Church (UPC, 1931), and the Pentecostal Church of God (1919)."[21] There have been position papers on the subject released by the Assemblies of God and the International Pentecostal Holiness Church; the Pentecostal Church of God (PCG) is currently[22] in the process of putting one together.

Even though the founder of the Church of God in Christ, Bishop Mason, was originally a Baptist before becoming a Pentecostal, the structure of the Church of God in Christ is Episcopal in nature and gives a prominent place to bishops. So prominent in fact, that the presiding bishop sees himself as "seventh" in the "apostolic succession,"[23] and they often call the bishops "Apostles." Yet it seems that they do not limit the charismatic apostolate to that of the episcopate; one of their own bishops, Bishop C.

---

19. Gee, *Wind*, 105.

20. Synan, "The 'Finished Work' Pentecostal Churches," 123–48, in Synan, *century*, chap. 6.

21. Anderson, *Introduction*, 52.

22. Charles G. Scott, General Bishop of Pentecostal Church of God, e-mail message to author, September 8, 2009.

23. See Blake, "An Apostolic Missive," where Blake writes: "The seventh in apostolic succession, I am humbled by the providence of God and the blessings He has secured for the Church of God in Christ."

Apostles Today: USA

Moody states, "Yes, there are Apostles today! They manifest extraordinary spiritual leadership, and are anointed with the power of the Holy Spirit to confront the powers of Satan, by confirming the gospel by signs and miracles and establishing churches according to the New Testament pattern and doctrine of the apostles."[24]

The Assemblies of God USA has a tumultuous history in regards to this issue, and it is a history that in large measure still determines their current stance. As an international denomination it has reached differing conclusions on the matter in different countries of the world. Its original stance was that although Christ still gives apostles to the church they did not carry the same kind of authority seen in the ministries of the Twelve or Paul; they were not to be addressed as apostles nor should there be a recognised institutional position of "apostle"; nor was it necessary for every local church to have one. In the wake of the Canadian Latter Rain revival of 1948 there were hopes by some members that Assemblies of God USA would make space for charismatic apostles and prophets in the local church, however this type of teaching was declared in error by the 1949 General Council of the Assemblies of God USA which met in Seattle. Even so, there has been a shift in recent decades within some quarters of the worldwide Assemblies of God to embrace charismatic apostles as an essential part of the local church's make up, and see them as visionaries and pioneers in the church's mission. A clear example of this has been the Assemblies of God Australia.[25] Peter Wagner applauds their example of being willing to drop the old way of doing things where authority was vested in the congregational government, and to embrace the authority resident in the charismatically empowered apostle.[26] David Cartledge, who spearheaded this change, has argued that the resulting growth of Assemblies of God Australia has been due to their change of structure and their acceptance of the offices of apostles and prophets.

As a result of the Assemblies of God Australia and the influence of Wagner in the USA (and beyond), there has been increasing pressure in other Assemblies of God networks to shift their understanding of apostolic ministry. However, in America and Canada this has not happened. Assemblies of God USA have responded by repeating a similar judgment

---

24. Bishop C. L. Moody, *World Pentecost*, Autumn 1996, 18. Quoted in Ross, "Apostolic Reformation," 61.

25. Cartledge, *Apostolic Revolution*.

26. See Wagner, *Churchquake*, 149–52.

PART ONE—Where We Are

made sixty years ago to apply to their church today.[27] In their 2001 statement Assemblies of God USA reaffirmed that Christ was still giving apostles to the church; however, they were not on the same level as the "foundational" apostles that are present in the New Testament and were more akin to the "apostles of the churches" that are mentioned in 2 Corinthians 8:23. Therefore, they stated: "Since the New Testament does not provide guidance for the appointment of future apostles, such contemporary offices are not essential to the health and growth of the church, nor its apostolic nature." They did concede that although they were opposed to using the title "apostle," that "some church bodies may in good faith and careful biblical definition choose to name certain leaders apostles" but were adamant that if this was the case the only form of "apostle" that could be biblically justified was that of the "apostles of the churches."[28]

In correspondence with Professor Jerald Daffe of Lee University—he made the following helpful observations and points about the previous stance of his church, The Church of God (Cleveland) as well as the contemporary one in regards to apostles:

> The Church of God recognizes the current operation of spiritual gifts. We do not believe there to have been a cessation of their operation in the current church. Since we do not have a specific doctrinal manual or pastoral theology manual our positions are basically outline without any specific expansion on specifics. That usually occurs through articles in *The Church of God Evangel*, our official denominational paper.... Like many other Pentecostals our history has been one of not believing in current apostles due to seeing them in a very localized position in terms of writers of the New Testament and disciples who were founders of the church. However, the *Apostolic Restoration Movement of the 1990s* has caused many denominations to rethink their verbal positions. Within the Church of God there are a growing number of individuals like myself who see the reality of the continuance of the office of apostle. This is a necessity. Otherwise, we are guilty of accepting only a part of Ephesians 4:11. The denomination does not have a posted paper detailing this view.[29]

Daffe's point that there was a growing number of people in CG who were happy with the New Apostolic Reformation "apostolic paradigm" would

27. General Presbytery of the Assemblies of God, "Apostles and Prophets."
28. Ibid., 10. They draw upon renowned New Testament scholars to make their case: Dunn, Kruse, Brown, Fee, and Stronstad.
29. Jerald Daffe, e-mail message to author, October 6, 2009, emphasis mine.

seem to be confirmed by the fact that the denomination's publishers had published a book by Daffe and Dr John A. Lombard Jr called *Spiritual Gifts for Today? For Me*, which was distributed to Church of God leadership as well as being placed on sale for the general public. He told me that "in it is a specific chapter which deals with apostles. We see them as current in today's church but with some defined identifications. Our position is that most who place the title, Apostle, by their name very likely are not."[30]

What is very revealing about the Church of God's current position is that by admission they were being pressured to reevaluate their doctrine in light of the "Apostolic Restoration Movement,"[31] however, unlike Wagner,[32] they are reticent to make much of the title.

The International Church of the Foursquare Gospel does not have a "specific statement in regard to the ministry of the apostle"[33] but affirm the ongoing need and presence of apostles on the basis of Ephesians 4:11–13. One of the representatives of their international office explained their current position on the matter in the following way:

> Generally, an apostle is understood to be one that is "sent out" with a particular message; the apostles in the New Testament were often the primary proclaimers of the Gospel and frequently established initial church efforts. Based on the Ephesians passage, it seems that an apostle would be different from a pastor, but there does not seem to be general consensus in regard to the specific nature of the difference. If a person designates himself as an apostle, he should be able to give a clear explanation of how he perceives his ministry fits that role.[34]

The International Pentecostal Holiness Church at their General Conference in 2005 made an assignment for appointed scholars and theologians to do a "biblical/theological study of the Apostolic Movement."[35]

---

30. Ibid. Jerald Daffe helpfully summarized the identifying marks of an apostle in the same e-mail: "Humility dominates as they genuinely love and serve people. Signs, wonders, and miracles are evident in their sphere of ministry. Financial relationships are handled with wisdom and personal integrity. The authority and covering of the church is valued. Christian ministry is being established among the unevangelized as they are brought to salvation and discipleship. Personal glory is shunned and the title rarely used."

31. A clear reference to Wagner's movement.

32. See chap. 3 for an overview of Wagner's teaching on apostles.

33. IFGC main office, e-mail message to author, October 6, 2009.

34. Wanda Brackett, e-mail message to author, October 6, 2009.

35. IPHC, "Apostolic Biblical Statement," 19.

Part One—Where We Are

The result of this was the paper they produced in 2007. In summary it affirmed the ongoing validity of apostles today; however they made a clear distinction between what they term "foundational apostles" and "functional apostles." Foundational apostles are a non-repeatable gift of Christ to the church and had divinely given inspiration in interpreting the Old Testament and being able to write or be responsible for the New Testament; these individuals had also personally "seen the Lord in the flesh." However, the paper argues that there are other apostles mentioned in the New Testament who do not share these qualities but are validly called apostles—they exhibit some similar characteristics evident in the foundational apostles' ministry; namely: "they could then and can today equal those at the second level in the area of anointing and power for ministry. . . . In addition, functional apostles to this day have a strong foundation-laying ministry, establishing the faith in the new areas they open up for the gospel. The base they build must always square with the historic faith laid by the foundational apostles who wrote the New Testament."[36]

The United Pentecostal Church has not released a paper on the subject and the following response from their main office explains their current understanding: "The United Pentecostal Church International has no official teaching on Ephesians 4:11–13. The most widely held position by members would be that the Ephesians passage describes the five-fold equipping ministry of the church. The UPCI has no official designation or office of an apostle or prophet and remains skeptical of people who self-designate themselves with either title. That being said, in an unofficial way certain individuals are seen to hold apostolic or prophetic ministries."[37]

The Pentecostal Church of God is in the process of addressing the issue afresh; however, their official doctrinal statement indicates that they do allow for the charismatic apostolate on the basis of their reference to 1 Corinthians 12:27–8 and Ephesians 4:11–12: "To the Church, through its members, are delegated the various gifts and offices of the Holy Ghost (1 Corinthians 12:7–11, 27, 28) which are necessary for the successful evangelization of the world and the perfecting of the Body of Christ (1 Corinthians 12:7; Ephesians 4:11, 12)."[38]

Nevertheless, they do not have an "office" of apostle in their church structure.

---

36. Ibid., 1ff.
37. UPC, e-mail message to author, September 8, 2009.
38. Pentecostal Church of God, "What We Believe."

In summary the American Historic Pentecostals are feeling a challenge from the New Apostolic Reformation to reevaluate their perspectives on apostles, which they all accept as still being given to the church. Some are responding by repeating judgments from an early period arguing for a functional apostolate not a church position, others are moving toward embracing a higher view of this ministry and highlighting the unusual "spiritual authority" that these individuals are demonstrating.

Historic Denominational Charismatics: USA

Dennis Bennett's sermon at Van Nuys in 1959 is seen by many historians as the event that set the Charismatic Movement off. Bennett was an Episcopalian and remained so until his death; he developed an itinerant ministry and was a recognized leader of the Charismatic Movement. A number of Episcopalian leaders followed in his footsteps and as a result during the 1960s, 70s, and 80s there were some notable Episcopalian leaders at the forefront of Charismatic Renewal.[39] Nevertheless, it is apparent that although many Episcopalians were affected by the Renewal it never properly infiltrated the institution.[40] The ministry organization, Acts 29, that Bennett and his wife, Rita, started to promote Renewal is still going, and seeks to continue Bennett's legacy in both the mainline Episcopalian Church (ECUSA) and the newly formed Anglican Church of North America (ACNA). The present CEO and President of Acts 29, Rev Alan Hansen, informed me that the five-fold ministry was promoted via their organization. They used a "spiritual gifts" questionnaire to help people identify their charisms. He believed that the charism of apostle was still evident today, and that although the office of apostle was directly related to the office of bishop it was not tied to that office; furthermore, he felt that many bishops did not function as apostles with the signs that Paul said would accompany their ministry. He did however believe there were bishops in the USA who were operating in a genuine apostolic ministry. He also thought that this gift could operate apart from the clergy, but he saw this as unusual.[41] What was clear is that for this Charismatic

---

39. E.g., Terry Fullam.

40. This is the informed opinion of Rev Alan Hansen, who leads Acts 29 Ministries and has been involved in fostering renewal within the Episcopalian Church since the 1970s. Alan Hansen, telephone interview with author, October 27, 2009.

41. Alan Hansen, telephone interview with author, October 27, 2009.

organization the possibility of apostles today is not being debated, it is an accepted teaching.

Despite the overt move into a more liberal expression of the faith there were still Episcopal parishes and dioceses eager for Acts 29's input; similarly, the newly formed Anglican Church of North America, which has emerged as a result of the increasing liberalism in the Episcopalian Church United States of America (ECUSA), is very open to this organization and to Charismatic impulses in general. It is well known that the Anglican Church of North America (ACNA) has tried to hold together the sacramental, Evangelical and Charismatic, and as a result has imbibed many Pentecostal and Charismatic convictions concerning the ongoing gifts of the Spirit. Although fully in accord with the Jerusalem statement released by the Global Anglican Future Conference (GAFCON), which was overtly Evangelical with no reference to the historic episcopate as being a God-given order, the Anglican Church of North America (ACNA) has affirmed its commitment to apostolic succession: "We confess the godly historic Episcopate as an inherent part of the apostolic faith and practice, and therefore as integral to the fullness and unity of the Body of Christ."[42] Of special interest has been the appointment of Todd Hunter, former head of Vineyard and a former leader in the Emerging church movement, to bishop elect with the vision of planting 200 churches on the West Coast of America.[43] Furthermore, the current Archbishop of the Anglican Church of North America (ACNA), Robert Duncan, has pledged to plant 1,000 churches in five years[44]—this initial vision is beginning to take shape and a whole initiative called Anglican 1000 has come out of it with various conferences and websites promoting it.[45] They are encouraging church-planting bishops, priests, and laity—Anglican 1000 does not categorize how this gift can operate, but believes it can be present amongst ordained or unordained members of the church.[46] In their official websites they do not use the terminology of apostle; however, within Charismatic circles the idea of "church planter" is often seen as synonymous with apostle.

Larry Christenson has been, and continues to be, a significant figure in Lutheran Renewal.[47] He was one of the pioneers of Charismatic Re-

42. ACNA, "ACNA—What We Stand For."
43. Viola, "Interview with Todd Hunter."
44. For the full proclamation see ACNA, "The 1,000 Churches Proclamation."
45. See Anglican 1000, "Anglican 1000."
46. For more information on this organization see Anglican 1000, "Who We Are."
47. Due to its very small presence in the UK I will not consider Lutheranism in

newal within the Lutheran Church and has remained an influential voice within Charismatic Lutheran circles. He drew attention to the ministry of apostles, in his warm appraisal of the Catholic Apostolic Church in his book, *A Message to the Charismatic Movement*.[48] Even though he personally saw that church as one that had an important message for the Renewal movement and saw no issue with the possibility of modern day apostles, in an e-mail correspondence with me he stated, "To my knowledge, the theology and experience of a modern day apostolate has never been vigorously pursued in the Charismatic Renewal among Lutherans."[49] However, things have moved on since Christenson was at the helm of Lutheran Charismatic Renewal; he was the director of the International Lutheran Renewal Center, but passed this role to Paul Anderson in 1995.[50] Anderson is also the director of Lutheran Renewal, an organization that is very active amongst Lutherans, although it has been distancing itself from the institution. Anderson has adopted a "call out" stance, affirming the worthiness of coming out of the institutional structure and networking with other likeminded Lutherans in a loose network known as The Alliance of Renewal Churches. Although he recognizes that some may feel bound to the institutional expression of Lutheranism, there is a general conviction seen in his writing that coming out and networking would be better.[51]

With the decision to branch out and form a loose network of Renewal-minded Lutherans and Lutheran churches, it is hard not to see the influence of the New Apostolic Reformation on this band of Christians. Prior to the formation of the Alliance of Renewal Churches they were in conversation with Wagner and reported what they were planning to do; significantly, Wagner was very pleased as it was the first "network" to emerge out of a "denominational framework" that he had encountered.[52] Although Anderson clearly esteems Wagner, he is not as ready as Wagner to use the noun "Apostle." He writes: "We at LR (Lutheran Renewal) are more comfortable with the adjective than the noun. We do have an apos-

Britain in chap. 2; however, it is a substantial denomination in the USA and therefore it is appropriate to look at it in that context.

48. Christenson, *Message*.
49. Larry Christenson, e-mail message to author, September 18, 2009.
50. Christenson and Anderson, "Lutheran Charismatics," 848.
51. See his bulletin written in 2004 titled "To Stay or To Leave." Nevertheless, according to Larry Christenson, he does not believe there will be a substantial exodus of conservatives and Charismatics from the Evangelical Lutheran Church even in light of its current stance on homosexuality (Christenson, e-mail message to author, September 19, 2009).
52. Information retrieved from the Alliance of Renewal Churches, "History."

PART ONE—Where We Are

tolic ministry of sorts. We started a seminary in 2001 called The Master's Institute and a network of churches in 02 called The Alliance of Renewal Churches (allianceofrenewalchurches.org). We do, however, have no one that we have identified as an apostle."[53]

The conception at the Alliance of Renewal Churches is that they are an "Apostolic Network," they understand these terms and their significance in the following manner:

> *We are a network.* We are decentralized rather than centralized, flat rather than hierarchical. We believe that one size does not fit all, so we enjoy unity without uniformity, coordination rather than control, and flexibility over rigidity every time. We like to reward risk-taking and innovation because we don't have all the answers. We trust what God does in a local church. At the same time . . .
>
> *We are apostolic.* We recognize that God raises up leaders, gifted in casting and communicating vision. We trust leaders, which also means that we don't do much voting. And it means that we might do the leadership thing differently than we've known in the past.[54]

Although the Alliance of Renewal Churches is not representative of all Lutheran Charismatics, it does highlight that New Apostolic Reformation thinking has become more commonplace within Lutheran Charismatic circles.

Vinson Synan contends that the Presbyterians have often been "pioneers in renewal and revival movements" and that the Charismatic Movement's interaction with the Presbyterianism in the USA was of decisive significance for other denominations and their response to it.[55] The leading Charismatic Presbyterian theologian, J. Rodman Williams, was not only looked to by people within Presbyterianism[56] but by others involved in Renewal across the denominational spectrum. His writings on the gifts and ministries of the Spirit are foundational for the Presbyterian and Reformed Ministries International (PRMI) who incorporate it in their teaching material.[57] His teaching affirmed the ongoing ministry of apostles, but

53. Paul Anderson, e-mail message to author, September 16, 2009.
54. Alliance of Renewal Churches, "About."
55. Synan, "Presbyterian," 995–97.
56. The Presbyterian and Reformed Ministries International have incorporated his teaching on the gifts of the Spirit.
57. I am grateful to the leader of Presbyterian and Reformed Ministries

made a fundamental distinction between the "foundational" ministry of the Twelve and Paul which can never be repeated, and the ongoing "sent" ministry gift of individuals who are appointed by God and whose ministries can be equated with New Testament characters such as Barnabas, Andronicus and Junia amongst others.[58]

Brian Harley, the UK based leader of GEAR (Group for Evangelism and Renewal), who has received much input from the Presbyterian and Reformed Ministries International (PRMI), which is based in the USA, informed me that "apostolic ministry" talk had become very commonplace within Presbyterian and Reformed Ministries International.[59] Harley thought that the current leader, Reverend Brad Long, would be an example of someone with an apostolic ministry. As an organization their conviction to apostolic ministry is borne out in their teaching material which is committed to seeing all five ministries functioning alongside the other charismata mentioned in the New Testament. Long is clearly aware that he is going against Calvin's viewpoint in this regard and makes the following critique of Calvin's ecclesiology:

> Unfortunately for the Presbyterian and Reformed Tradition our founder John Calvin believed that only the office of teacher and pastor has persisted to the present day. Calvin did not even see the need for the evangelist except in extreme circumstances where there had been such a "decay of religion" that evangelism was made necessary. . . . This neglect of these important offices established by Jesus Christ reflects the immediate challenges of the days in which Calvin lived. The challenge of the Reformation was the establishment of the Bible of the Word of God and the restoration of the priesthood of all believers. This required offices of teaching the people true doctrine and pastoring the flock. From the vantage point of the reformers nearly as far as they could see was the vast land of Christendom.[60]

The impact of the Charismatic Movement on the United Methodist Church can be seen by the fact that the general conference of 1972

International, Brad Long, who e-mailed me excerpts from their manuals on the gifts of the Spirit that quote extensively from J. Rodman Williams. The unedited chapters were from the Dunamis Project series, *In the Spirit's Power*, chap. 2, and *Listening Evangelism*, Unit 6, chap. 7. Brad Long, e-mail message to author, October 1, 2009.

58. Williams, *Renewal Theology*, 2:165–70.

59. Brian Harley saw it as a good example of an "apostolic network." Brian Harley, e-mail message to author, September 13, 2009.

60. Long, *Listening Evangelism*, 89.

PART ONE—Where We Are

requested that "a position statement be prepared on the Charismatic renewal" which resulted in a conciliatory report that was "presented to the 1976 general conference."[61] Notable Charismatic leaders were members of the United Methodist Church such as Oral Roberts, Robert Tuttle, and Tommy Tyson.[62] The United Methodist Renewal Service Fellowship was set up in 1977; in time it has changed its name to the Aldersgate Renewal Ministries. It is a fellowship that seeks to promote Renewal within the United Methodist Church but under the authority of the United Methodist Church.[63] In conversation with the Reverend Frank Billman,[64] the director of church Relations at Aldersgate Renewal Ministries, it was clear that it had always been and remains the conviction of those in Aldersgate Renewal Ministries that Ephesians 4:11 applied to today and therefore apostles were to be expected. However, he acknowledged that even though this was the belief, which they have taught and continue to teach, it was not a major feature of their teaching. At present he was not aware of any "apostolic networks" within the United Methodist Church and claimed to be quite ignorant of the New Apostolic Reformation, although he had noticed that there were many more people in Charismatic circles calling themselves apostles. Even though Aldersgate Renewal Ministries and the United Reformed Church have not majored on this issue, Aldersgate Renewal Ministries clearly draws on some leading Renewal ministries that have done so for when I spoke to Rev. Billman he had just returned from a "Voice of the Apostles" conference which had speakers such as Randy Clarke, Bill Johnson, Ché Ahn and John Arnott; furthermore, Johnson and Clarke along with Mike Bickle had all been or were going to be speakers at the main Aldersgate Renewal Ministries 's conference.[65]

There are five main Baptist groups in the USA: Southern Baptists; American Baptists; Conservative Baptists; General Baptist Conference; Independent Baptists; National Progressive Baptists.[66] In none of these groups has there been a widespread acceptance of the Charismatic Movement. The opposite has been the case in the Southern Baptist Convention

61. Bundy, "Methodist," 1159.
62. Much of this information comes from ibid.
63. See the history of Aldersgate Renewal Ministries, which details its history and its main characteristics in Aldersgate Renewal Ministries, "History."
64. Frank Billman, telephone interview with author, November 3, 2009.
65. Frank Billman, telephone interview with author, November 3, 2009.
66. Thanks to Dr Clay Ford, Chairman of Holy Spirit Renewal Ministries, for outlining and naming the differing main Baptist groups in the USA. Clay Ford, interview and e-mail message to author, December 12, 2009.

where there has been some disfellowshipping as the result of Charismatic convictions and practices.[67] Yet, as a whole, the Baptist Church has produced influential Charismatic leaders such as Jack Taylor, Ron Phillips, and Gary Folds, as well as the prominent Christian television presenter, James Robison[68] who have enthusiastically embraced other ministries who are at home with five-fold ministry theology.[69]

Nevertheless, there has been more openness to this movement recently amongst the American Baptists. One organization in particular has been instrumental in spreading Charismatic Renewal within this branch—the American Baptist Charismatic Church fellowship. It emerged from an informal fellowship of Charismatic Baptist leaders, who initiated Renewal gatherings; in 1982 under the leadership of Gary Clarke it changed its name to Holy Spirit Renewal Ministries in American Baptist churches, and continued its focus on bringing Renewal throughout the American Baptist Church. More recently it has broadened its vision to be more ecumenical in its endeavors and has sought to be a Renewal Ministry for the wider church and hence has become Holy Spirit Renewal Ministry. They are however keen to make it clear that they have not abandoned their previous calling to foster Renewal amongst the American Baptist churches.[70] In conversation with their current chairman, Dr Clay Ford, it became apparent that as a group they were now gaining the attention of the denominational leaders—including the President of the American Baptist Ministers Council who recently stated that "what HSRM (Holy Spirit Renewal Ministry) offers is what the whole denomination needs." In the near future Dr Ford will be addressing a large conference where ten executives will be present who collectively oversee a large number of churches. Dr Ford specified that they did not as an organization focus talks on the five-fold ministry, but he acknowledged that there were members of his team who were committed to that doctrine. Furthermore, he would teach on modern-day apostles but not necessarily use that ter-

---

67. Hewett, "Baptist," 365–66. Hewett gives the names of a number of influential Charismatic leaders who ended up leaving the Baptist Church.

68. For an insight into the influence of the Charismatic Movement within the Southern Baptist Church USA see the negative appraisal by David Cloud, "Charismatic." It was David Cloud who made me aware of the various influential Charismatic leaders in the Baptist Church.

69. Jack Taylor has been very involved with the Toronto leaders, and was one of the main speakers at a *Catch the Fire* conference in Texas in 1996 alongside Randy Clarke, Marc DuPont, John Arnott, and Mike Bickle.

70. Holy Spirit Renewal Ministries, "Introducing."

minology—he was very suspicious of some who claim to be apostles and saw signs of a repetition of the Shepherding movement that had caused such devastation.

As an organization they were clearly drawing upon some of the most prominent current Charismatic leaders—Bill Johnson had addressed them, and Randy Clarke was coming in 2010. He was very complementary about Johnson and emphasized that he was having a "very large impact" on the Charismatic scene in the USA. Although not embracing all the developments coming from the New Apostolic Reformation, he did not downplay its influence and recognized that many within his team were committed to it, but was clear that emphasizing it was not sensible in their mission field amongst the American Baptists. Dr Ford was not aware of any other Charismatic Baptist organizations within the other Baptist branches, but did not think it an impossibility. In his opinion some branches were more receptive to Charismatic Renewal than others—so he stated that the American Baptists were more open than the Southern Baptists who in turn were more open than the Conservative Baptists. In spite of organizations such as HRSM and individuals' own theologies, the Baptist Church USA does not make room for a charismatic apostolate, and in the main is still working with a cessationist perspective. However, it is a church that has never been short of missionary endeavors.

Although many of the Renewal groups that I have mentioned have a strong sense of their denominational identity, it is also fair to say that many of them are self-consciously Evangelical/Charismatic first. Therefore if something is seen to be biblical they will often espouse it even if it cuts against their denomination's traditional teaching—a good example of this is Presbyterian and Reformed Ministries International's repudiation of Calvin's view, and their incorporation of Charismatic exegesis on Ephesians 4:11–13. As we have seen in this review, many of these groups will look to Evangelical/Charismatic leaders outside their tradition to influence them and help formulate their position. This happens to a much lesser degree in the Roman Catholic and Orthodox Charismatic Movements in the USA.

The Catholic Charismatic Movement had its origins in the USA, and has had a large following there; it has been a movement characterized by openness to other Charismatic communities—whether it be from older denominations or newer expressions of church. There has been some notable interaction between significant independent Charismatics with Catholic Charismatics—notably between the Fort Lauderdale Five, and the Word of God community;[71] more recently between non-Catholic Charismatic "prophet" Rick Joyner and longtime Catholic Charismatic Ralph Martin.[72] Nevertheless, Charismatic observer and historian, Father Peter Hocken offered the following perspective on the matter: "As far as I know, the 5fold ministry issue has hardly surfaced in the Catholic Charismatic renewal";[73] "the idea that such charismatic apostles are for today is just not being discussed in CCR (Catholic Charismatic Renewal)."[74] Hocken's perspective was confirmed by the current executive director of the National Service Committee of the Catholic Charismatic Renewal USA, Walter Matthews, who informed me that there was no one he was aware of who was teaching the five-fold ministry within Catholic Renewal circles. He was clear that some might function in the kind of gift that Wagner and others ascribe to "apostles" but that term would never be used due to their understanding of apostolic succession.[75]

It has often been noted that of all the different churches that have encountered the Charismatic Movement, one of the staunchest opponents has been the Orthodox Church. Yet it too has been affected in places by the Pentecostal Charismatic Movement.[76] Father Eusebius Stephanou has been an outspoken advocate of Orthodox Charismatic church Renewal, finding justification for his Pentecostal perspective in the writings of St Symeon the New Theologian. He told me that the restoration of the five-fold ministry was not prominent in Orthodox Renewal and that it was not realistic under the current system of church administration.[77] As with the

71. For both the history of the Catholic Charismatic Movement in the USA and information about its links with other Charismatic Movements see Hocken, "Charismatic Movement," 481–87.

72. Thanks to Peter Hocken for the information about contact happening between Martin and Joyner. It is worth mentioning that there is not the same cordiality between Wagner and Catholic Charismatics as there was between Wimber and the Catholic Charismatic Renewal. This is undoubtedly due to Wagner's sustained attack on the Catholics' veneration of Mary which was given much exposure due to his galvanizing of a concerted intercessory "warfare" against "the Queen of heaven."

73. Peter Hocken, e-mail message to author, September 9, 2007.

74. Peter Hocken, e-mail message to author, September 28, 2009.

75. Walter Matthews, telephone conversation with author, November 3, 2009. Significantly, the Catholic Charismatic Renewal does not seem to have bought into the language used at Vatican II in describing the laity as "apostles."

76. A notable pocket is the Renewal movement associated with Father Iosif Trifa who founded "The Lord's Army" in Transylvania—it actually started before the Charismatic Movement, but has had a "revivalistic" impulse that has not been thwarted despite persecution. See J. Brown, "Divisions."

77. Father Eusebius Stephanou, telephone conversation with author, October 21, 2009.

Catholics in the USA, it appears that talk of "charismatic apostles" is not in the vocabulary of Orthodox Renewal. However, he did see a direct correlation between missionary work and apostolic ministry which is universally recognized by the Orthodox Church.[78]

In summary, there is a conscious effort by many denominational Charismatics to see the charismatic apostolate operate within the structures that are already in place; some, like the Charismatic Episcopalians, see it as naturally suited to the episcopate; others recognize elements of the charism within their church but cannot embrace the present popular conceptions due to their own established categories (Roman Catholic and Orthodox). Many denominational charismatic apostolate advocates are avoiding charismatic apostolate language whilst promoting Renewal and the various charisms to make their message more palatable (e.g., Holy Spirit Renewal Ministry within the Baptist Church). Nevertheless, high profile independent Charismatic speakers who are advocating apostles today are impacting those involved with the Pentecostal Charismatic Movement in most denominational churches with that message.

Independent Charismatic Churches/ Neo-Apostolic Churches/Modern Independent Pentecostal Churches: USA

> According to David B. Barrett, author of the *World Christian Encyclopedia*, contemporary Christianity has experienced an explosion of what he calls "neo-apostolic" movements. Distinct from traditional Protestants, and numbering about 400 million Christians in 20,000 "movements," neo-apostolic believers "reject historical denominationalism and restrictive or overbearing central authority."

In Barrett's estimate they will constitute 581 million members by the year 2025, *120 million more than all Protestant movements*. In two decades these sectarian movements will outnumber Orthodox and Protestant Christians and be almost half the size of worldwide Catholicism."[79]

A Roman Catholic writer, relying on Barrett's statistics, commented concerning independent Charismatic churches: "We can't simply dismiss

---

78. Father Eusebius Stephanou, e-mail message to author, September 28, 2009.
79. Clendenin, "Journey."

these people, no matter how uncomfortable they make us. For one thing, the United States is the Western epicenter of Independent Christianity. There are some 80 million Independent Christians in this country. They are, by far, the largest bloc (as opposed to denomination) of Christians."[80]

If Barrett's estimations are to be believed, independent Charismatic Christianity will become the second mega-bloc in world Christianity after the Roman Catholic Church. The main hallmarks of these Independent Charismatic churches are that they have begun recently; Donald Miller in categorizing this group identifies them as having started post-1950,[81] and being unconnected to an older church. A number of these independent churches have been active in church planting—a classic example being John Wimber's Vineyard Association of churches.

Dr Peter Wagner has named this movement of churches and networks associated with this mega-bloc the "New Apostolic Reformation" (NAR). He contends that the New Apostolic Reformation

> is an extraordinary work of God at the close of the twentieth century, that is, to a significant extent, changing the shape of Protestant Christianity around the world. For almost 500 years Christian churches have largely functioned within traditional denominational structures of one kind or another. Particularly in the 1990s, but having roots going back for almost a century, new forms and operational procedures are now emerging in areas such as local church government, interchurch relationships, financing, evangelism, missions, prayer, leadership selection and training, the role of supernatural power, worship and other important aspects of church life. Some of these changes are being seen within denominations themselves, but for the most part they are taking the form of loosely structured apostolic networks. In virtually every region of the world, these new apostolic churches constitute the fastest growing segment of Christianity.[82]

One of the key aspects that Wagner has identified with those churches/networks that fit into the New Apostolic Reformation is the amount of authority invested in a leader rather than an institution: "The biggest difference between New Apostolic Christianity and traditional Christianity is the amount of spiritual authority delegated by the Holy Spirit to individuals. . . . In traditional Christianity, authority resided in groups such

---

80. Weddell, "Challenge."
81. See Miller's categories in Rowell, "New Apostolic Reformation."
82. Wagner, "New Apostolic Churches."

as church councils, sessions, congregations, and general assemblies. New Apostolic Christianity sees God entrusting the government of the church to individuals."[83]

In America, it is a movement that has stressed the ministries of "so-called" apostles. Although there are exceptions[84] most groups associated with the "New Apostolic Reformation" do advocate present-day apostles. For many involved in this movement, the Post-denominational symposium of 1996 at Fuller organized by Wagner was a watershed mark when those present affirmed the ongoing ministry of apostles as being a valid "office" in the church today. Bill Hamon referred to it as a

> historical occasion in God's annals of Church history . . . prophetically orchestrated by the Holy Spirit. . . . Numerous denominational representatives were present with many delegates from other nations. The consensus of the panelists was that there are still apostles and prophets in the Church, and that there is an emerging Apostolic Movement that will revolutionize the 21st-century Church.[85]

Although a participant in the conference told me that there were some present that were more Evangelical than Charismatic, having reviewed the list of participants, the people I recognized were all involved in the Pentecostal Charismatic Movement (e.g., Bill Hamon, John Kelly, Ted Haggard).[86]

According to John Rowell, "Dr. Wagner estimates that in the US alone there are as many NAR (New Apostolic Reformation) churches as there are Southern Baptist congregations—something approaching 40,000."[87] Vinson Synan is very skeptical of Wagner's grouping these growing churches under this new heading "New Apostolic Reformation," as he sees them as fundamentally Pentecostal/Charismatic and flowing from that movement, rather than anything distinctively new. He wrote,

---

83. Wagner, "New Apostolic Reformation."

84. For example Bill Hybels is categorized as an apostolic leader by Wagner, but Hybels does not view himself in that light nor espouse a Restorationist paradigm.

85. Hamon, *Apostles*, 10. Having seen who was on the Panel it does not surprise me that they came to this conclusion.

86. Thanks to Nancy Gower of Fuller who provided me with the list of speakers and other helpful information about the event. Nancy Gower, e-mail message to author, March 13, 2009.

87. J. Rowell, "New Apostolic Reformation."

It seems that most of these networks were planted and inspired by the Pentecostal/Charismatic Movement in the first place since almost all of them operate in the gifts of the Spirit. Most of them were previously listed as "denominational Pentecostals" by David Barrett until his *New World Christian Encyclopedia* (2000) began to designate them as "neo-Charismatic." Rather than being part of a "New Apostolic Reformation," most of them are actually part of the "Pentecostal/Charismatic reformation." It seems that Wagner has tried to impose a new title for movements that were already dynamic churches originally inspired by the Pentecostals and to create an artificial apostolic structure with himself as "presiding apostle."[88]

I think Synan is in the main correct in his assessment, however, Wagner is right in recognizing something new within that stream that is self-consciously more embracing of apostles and prophets. Synan thinks that Wagner has vastly over emphasized the phenomenon and sees it as insignificant and only really affecting the independent Charismatic sector.[89] He is right in that the majority who are associating with Wagner are from independent Charismatic churches, but wrong in his estimation of Wagner and the New Apostolic Reformation's influence. From talking to those involved in Charismatic Renewal within some of the older churches they clearly have an ear to what is happening, and are taking on board ideas from Wagner and those associated with Wagner's New Apostolic Reformation (e.g., see my earlier section on both Lutheran and Baptist Renewal in the USA). The personalities associated with it such as Bill Johnson are influential across the board in the Pentecostal Charismatic Movement and Wagner's views are percolating into a number of denominational settings not only independent churches. Many of these New Apostolic Reformation churches have become household names in Christian circles due to their popularity.[90]

Notable prominent independent churches and ministries exerting a wide influence not only in the USA but internationally as well[91] are the

---

88. This was an article entitled "Apostolic Practice" that Professor Synan contributed to an Assemblies of God publication on Apostolic Ministry published in 2004. Professor Synan forwarded the article onto me via e-mail, October 27, 2009.

89. Vinson Synan, telephone conversation with author, December 15, 2009.

90. Examples of this would be T. D. Jakes' Potter's House Church or Joel Osteen's Lakewood Church.

91. One only has to have access to Christian satellite television to get an appreciation of how influential these churches and ministries are.

PART ONE—Where We Are

Toronto Airport Fellowship Church;[92] the churches associated with MorningStar ministries;[93] Mike Bickle's International House of Prayer (IHOP) movement;[94] and Bill Johnson's Bethel Church in California. According to Rev Frank Billman who works with Aldersgate Renewal Ministries (an organization promoting Renewal in the United Methodist Church), all of these churches and ministries are seen as epicenters for Charismatics in the USA.[95] It is noteworthy that John Wimber's influence has been felt in each of these circles. Toronto Airport Fellowship Church was originally part of the Vineyard; Kansas City Fellowship where Bickle was senior pastor became part of the Vineyard for a number of years; although Bethel was part of Assemblies of God, Bill Johnson had attended a John Wimber conference in 1987 on Signs and Wonders which affected him profoundly.[96] Toronto Airport Fellowship Church, MorningStar, International House of Prayer and Bethel have all advocated the five-fold ministry and promoted the idea of modern apostles and prophets. For those involved with them it is a non-issue, viewed as accepted Scriptural teaching. These type of churches/ministries, according to Wagner, incorporate apostles into their leadership structure—sometimes they do this overtly, other times discreetly, and other times not even recognizing that that is what they are doing.[97]

The Vineyard would be an example of a network of Charismatic churches that although classified as part of the New Apostolic Reformation are reticent about some of the emphases about "apostles" that have emerged. During a sizeable period of his ministry Wimber joined forces with the Kansas City Prophets who were looking for the rise of "apostles and prophets." According to Clifford Hill, Wimber embraced this teaching.[98] If Hill is correct—and the evidence he collates points that way—this embracing was short lived as Wimber categorically repudiated this per-

92. Home of the now infamous "Toronto Blessing."

93. Rick Joyner is the influential leader of this ministry.

94. IHOP stands for International House of Prayer and has as its founder Mike Bickle who previously headed up the Kansas City Fellowship. For more information see International House of Prayer, "International."

95. Frank Billman, telephone conversation with author, November 3, 2009.

96. Johnson, *Heaven*, 88.

97. Examples of these different types can be seen in his book, *The New Apostolic Churches*. A notable example of one who contributes to the book who does not see himself as an "apostle" and refrains from using that kind of terminology in regards to church leadership is Bill Hybel, leader of Willow Creek.

98. Hill, "Here Today," 200–201.

spective after the "marriage" ended.[99] According to Bill Jackson it was at the 1995 Pastor's Conference in Anaheim that Wimber told the leaders "that he regretted leading the Vineyard into the prophetic era";[100] Wimber was wary of the Latter Rain emphases[101] that were coming through via Bob Jones, Paul Cain, and Mike Bickle. Don Williams (co-worker with Wimber in the Vineyard, and one of that movement's most recognized theologians) believed that there was a clear attempt by the Kansas City folk to make Wimber into an apostle, which was another reason for the tension between them. Apparently, Wimber "personally rejected all attempts to make him one" and said "that he would only accept the title if the Lord himself told him and he never did."[102] John Wimber became very suspicious of talk about the "office" of apostle. Nevertheless, Wimber did believe Ephesians 4:11–13 predicted that apostolic "functions" (Wimber did not like people talking about the office of apostle, rather he talked about someone having an apostolic function) would continue in the church until it reached maturity in the faith, and therefore was keen that the church encouraged that function alongside the other three/four mentioned in those verses. Wimber admits that "Ephesians 4:11–16 has been foundational for the ministry of the Vineyard since its inception." He further states, "It lies at the very heart of our emphasis on equipping and releasing the Body to do the works and words of Jesus."[103]

Wimber's understanding of a modern charismatic apostolate was governed by his conviction that it was of a different order to the twelve apostles and Paul's authoritative ministries, and that people who were so gifted should not be thought of as apostles. Wimber indicated this distinction by using capitalization: there are no Apostles today (with a big "A" to suggests an authoritative "office") but there are "apostles" (with a small "a"), who were akin to missionaries and church planters. He wrote:

> While I believe there is lower-case apostolic ministry today, 1. I don't presume that they are going to displace the leaders of existing ecclesiastical structures today; 2. I don't believe any of them will write a new Bible or communicate anything equal

---

99. For a helpful description of the interaction between KCF and Vineyard including their parting of the ways see Jackson, *Quest*, chaps. 13 and 19.

100. Ibid., 234.

101. One of the Latter Rain emphases was looking for the new thing that God was doing; Wimber reacted against this declaring that God was not doing anything new, "only drawing attention to facets of the old." Ibid., 246.

102. Don Williams, e-mail message to author, February 6, 2008.

103. Wimber, "Five-Fold," 11.

> with Scripture since the canon is complete . . . 3. I also don't see them ruling or usurping power or even influence over the whole church (Rev. 4:9–11), and finally 4. I believe the purview of the apostolic function today is the same as in the New Testament: to win souls, make disciples and plant, nurture and set things right in churches over which they have spiritual authority.[104]

He actively discouraged the Vineyard from embracing the Latter Rain beliefs that a "super-breed of Apostle" were to emerge in the church and was against anyone being titled an "Apostle."[105] Even though Wimber had these views, a number who were his disciples and close associates have been instrumental in advocating what Wimber called Apostles with a big "A"—most notably, Peter Wagner.

The independent Charismatic sector does not have a united viewpoint on what type of apostle/Apostle (to borrow Wimber's use of capitalization) is still being given to the church, but the evidence suggests that it is a settled conviction that Christ is still giving them.

Another Noteworthy Independent Stream: House Church

At this point it is worth highlighting an increasingly noticeable independent movement associated with Gene Edwards[106] and Frank Viola. They have been attempting to recover a purer expression of the Christian faith devoid of all the trappings, as they perceive it, of tradition and paganism that they see pervading older forms of church whether that be Orthodox, Roman Catholic or Protestant. It is a movement that owes much to Watchman Nee's nuanced organic Brethren, higher-life ecclesiology. Nee was committed to the charismatic apostolate, and they were fundamental to the spread of his Little Flock movement.[107] Although critical of how Nee's Little Flocks had developed in China, and also of Nee's co-worker Witness Lee's "local churches," Edwards has championed Nee's anti-denominationalism and organic view of the church. Although his teaching

104. Ibid., 6.

105. Information gained from Jackson, *Quest*, and John Mumford, the head of Vineyard UK, telephone interview with author, September 15, 2009.

106. He is described by the Tyndale website as "one of America's most beloved Christian authors." http://www.tyndale.com/authors/authorbio.asp?id=184, accessed December 8, 2010.

107. See fuller discussion of Nee and the charismatic apostolate on 161–2.

on the House church was emerging at the same time as the Shepherding movement, he never joined forces with them and was very critical of the authoritarian concepts inherent within their teaching.[108] Edwards sees the apostle, or church planter, as fundamental to the development of the local church. Ephesians 4:11–13 is the key text for Edwards to support his view that there can be modern day apostles/church planters. One of his disciples, Frank Viola, has built upon Edwards' vision and his material unpacks further Edwards' ideas. Viola has become increasingly acceptable in emerging church circles and is now making waves further abroad with his influential book, *Pagan Christianity*, recently re-released and co-authored with George Barna (of church growth fame). He does not appear as exclusivist as Edwards or Lee, but is equally denouncing of "institutional" Christianity. His work is well informed with frequent references to reputable scholars; nevertheless, his writing betrays an obvious bias toward house churches and perpetuates a "blue print" pattern ecclesiology[109] even though he tries not to do so. Viola contends that when the church is allowed to form in an organic manner under the headship of Jesus Christ, these ministries will emerge in time; however, since most of Christendom and even the New Apostolic Churches do not operate in this fashion, New Testament apostles have not been emerging.[110] Nevertheless, he clearly sees himself as being a part of a New Testament styled church, and has been instrumental in founding this type of house church, which begs the question whether he sees himself as an apostle.

Viola rejects as unbiblical any ossification of this function into a titled position, and is critical of any apostleship that diminishes the "headship" of Christ—in his opinion, that happens when someone leads a meeting or a church. He is opposed to any clergy/laity division and argues for an organic conception of church rather than an "institutional" one. In his exegesis of 1 Corinthians 12:13–14 Viola comments:

> Paul is saying that within the scope of church building, the apostle's ministry is the most fundamental. That's because apostles give birth to the church and sustain it during its prenatal development. Apostles break the ground and plant the seed of ekklesia. Since apostles lay the foundation of the church, they're also ranked first (chronologically) in the work of church

---

108. For a helpful view of Edwards' ecclesiology and indebtedness to Nee see Lie, "Ecclesiology."

109. Normative church life for Viola is based on 1 Corinthians 12–14. For some insightful criticisms of Viola's views see A. Rowell, "Pagan Christianity."

110. See Viola, "Rethinking."

building (Rom. 15:19–20; 1 Cor. 3:10; Eph. 2:20). Significantly, while apostles are placed first in the church-building scheme, they rank last in the eyes of the world (Matt. 20:16; 1 Cor. 4:9).[111]

To summarize, we find in the Independent Charismatic sector a diversity of views, some happily embracing both title and office of apostle (prominent amongst independent New Apostolic Reformation churches), others wary of such, preferring to focus on the function yet still at home in using apostolic terminology (e.g., Vineyard, house church). Yet all agree that Ephesians 4:11–13 justifies their belief in an ongoing charismatic apostolate.

Conclusion

From this survey it can be seen that Apostles/apostles and A(a)postolic ministry is firmly on the agenda in the independent Charismatic churches, the Pentecostal denominations and has made substantial inroads into the Charismatic contingents in the mainstream Protestant churches. Although not affecting the *opus operandi* of the Catholic Charismatic Renewal and the Orthodox Renewal movement, they themselves are both aware of five-fold ministry, and whilst not embracing it are content to recognize Charismatic apostolic ministries but by a different name. The proliferation of Charismatic views on ministry has been spread far and wide through Christian television, radio, books and publications like *Charisma*. The understanding of apostolic ministry and apostles differs from group to group, but the underlying conviction that Christ is still giving apostles to the church would appear to be the majority view within the Charismatic sector in the USA.

How important the apostolic has become within Charismatic circles can be seen from the results of a meeting convened in 2004 amongst a "who's who"[112] of Pentecostal/Charismatic leaders which addressed the subject of the five-fold ministry head on. The event was chaired by respected and influential pastor, Jack Hayford. Its stated objective was "to promote relational harmony and ministerial partnership" in "light of the current misgivings concerning the awakening and release of the five-fold minis-

---

111. Viola, *Reimagining*, 285–86.

112. Those present included: Jack Hayford, Reinhard Bonnke, Peter Wagner, R. T. Kendall, Joyce Meyer, Rick Joyner, Bill Hamon, John Bevere, Cindy Jacobs, Keith Butler, Rod Parsley, Ted Haggard, and Myles Munroe—amongst many others. See anonymous, "Ministries Today Update."

Apostles Today: USA

tries in the Charismatic/Pentecostal movement." As a result of their meeting, they have seen "six distinct areas of general agreement."[113] The most pertinent, in relation to this study, were the following two: "Continuation of the Fivefold Ministries: We affirm that there is an ongoing post-New Testament activity of the charismata of 1 Corinthians 12, as well as the ministries of the pastor, teacher and evangelist described in Ephesians 4. Therefore, it would naturally follow that we affirm the ongoing post-New Testament activity of apostles and prophets."

They also affirmed "that, while all of the fivefold ministries have been active since their bestowal by the ascended Christ, that the last thirty years has evidenced an increase of apostolic and prophetic ministry, resulting in substantive growth of the church in the developing world and a resulting influence on the Charismatic church in the United States and Europe."[114]

This is a remarkable consensus amongst leaders who are not all actively in partnership with Wagner, and highlights how mainstream the five-fold ministry is in Charismatic circles in the USA. The perception is that this gift is widely needed. The General Editor of Charisma, Dr J. Lee Grady, confirmed this in an e-mail (October 6, 2009) to me, "There are MANY Charismatic/Pentecostal/Renewal groups in the US that believe apostles are needed today to pioneer and advance the work of church planting, missionary activity and missions." What happens in America has huge repercussions upon other parts of the world in the religious sphere as well as in the economic; therefore, trends we find there often arrive on these shores too, and therefore it is a vital scene to be aware of in considering the future of the charismatic apostolate in Britain. Whether the British church scene emulates the American one is what will be looked at in the next chapter.

---

113. Ministries Today Symposium, "Orlando Statement."
114. Ibid.

2

Apostles Today

Britain

INTRODUCTION

BRITAIN HAS HISTORICALLY HAD its share of titled "apostles" with the Catholic Apostolic Church, the Apostolic Church, the radical House Church movement and today's apostolic networks. Although Britain and the USA have marked differences, many of the same currents, trends, and cultural shifts that have happened on the American side of the Atlantic have occurred on the British side too. Therefore, it is unsurprising that the increased attention given to apostles in the USA is finding a similar expression in the different sectors of the church in Britain. As in America, Evangelicals and Charismatics are often more in tune with the latest Evangelical or Charismatic fad and opinion then their own denominational view. They will often go to interdenominational Charismatic or Evangelical conferences, read and listen to Evangelical/Charismatic speakers online or via satellite or radio and use material from flagship Evangelical or Charismatic churches. Before looking at the different groupings of churches, it is important to highlight certain trends that are affecting Evangelicals and Charismatics of all churchmanships; whether it is through gift courses, or books on leadership, the word about apostles and apostolic ministry is being propagated amongst Charismatics and Evangelicals of all stripes across Britain.

One of the most recent "successful" initiatives aiming to help churches grow qualitatively has been Christian Schwarz' Natural Church Development. Schwarz has purposefully moved away from the numerical emphasis of the Church Growth Movement and focused on qualitative growth—which (in his opinion) inevitably leads to numerical growth. His organization has done extensive research across the world looking at the principles which lead to a healthy church and showed the importance of being "gift-oriented."

Schwarz's finding has been reflected in a popular development within the British church, which appears to be the same in the USA, of spiritual gift inventories being utilized in many Evangelical churches. At my London church (Anglican/Charismatic/Evangelical), at theological college in Cambridge (conservative to Liberal Evangelical), in a church placement in Hampshire (Anglican/Conservative Evangelical), and at my current place of worship in Guildford (conservative to Liberal Evangelical) differing gift courses (Bodywork; Network; LifeShapes; SHAPE) were used to enable people to discern their spiritual gifts and talents. All four of these courses were not self-consciously Pentecostal as there was no teaching focused on "baptism in the Spirit"; nevertheless, all of them incorporated all the gifts and ministries of the Spirit mentioned in Romans 12, 1 Corinthians 12, and Ephesians 4. It surprised me to find the Conservative Evangelical church in Hampshire running LifeShapes which majors on Ephesians 4:11–13 as being central to discovering one's "base ministry," one of which is that of "apostle." When I quizzed the incumbent on this he was very comfortable with the interpretation the author gave on the matter and seemed convinced by it. How widespread these courses are is beyond the remit of this study; they are not universally used by Evangelical churches as some have misgivings about them. Nevertheless, the fact that I have unintentionally come into contact with these courses in four different places in England in a variety of Evangelical churchmanships indicates that they are common. Furthermore, three of these four courses are linked to very influential churches. LifeShapes was originally limited to discipleship training at St Thomas Crookes, Sheffield, under Mike Breen; it has now become an international phenomenon due to its mass publication and promotion in the USA and Britain. Likewise, numerous churches which look to Willow Creek as a model and resource church have incorporated their Network gift course. Then there is the SHAPE[1] course that is linked

---

1. Rees, *S.H.A.P.E.* "SHAPE" stands for "Spiritual gifts, Heart, Abilities, Personality, Experience."

PART ONE—Where We Are

to Rick Warren's hugely popular books, *The Purpose Driven Life* and *The Purpose Driven Church*.[2] C. Peter Wagner's series on spiritual gifts has also been popular, and it was an integral feature of his Church Growth material which was highly influential both in the States and Britain.

A sample of these courses will highlight how the "gift of apostle" is being presented. It is, in my opinion, interesting (and telling?) that the controversy surrounding the topic is not mentioned at all—it is taken as a given that this charism is operative today. Bodywork: this was a course specifically designed and developed at St Barnabas Kensington under the leadership of Reverend John Irvine. In the description of apostleship the author writes the following: "The special ability given by the Holy Spirit to initiate new Churches or ministry projects to extend the mission of God in Christ. . . . People with this gift are pioneers, are flexible and able to adapt to different people and situations, and are concerned with extending God's work to unreached people."[3]

The biblical references given to help explain this gift were 1 Corinthians 12:28–29; Ephesians 4:11–12; Romans 1:5; and Acts 13:2–3.[4]

In the LifeShapes *Passionate Life Workbook*, the apostle is described in the following way: "An apostle is one who is 'sent out.' Apostles are visionary and pioneering, always pushing into new territory. They like to establish new churches or ministries. They come up with new, innovative means to do kingdom work. They enjoy dreaming, doing new and challenging tasks. Paul is a good biblical example of an apostle. Words that describe someone with this ministry role would include: excites, envisions, challenges, bridges. Apostles make good entrepreneurs and explorers."[5]

According to SHAPE:

> Apostleship: The God-given special ability to serve and strengthen the body of Christ by launching and leading new ministry ventures that advance God's purposes and expand his kingdom. The original Greek meaning of the word is "sent one" (literally, one sent with authority, or as an ambassador. People with this gift . . .

---

2. Other influential materials are C. Peter Wagner's series on spiritual gifts, and the material connected to Christian Schwarz' Natural Church Development.

3. Bodywork seminar notes, 21. The course was developed at St Barnabas Church specifically for use there.

4. Ibid.

5. Breen and Kallestad, *Workbook*, 56.

- Are driven to start new endeavors for God, most often churches.
- Often welcome risky new challenges.
- Enjoy making a difference in the lives of believers and unbelievers alike.
- Are eager to be known as ambassadors for Christ in the world.
- Willingly work hard to see churches reach their full potential for God.[6]

Willow Creek's Network Course states: "The gift of Apostleship is the divine ability to start and oversee the development of new churches or ministry structures." It lists the "Distinctives" of this gift in the following way:

> Pioneer and establish new ministries or churches. . . . Adapt to different surroundings by being culturally sensitive and aware. . . . Desire to minister to unreached people in other communities or countries. . . . Have responsibilities to oversee ministries or groups of churches. . . . Demonstrate authority and vision for the mission of the church. The traits of such a person are: Adventurous, Entrepreneurial, Persevering, Adaptable, Culturally sensitive, Risk-taking, Cause-driven.[7]

The references given to support these ideas are "1 Corinthians 12:28–29; Ephesians 4:11–12; Romans 1:5; Acts 13:2–3."[8]

Church leadership books have also been drawing attention to the charismatic apostolate. On top of Charismatic/Pentecostal publications, there are well-regarded Evangelical publishers such as InterVarsity Press, Hendrickson, Paternoster, and Grove that have released positive books on the subject. The writers are from a variety of denominational backgrounds, yet they are all Evangelical and writing primarily for that audience. Professor Eddie Gibbs has argued, in an InterVarsity Press publication, for a shift in how we do mission, and the desperate need for "apostolic leadership."[9] Frost and Hirsch, in a Hendrickson publication, contend that the Western church mobilize and train a new "apostolic" type of leader. They believe that this is demanded theologically and sociologically, and the church

---

6. Rees, *S.H.A.P.E.*, 38–39.

7. Bugbee et al., *Network*, 74.

8. Ibid.

9. E.g., Gibbs, *Leadership Next*, 20: "The church of the twenty-first century needs missional thinkers and apostolic leadership."

PART ONE—Where We Are

must embrace this change for the sake of her mission: "The issue of the development of a new kind of leadership is possibly the single most important question of strategy in this decade, and whether the church responds correctly or not will determine to some extent its survival as a viable expression of the gospel in years to come."[10]

The Anabaptist Stuart Murray-Williams in a Paternoster book has argued that we are in a Post-Christendom society, and therefore share features with the Pre-Christendom world when Christianity was not established; as a result it is imperative that we rethink how we are church in this day and age.[11] As part of this he has argued for the inclusion and embracing of the gift of apostle, seeing it as essential for the church in order to metamorphosize into a missional church: "The recovery of apostles, prophets and evangelists (in Christendom only pastors and teachers were recognized) is critical for the emergence of a missional church. These neglected gifts must be restored if churches are to be healthy and properly balanced."[12] Martin Garner, a Church Army Officer, has made an impassioned plea for apostles today in a Grove booklet arguing that the "first stage in pioneering mission is not a programme, a structure, or a plan but a person—a person called an apostle."[13] He concludes his booklet with a prayer "for the release of God's pioneers to lead a new wave of advancement in the cause of Christ in this country," and states that "we need many more apostles to be raised up and released if this nation is going to be reached again with the amazingly good news of Jesus Christ."[14] The fact that these highly regarded publishers, which are taken note of by Evangelicals of all colors, are publishing these works shows the increasing acceptability of talk about apostles and apostolic leadership.

One interesting development that has its roots within the radical House Church movement which involves Charismatic leaders from across the churches is Gerald Coates' Charismatic Evangelical Round Table—privately it is known as "the apostolic and prophetic forum."[15] Initially this was a meeting called together by Coates for those who were the "Restora-

10. Frost and Hirsch, *Shaping*, 165.

11. Murray-Williams, *Post-Christendom*.

12. Ibid., 89. Murray is quick to point out, though, that the way in which these gifts are manifested will determine their effectiveness.

13. Garner, *Apostles Today*, 3.

14. Ibid., 27.

15. Coates, "Growing," 9. This whole concept of the "round table" seems quite a popular one in Prophetic groups, and is a regular feature in the USA Prophetic movement.

Apostles Today: Britain

tion" leaders who had fallen out previously; over time it grew to include significant Charismatic and Evangelical leaders from a variety of differing church backgrounds. It currently meets twice a year and offers opportunity for those present to share what they perceive God has been doing—the likes of Sandy Millar, Nicky Gumbel, Stuart Bell and Colin Urquhart have been present at these occasions.[16] So it is a mixture of people from old and new churches; however, a significant omission so far has been the presence of a Roman Catholic leader; nevertheless, Gerald Coates did indicate to me that this might change and he had in mind one particularly significant Catholic Charismatic lay leader whom he might invite.[17] These developments within the Charismatic and Evangelical sector of the British church are furthering a cause that is becoming more common in various Historic Pentecostal churches, Denominational Charismatic churches, and in Independent Charismatic churches/networks.

HISTORIC PENTECOSTAL DENOMINATIONS: UK

According to statistician Rob Powys Smith,[18] the following are currently the largest groups of Pentecostal churches in Britain: "1) Assemblies of God; 2) Elim Pentecostal; 3) New Testament Church of God; 4) Apostolic Church; 5) Church of God of Prophecy."[19] All of these denominations were formed pre-1950, and although sharing similar DNA to one another have developed their own understandings of the charismatic apostolate.

Elim is and has always been committed to the full range of gifts and ministries of the Holy Spirit; their commitment to this is highlighted on their website: "We believe in the ministries that Christ has set in His Church, namely, apostles, prophets, evangelists, pastors and teachers and in the present operation of the manifold Gifts of the Holy Spirit according to the New Testament."[20] Influential Elim Pastor, Colin Dye, has written and spoken on this topic. Dye himself is viewed as an apostle by many; I

---

16. Gerald Coates, interview with author, September 1, 2009, and Coates, "Growing."

17. Gerald Coates, interview with author, September 1, 2009. I never asked whether any Orthodox leaders were ever present or had been invited, but as they do not seem to have any notable Charismatic figures in the limelight in Britain at the moment, I would imagine not.

18. He is the Research Executive at Christian Research.

19. Rob Powys Smith, e-mail message to author, August 10, 2009.

20. Elim UK, "What We Believe."

PART ONE—Where We Are

happened to be present at a meeting where Bill Hamon prophesied Dye into an apostolic ministry. His commitment to the five-fold ministry is central—according to an advert for his International Bible Institute of London, Dye's "heart is to see the fivefold ministry releasing the church to fulfil their potential in Christ."[21] Within Elim as a whole there has not been much shifting from their original stance which was set in opposition to the Apostolic Church's view that apostles were integral to the local church and should be titled. The present superintendent John Glass explained the current view in this way:

> Elim churches would recognize the contemporary role of Apostle as those who plant churches and oversee them. We have five Regional Leaders who each oversee around a hundred churches in the UK and we would recognize an apostolic ministry in them. I have planted three churches during my forty years of ministry and have overall responsibility for the 550 churches in our denomination. My role would be seen as apostolic.... What we do not do is append titles to individuals as we deem that function is more important than office.[22]

I enquired of Glass whether Elim had felt any pressure to change their stance in light of Wagner's New Apostolic Reformation, to which he replied "No."[23] Even though there is antipathy within Elim to people calling themselves "apostles," it is well known that there are two individuals that have often been referred to as apostles by Elim generally: George Jeffreys and Percy Brewster.[24] Nevertheless, Elim UK has not officially shifted from the views it inherited from its forefathers.

The New Testament Church of God is part of the Church of God, Cleveland and the Church of God of Prophecy that split from it; as a result their doctrinal positions are in accord with that church. This was confirmed in discussion with a New Testament Church of God minister in the UK who told me that there was an interesting ambiguity in their thinking as they recognized and encouraged the function but did not have a set position in the church for charismatic apostles,[25] which was the same situation I had encountered with Church of God, Cleveland.

---

21. Taken from a full-page advert on the back of *Christianity* magazine, August 2009.
22. John Glass, e-mail message to author, August 21, 2009.
23. John Glass, e-mail message to author, August 25, 2009.
24. Neil Hudson, Pentecostal scholar, discussion with author, October 13, 2009.
25. Anonymous NTCG minister, telephone conversation with author, October

In Assemblies of God UK there is general agreement, based upon their statement of faith, that apostles are still being given today. According to David Petts, "In practice we have always believed in apostles today, although have sometimes been hesitant in recognizing them. Nevertheless there has been more talk in recent years of the need for apostolic ministry today and although opinions vary there is certainly general agreement as to the existence of these important gifts in our churches."[26]

As a result the Assemblies of God in Britain seem perfectly content to speak of their National leader as having been "a pastor and apostolic leader."[27] And their casual reference to Ephesians 4:7–16 highlights their historic commitment to the five-fold ministry.[28] In comparison the Apostolic Church has always had apostles as a central feature of their denomination and there has been no change in this regard; there is a specific office of apostle within their church structure, and they are viewed as the highest authority within the church.[29]

In summary, the influence of the New Apostolic Reformation appears less in the Pentecostal sector in Britain than in the USA, nevertheless, aside from the Apostolics, where it has always been majored on, historic Pentecostal churches have started to think and speak more about this ministry.

Historic Denominational Charismatics: UK

The historic churches which embraced Charismatic Renewal have had a mixed relationship with the five-fold cause. This is undoubtedly due to a more positive view of the church's history and traditions than that held by their Restorationist brethren who believed that the church had been falling away from the pristine structures of the New Testament and had incorporated ungodly traditions and structures. Renewalists did not see church history like that and were open to the idea that God might be

---

21, 2009.

26. David Petts was Principal of Mattersey Hall, the Assemblies of God Bible College, for 27 years, and for 20 years the Chairman of its Executive Council. He e-mailed this to me on August 25, 2009.

27. A description of John Partington, national leader of Assemblies of God. Quote taken from Assemblies of God UK, "Meet the Leaders."

28. Assemblies of God UK, "Statement of Faith": "We believe in the operation of the gifts of the Holy Spirit and the gifts of Christ in the Church today (1 Cor. 12:4–11, 28; Eph. 4:7–16)."

29. For more information on the Apostolic Church see chap. 4.

Part One—Where We Are

behind some of the developments that occurred which were not contra apostolic teaching and practice. As a result, within England debate about modern apostles was particularly played out between those involved in the Anglican Renewal and those who were part of the House Church Movement. *Renewal* magazine set forth the arguments from a typical Renewalist perspective, that of the then Anglican Michael Harper, and a Restorationist one, that of Terry Virgo. All of this being debated amongst those who argued that Charismatics should "come out" of the corrupted structures, and those who thought they should stay and reform them.[30] Influential figures involved in the Anglican Renewal movement opposed the House Church theology of apostles, arguing on the basis of church history as well as Scripture.[31] Nevertheless, Anglicans Tony Higton and Gilbert Kirby challenged the historic church to consider the strengths of the House Church movement, particularly its emphasis on apostles, and made a case for incorporating apostles into Church of England structures.[32] Alongside this, there was an influential book on spiritual gifts written by a Baptist pastor, Donald Bridge, and a lay Anglican, David Phypers, which made a strong Scriptural case for the continuation of a charismatic apostolic office.[33]

More recently the New Wine network has been significant in promoting the five-fold ministry. It is interesting to note that Kay believes that David Pytches (the founder of New Wine) and John Coles (the present leader of New Wine) lead in an "apostolic capacity"[34] through this network. There are books by influential Charismatic Anglicans—Mike Breen, David Pytches and John Peters—all of which promote apostleship today. The idea of charismatic apostles working in the mainstream churches has been given more credence through the influence of St Thomas Crooke's LifeShapes Material, as well as a recent Grove publication[35] on the need for

---

30. H. I. Lederle outlines David Watson's criticisms of Restorationist ecclesiology and Arthur Wallis' arguments against remaining in the polluted denominations in *Treasures*, 50–53. In discussions with both Michael Harper (interview with author on September 10, 2009) and John Gunstone (e-mail to author, Jan–Feb 2009), it was clear that amicable relations were always sustained amidst the discussions about issues of ecclesiology.

31. See the articles by Edward England, Clifford Fryer, John Gunstone, and Michael Harper in England et al., "House Church."

32. See *The Challenge of the House Churches* (Oxford: Latimer House, 1988) 16–20.

33. Bridge and Phypers, *Spiritual Gifts*.

34. Kay, *Networks*, 237.

35. Garner, *Apostles Today*.

apostles today, as well as all the "discovering your gifts" courses that have been popular in churches.[36]

One of the most significant and widely read Church of England documents has been *Mission-Shaped Church*. This provided fresh impetus for mission, and challenged the view that there is only one form of church, suggesting that the structure should be flexible for the sake of mission. As a result there was an encouragement to pioneer and support "Fresh Expressions" of church. What was particularly striking was the use of Ephesians 4:11–13. The report said the following: "Ephesians 4 lists Christ-given ministries: apostles, prophets, evangelists, pastors/teachers. Although the term has wider meaning, apostles plant churches. Planting establishes the community from which further apostolic, prophetic, and evangelistic ministry proceeds and which, through pastoring and teaching grows to maturity in Christ."[37]

In so using this passage there is an implicit support for a "charismatic apostolate"; obviously the form of this apostolate was not a replacement to the Anglican bishop as successor to the apostles, but a form of ministry that could run alongside it. Furthermore, the report challenges bishops to own their role as "missionary": "The bishop's role as missionary, focus of unity and guardian of the faith, places him necessarily in a key strategic role.... In council and in synod the bishop leads the Church in its decision making and he licenses ministers. This is a missionary role, necessarily responsive to cultural change."[38]

The report has spurred on the Fresh Expressions movement, and promoted an "apostolic" ministry—the "pioneer" minister. Significantly, Steven Croft, who headed up the Fresh Expressions movement, told me that he was keen to use the title pioneer, rather than apostle so that there was no confusion in regards to who has the apostolic authority within the Church of England—that is, the bishops. It appears that this terminology of "pioneer" minister/ministry is now being accepted and used by a number of different denominations in Britain who have bought into Fresh

36. E.g., Bugbee et al., *Network*, and Rees, *S.H.A.P.E.*

37. Cray et al., *Mission-Shaped Church*, 95.

38. Ibid., 101. An area the report does not consider but which is a reality in other parts of the Anglican Church is the possibility of the bishop being an apostolic church planter. Michael Green records how in "1992 the Archbishop of Lagos consecrated Bishop Emmanuel Nglass to a see with no churches, no clergy and no resources.... Six years later the Diocese of Uyo had twenty congregations, twenty-nine clergy and several thousand communicants. It all began, as in the early days of the church, with Bishop Emmanuel preaching to the people in the town square." Green, *Holy Spirit*, 315–16.

Part One—Where We Are

Expressions. The following groups have climbed on board: "The Church of England; The Methodist Church; The United Reformed Church; The Congregational Federation; Anglican Church Planting Initiatives; Church Army; CMS (Church Missionary Society); The Lambeth Partners and the Lambeth Fund."[39]

Not everyone involved in Fresh Expressions is happy to call church planters and pioneers "apostles," nevertheless, in conversation with the Guildford diocesan director of Mission, Evangelism, and Parish development, Reverend John Gooding, he felt it was appropriate to do so in certain contexts;[40] likewise Dave Male, who is the Fresh Expressions tutor at Anglican training colleges in Cambridge, Ridley Hall and Westcott, believed that was the way many of the pioneer ministers viewed themselves particularly if they had a Charismatic/Evangelical background.[41] Mike Moynagh, a renowned spokesperson on Fresh Expressions, was much more hesitant on equating the two—although he thought there may be a valid place for it in reference to serial church planters, yet even there he would be cautious of using the language.[42] The leader of Anglican Church planting initiatives and a member of the Fresh Expressions team, Bob Hopkins was clear that there were people within the Fresh Expressions movement who were happily using the language of "apostle" and "apostolic." His own opinion was that there was no real distinction between the church planting movement that he had been involved in over the last thirty years and the Fresh Expressions movement. Within that time span he had noticed a dramatic increase in the terminology of "apostle." He stated that within this movement (joining the two together), about twenty years ago less than 5 percent would have been comfortable with this language, whereas today he estimated about 40 percent would be. He thought the Charismatic sector within this were the most accepting, whereas the more Evangelical groups would be happier to use "apostolic" instead. Gooding similarly believed that the theme of apostolic ministry was returning.[43] Hopkins believed Steven Croft had been particularly influential in making the five-fold ministry more acceptable to an Anglican ecclesiology and to a wider constituency as he has done much to relate the three fold order to

39. Fresh Expressions, "Big Night."
40. Rev John Gooding, interview with author, July 17, 2009.
41. David Male, e-mail message to author, May 18, 2009.
42. Mike Moynagh, interview by author, August 21, 2009.
43. Rev John Gooding, interview with author, July 17, 2009.

the five-fold ministry, and considered ways in which bishops, priests, and deacons should exhibit the charisms of Ephesians 4:11–13.[44]

Croft's perspective is in accordance with a broader movement within the Church of England to reclaim the "apostolic" dimension to these orders in light of our increasingly post-Christendom situation. The Anglican, Rev Mark Mills-Powell similarly has called for a new apostolic leadership in light of the era in which we live: "The difficulty is that if the rapid decline of the Church is to be reversed, the Church in Western Europe needs the apostolic ministry far more urgently than any other form of ministry. As Robert Brow has written, 'The apostolic function is the most neglected and yet most necessary gift for the world-wide church.' The pastoral ministry is simply too blunt a tool to be able to make the impression that is needed in what have become post-Christian societies."[45]

In this regard he argues that "the Episcopal ministry must become apostolic again."[46] Likewise Trevor Beeson:

> The Church has been pushed to the margins of society: this is precisely where the Church stood during the earliest centuries of its existence, yet with the crucial difference that its Episcopal leaders were seen as missionary pioneers, rather than as crisis managers. It is this role that needs to be revived, but this can only happen if there is a bold facing of the facts and a determination to change those aspects of the Church's life that are no longer appropriate to a missionary situation.[47]

Linking into this general trend but also re-affirming the historic succession is Bishop Christopher Cocksworth's contention that the bishop is "ordained to signify the apostolic mission of the church by their historical connection to the ministry of the originating apostles, and to enable the church to be effective in mission by fulfilling the apostolic functions handed over to them at their ordinations."[48]

All of these happenings confirm Hopkins' impression that there had been a remarkable shift toward incorporating and promoting "apostolic" ministry within the Church of England over the last four years as a result

---

44. An example of where Croft does this is in Croft, *Ministry*, 208.
45. Mills-Powell, "Leadership," 223.
46. Ibid., 218.
47. Beeson, "Liberating," 230.
48. Cocksworth, *Holding Together*, 259.

PART ONE—Where We Are

of the General Synod's acceptance of the *Mission Shaped-Church* and its promotion of pioneer ministers and ministry.[49]

During the Charismatic Movement's heyday in the 1970s and 80s there were some influential Baptist leaders and churches affected by it: in particular David Pawson at Millmead, Guildford, and Douglas McBain at Lewin Road Baptist in Streatham. Pawson argued for the five-fold ministry and identified himself as a prophet. Douglas McBain was "ordained" as an apostle within the Baptist Church[50] and was viewed as such by a number of people. Nigel Wright thought that his unofficial role as an "apostolic" leader was recognized by the denomination that in turn made him the General Superintendent of the London area—thereby facilitating and incorporating his "apostolic" gift.[51] Notwithstanding these men's influence, "apostleship" has become more common within Baptist circles in the UK today via an organization known as Baptist Mainstream.[52] It views itself as an apostolic network and promotes "apostleship" as a central feature of their association. According to the leader of Baptist Mainstream, Rob White, the organization was originally set up to help support Evangelicals within the Baptist Church and to enable them to inhabit influential positions within the Union. When this was achieved, the leaders of Baptist Mainstream met together to ask the question of whether its day was now over. They sensed through prayer and fasting that this was not to be the case but that they were to take on a different emphasis—namely that of Charismatic Renewal. Central to that vision was for them to become an "apostolic network," and promote apostolic ministry. They believed the terminology of apostle and apostolic network was very important and in some sense "inspired."[53]

There are strong similarities with Anglican-led New Wine, although New Wine has never promoted this kind of terminology on its web page, unlike Baptist Mainstream. This may be because the Baptist set-up is very different to the Anglican one and sensibilities are likely to be more offended in a church where "apostolic succession" is highly prized by many of its members. Even though Baptist Mainstream is very up front about

49. Bob Hopkins, telephone interview with author, November 1, 2010.

50. Tom Smail (a close friend of McBain), interview with author, 8 April 2009. This was confirmed to me by Nigel Wright who was actually involved in the service. Nigel Wright, interview with author, 11 November, 2009.

51. Nigel Wright, interview with author, 11 November, 2009.

52. It has now been renamed, Fresh Streams, and Rob White has stepped down from leading it in 2013. Fresh Streams "How Fresh Streams was launched."

53. Rob White, telephone interview with author, August 13, 2009.

its conviction concerning modern day apostles, it does not promote an authoritarian-type apostle as they are committed to the Baptist Church and therefore involved with the Baptist Union. They in no way seek to undermine the Baptist Union, despite their ecclesiology being at odds with the usual Baptist one which has no apostolic leadership.[54]

Nigel Wright believes that "apostolic" language is becoming much more common in Baptist UK circles, and regional ministers are now more "bishop-like" and therefore have a translocal apostolic role. From Wright's perspective the correct focus should be on apostolic function rather than status. He did acknowledge that much of this development concerning apostolic ministry within the Baptist Church is as a product and provocation of the House Church emphases. From his experience the Baptist Church was much more impacted by the radical House Church movement, and there were about twenty to thirty churches that became Restorationist; therefore, it makes sense that as a denomination they were having to tackle the issues raised much more than the Anglican Church.[55]

The organization that has been fostering Renewal within the United Reformed Church (URC) in Britain has been GEAR (Group for Evangelism and Renewal). The current chairman of that organization is a United Reformed Church minister, Brian Harley, who oversees a local church on the Isle of Wight. Although there is no doctrinal position on apostles from the organization as a whole, they have not been untouched by the emphasis. Brian Harley himself was prophesied over as having such a ministry, and in communication with me he made it clear that some do view him in that manner—although he was keen to add that he "may be shy to employ such a term to myself"; he also thought it inappropriate to do so in the context of his denomination. Harley pointed out that as an organization they had had considerable input from the American Renewal Ministry, Presbyterian Reformed Ministry International (PRMI), which had "increased the apostolic emphasis a bit." What has been clear from my communication with Harley, is that there is a clear consciousness within GEAR of apostolic-type ministry and an embracing of it, but no desire to name it in that way.[56]

---

54. A description of the issues at stake has been put into writing by one of the theologians representing Baptist Mainstream, Stephen Ibbotson, in "Apostolic Leadership." Interestingly, Baptist Mainstream do have some precedent for their ecclesiology in Baptist circles when that denomination had the ministry of the Messenger—see chap. 4 for more information.

55. Nigel Wright, interview with author, 11 November, 2009.

56. Brian Harley, e-mail message to author, September 13, 2009.

PART ONE—Where We Are

Methodists have been involved in the Charismatic Renewal since its earliest days[57] particularly through the experience and influence of Charles Clarke.[58] In more recent times, the most prominent Methodist advocating Renewal was the late Rob Frost.[59] He started the ecumenical Easter People and Share Jesus International. He appeared on the God Channel, a Christian television station, and Premier Radio and was highly regarded by Charismatics across the denominations.[60] His Easter Weeks have been very important in fostering Renewal in Methodist circles. The recent ECG yearly conference (ECG standing for Equipping, Calling, Going) has in many ways filled the gap that was left after the Easter Weeks finished.[61] Alongside these there has been the emergence of the Methodist Evangelicals Together (MET) which is committed to the Evangelical faith and prayer for Revival.

A Methodist network that is more overtly charismatic is Ignite Revival; it is headed by William Porter. The beginnings and development of this network is described on their website:

> In 1998 a group of church leaders in Methodism ran a tour called "Approaching Revival"—days of worship, teaching and prayer around issues of spiritual revival. For the next four years the group then organized yearly conferences under the banner "Church in Revival". Out of some prophetic visions in 2003, the group changed its name to Ignite Revival. It began to intentionally network leaders with a similar vision as well as others who were praying for revival. Ignite Revival has run leaders' days with an emphasis on worship & prayer ministry, and some major conferences: "Father's Heart" October 2005 with John & Carol Arnott & Scott McDermott, "Glory in the Nations" International Prayer Conference June 2006 with an international team of speakers, "Look to the Heavens" European Methodist

---

57. For a historical depiction of how Charismatic Renewal got going in Methodist circles in Britain see Hocken, *Streams*, chap. 12.

58. Ibid., and also see Scotland, *Charismatics*, 18–19.

59. In e-mail correspondence with Andy Frost, Rob Frost's son, he thought my assessment was correct in terms of his father's impact; however, he stressed that his father was first and foremost an evangelist and his focus was mission, of which renewal was a part. Andy Frost, e-mail message to author, April 28, 2010.

60. For an overview of his life and work see Horsley, "Obituary—Rob Frost."

61. Andy Frost pointed out three groupings that consciously represented Charismatics in the UK Methodist Church: ECG (Equipping, Calling, Going), Ignite and MET (Methodist Evangelicals Together). Andy Frost, e-mail message to author, April 28, 2010.

Prayer Conference November 2007 (in Slovakia) and "Glimpses of Heaven" June 2008. Ignite has also run regional leaders' days, led seminars at Easter People & ECG. Ignite has developed some resources for churches, including "If My People" prayer DVD, the book "Igniting Leadership" and a website.[62]

According to Porter, they have now "developed a network of some 250 folk, many of them church leaders, gathering around praying for revival and releasing people in Charismatic ministry." As to apostles and the five-fold ministry, Porter stated, "We don't really have a strong focus on the 5-fold ministries or apostles in particular. However we do recognize such giftings, and have brought at times in people to share in conferences who we would see having that gift."[63]

The associations that this group has with the Arnotts, and its affirmation of the Lakeland Revival,[64] would suggest that it is very much at home within the Charismatic stream that affirms apostles today.

The Roman Catholic Charismatic sector within Britain is very similar to its "sister" in America and has tended not to draw attention to modern-day apostles. Nevertheless, it is important to note that the British Roman Catholic scholar Peter Hocken has called the older churches, including his own, to be challenged by the resurgence of the Ephesians 4 ministries—including apostles: "Non-denominational Charismatic Christianity challenges the churches to allow space for the full functioning of all the manifold gifts and ministries of the Holy Spirit."[65] He sees it as one of the core reasons to why God has raised up the independent non-denominational Charismatic churches.[66] More recently in an e-mail exchange Peter Hocken stated, "In my writings I have been saying a few times that the historic churches need to reflect on the phenomenon of the 'reappearance' of the 5 fold ministries. It is true that I am seeing something from the Spirit here but I have not clearly called for a place to be made for them, at least I don't think so! It is more that I think a taking this phenomenon seriously will have practical consequences, though I have not tried to spell them out."[67]

62. Ignite Revival, "History."
63. William Porter, e-mail to author, November 5, 2009.
64. Their website has a link with Stephen Strader—the Pastor of the Lakeland Church—and testimonies emerging from his church. See Ignite Revival, "Testimonies."
65. Hocken, "Non-Denominational," 231.
66. See ibid., 221–38.
67. Peter Hocken, e-mail message to author, October 28, 2009.

Part One—Where We Are

Fellow Roman Catholic scholar Bernard Cooke has gone further and appealed for a revival and recognition of apostles.[68]

Charles Whitehead, an influential figure in the Catholic Charismatic Renewal in Britain,[69] had the following to say about the Catholic Charismatic stance on the issue which explains why it has not really infiltrated the Catholic Charismatic Renewal in Britain at all:

> Whilst I and other leaders in the Catholic Charismatic Renewal (CCR) are well aware of the description Apostle being used to describe key independent Charismatic leaders and planters of new streams of churches, our ecclesiology means that we do not use this title at all. Because we see the Catholic Church as universal, the question of establishing new churches does not arise. New parishes and congregations may be established, but not new churches. These will be approved by a bishop—a successor to the Apostles. When new ecclesial movements or communities are formed, we see those who carry and implement the vision as "founders." Similarly with new religious orders. . . . So whilst I understand how others may see certain people as having an apostolic anointing or ministry, this does not fit into Catholic understanding or practice. We recognize and honour the anointing which rests upon founders of new movements, communities, or religious orders, but would never see them as apostles, and the establishment of all new church congregations rests with the bishops.[70]

It is clear therefore, that the Roman Catholic Church in Britain does not officially recognize a "charismatic apostolate," and it would be hard pressed to do so.[71]

There is very little to report on Charismatic Orthodoxy as there is no real discernible group advocating Charismatic Renewal amongst the

---

68. Kevin Giles notes that the Roman Catholic scholar, Bernard Cooke, argues in his book, *Ministry to Word and Sacraments*, that "we need to encourage and recognise the ministry of apostle . . . in the church today." Giles, "Apostles Before," 256, n. 86.

69. For more detail on his place in the Catholic Charismatic Renewal, see Hocken, "Whitehead," 1194.

70. Charles Whitehead, e-mail message to author, November 18, 2009.

71. This is not to suggest that they do not affirm people's "apostolic gifts"—they clearly do, a number of communities have been initiated and have thrived; nor am I suggesting that the Catholic Charismatic Renewal will not be influenced by leading Pentecostals and Charismatics who very much espouse the five-fold ministry doctrine. In a recent article in the Catholic Charismatic Renewal's magazine, *GoodNews*, Dave Payne wrote at length on the impact that Bill Johnson and his church recently had on him. See Payne, "Learning."

Orthodox in Britain. One might have expected the late Michael Harper to have pushed this, but he purposely decided not to, and distanced himself from Father Eusebius Stephanou's Renewalist approach. As it is therefore, there is no attempt to advocate a contemporary charismatic apostolate; and the influence of the Pentecostal Charismatic Movement on Orthodoxy is negligible in this country.

To summarize: UK denominational Charismatics are increasingly at home with the idea of a charismatic apostolate, even those who do not embrace the concept due to ecclesiological factors are very aware of the phenomenon, and can see ways in which it dovetails with charisms already recognized within their own denomination. However, where churches are not inhibited by older structures there has been a greater freedom to incorporate new forms of ministry, and this has indeed been the case within the independent Charismatic sector.

Independent Charismatic Churches/ Neo-Apostolic Churches/Modern Independent Pentecostal: UK

Allan Anderson observed in 2004 that "The fastest growing churches in Britain today are the 'new churches,' mostly independent Charismatic churches, sometimes led by former Anglican ministers and forming loose associations. These have probably outstripped the classical Pentecostal churches in influence and extent."[72]

This observation may well be the case, but amidst the growth and success stories there have been splits and even decline amongst some of these new churches;[73] nevertheless, in relation to twelve prolific networks that William Kay has studied, the overall picture is one of growth: "Putting these figures together we can say that about two thirds of apostolic network congregations appear to be growing and about a third are either static or have suffered decline."[74] Kay traces the general pattern that he sees emerging within these new churches that enable them to become an "apostolic network": "Apostolic networks grew out of the Charismatic

---

72. Anderson, *Introduction*, 95.

73. In an e-mail sent to me on August 21, 2009, the renowned Christian researcher Dr Peter Brierley informed me that there has been further decline amongst the new churches due to splits.

74. Kay, *Networks*, 311.

Part One—Where We Are

Movement, though they also occasionally drew upon Pentecostals... and the networks began as churches that met within homes... before moving to schools and hired halls before eventually buying their own buildings. So they moved from being 'house churches' to being 'new churches' and eventually as they became configured under apostolic ministry, they became 'apostolic networks.'"[75]

Kay has identified the following twelve "apostolic" ministers and studied both them and their networks in depth: 1. Bryn Jones and Covenant Ministries International; 2. Terry Virgo and Newfrontiers International; 3. Barney Coombs and Salt and Light; 4. Tony Morton and Cornerstone; 5. Roger Forster and Ichthus; 6. Gerald Coates and Pioneer; 7. Stuart Bell and Ground Level; 8. Colin Dye and Kensington Temple; 9. Noel Stanton and the Jesus Fellowship; 10. John Wimber and Vineyard; 11. Colin Urquhart and Kingdom Faith; 12. Hugh Osgood and churches in Community. Many of these networks are directly related to the radical House Church movement of the 1960s and 1970s;[76] all of them have their roots within the Pentecostal Charismatic Movement. Aside from Wimber, they are all British; the majority of whom would happily call themselves apostles and all of them have been thought of as such due to their pioneering work, influence and estimated spiritual authority. Except for Colin Dye whose church, Kensington Temple, is still part of Elim, they stand alone as independent Charismatic networks. Nevertheless, most of them have a much wider influence than the network which they head up, being heard outside their networks due to their writings, Satellite TV, ecumenical conferences and radio. Colin Urquhart, for example, is a highly successful author who spoke regularly on Premier and also had a program on the GOD Channel. Terry Virgo has been a main speaker at the ecumenical Spring Harvest, and has written books that are recommended in Evangelical circles outside the new churches.

The situation is similar to that in the USA in that it depends on the particular church or network whether the terminology of "apostles" is used. Therefore, "non-denominational" Charismatic churches, such as Kingdom Faith, promote apostles today, whilst the Vineyard Church UK has no official line, although according to Vineyard Church UK leader, John Mumford, it takes Wimber's perspective by affirming the *function*

---

75. Ibid., 19–20.
76. For a detailed account of the rise of this movement see Walker, *Restoring*.

Apostles Today: Britain

of apostles but usually calling those who are operating in that way by a different name.[77]

Amongst the independent churches that have been started over the last half century, there has been a notable rise in Black churches. As Lynette Mullings points out in 2009, "statistics from the last Church Census in England show that the growth in Black Pentecostal Churches partly accounts for the slow rate of decline in churchgoing. Black people now account for 10% of all churchgoers in England and in inner London alone, 44% of churchgoers are now black."[78]

This is an area that Kay did not look at due to the lack of statistical data available from the official handbook on church statistics which his study was based on.[79] Many of these churches have their roots in Africa and are now a significant feature on the UK church landscape.[80] There are several notable black-majority mega-churches in England such as Kingsway International Christian Centre, Ruach Ministries, Glory House, New Wine Ministries, Jesus House, Everlasting Arms Ministry, House of Praise, Trinity Baptist Church, and House on the Rock.[81] Are these influential new black-majority mega-churches advocating modern day apostles? If so, we are then finding another pool of "apostles."

Kingsway International Christian Centre (KICC),[82] founded by Matthew Ashimolowo, has grown phenomenally since it first appeared over a decade ago. According to *The Guardian*: "It launched in 1991 in an east London school with 300 members. Now, led by the Nigerian TV preacher Matthew Ashimolowo . . . it attracts 12,000 worshippers every Sunday."[83] Not only does Ashimolowo have a worldwide television ministry,[84] his In-

77. John Mumford, telephone interview with author, September 15, 2009.

78. Mullings, "Future," 1.

79. William Kay, e-mail message to author, June, 2009.

80. For an insight into this new phenomenon, see Oloyede, "Black Church," which gives a portrayal of what is happening, as well as figures by Peter Brierley indicating the extent of Black majority churches.

81. These nine churches were the biggest black churches in 2005. The list of these churches with attendance numbers was recorded in anonymous, "Black Churches," 14.

82. Kingsway International Christian Centre now has a number of church communities that have been planted in other areas known as "chapels" and "branches." They also have a growing number of churches in Ghana and Nigeria. See Kingsway International Christian Centre, "Near You," for list of Kingsway International Christian Centre churches.

83. Booth, "Religion."

84. According to ibid, "his sermons are broadcast 24 hours a day on Sky and around the world."

51

PART ONE—Where We Are

ternational Gathering of Champions conferences are some of the biggest Christian events in Europe.[85] Kingsway International Christian Centre has also been branching out through the planting of "Chapels and Branches" in London, the West Midlands, and in the Home Counties.[86] Ashimolowo does not advertise himself as an apostle, yet he is often referred to as a "spiritual father," which in Charismatic circles can be a way of saying someone is an apostle.[87] Undoubtedly he would fit into Wagner's definition of an apostle due to the personal spiritual authority accredited to him and the phenomenal growth associated with his church and wider network. One of the pastors on staff at Kingsway International Christian Centre London confirmed that Matthew Ashimolowo is seen as an apostle by the church.[88] A fellow pastor at Kingsway International Christian Centre was just as clear about this; however, he underlined the fact that Kingsway International Christian Centre do not label people as apostles although they recognize apostleship as a function but do not ordain people as such. The three ministerial positions within Kingsway International Christian Centre are ministers, deacons and pastors. The five-fold ministry is clearly a belief held by Kingsway International Christian Centre but it is not one given prominence on Sundays; the place where it would be taught is at their Bible College and at their training for leaders where they will actively identify people's gifts and functions. Matthew Ashimolowo was theologically trained in the Foursquare Gospel denomination, and was associated with them for eighteen years. Therefore, it is unsurprising that Kingsway International Christian Centre holds a very similar perspective.[89]

Ruach Ministries is headed up by Bishop John Francis—one of the founders of the London Community Gospel Choir—who like Ashimolowo has a large television ministry, and a claimed attendance of about "5000+"

---

85. Robert Booth suggested that there were to be 12,000 people present at the final service in 2008. See ibid.

86. For more information see Kingsway International Christian Centre, "Branches."

87. It is picking up Paul's terminology in his exchange with the Corinthian church where he points out as proof of his apostolic credentials that although they have many teachers he is their spiritual father through the gospel—see 1 Corinthians 4:15–16. However, it is also used in other Christian circles to speak of a bishop or overseer—so this may not be conclusive either way.

88. Pastor Esther Dunmoye, telephone conversation with author, October 29, 2009.

89. Pastor Dipo Oluyomi, Resident Pastor Kingsway International Christian Centre South West and London District Superintendent, interview with author, January 12, 2010.

people each Sunday.[90] Unlike Kingsway International Christian Centre his church has not branched out in London and elsewhere in England. This ministry has propagated that Francis is an apostle: "Operating in his gift as an Apostle and speaking with a prophetic voice, Bishop Francis..."[91] This affirmation of the apostolic gift by Ruach ministries was made even more explicit in personal correspondence with the ministry where it stated that "we ordain ministers and recognize their gift as an apostle."[92] From what I have observed of Bishop Francis via satellite television, the five-fold ministry is not a major feature of his preaching ministry; but the fact that he sees himself as an apostle, and others recognize him as such means that "apostolic ministry" is a given within that church community.

Jesus House[93] and House of Praise[94] are part of the wider Redeemed Christian Church of God, a Pentecostal network founded in 1952.[95] The House of Praise in particular is very direct about its belief in apostolic ministry today, and uses apostolic network type language on its website, lauding "the apostolic ministry of Andrew Adeleke, founder of the Praise Mission."[96] The success of the Redeemed Christian Church of God has raised the profile of its current leader Pastor Adeboye, to worldwide fame: *Newsweek* included him in their list of the fifty most powerful people in the world and wrote the following about him:

> You may never have heard of E. A. Adeboye, but the pastor of The Redeemed Christian Church of God is one of the most successful preachers in the world. He boasts that his church has outposts in 110 countries. He has 14,000 branches—claiming 5 million members—in his home country of Nigeria alone. There are 360 Redeemed Christian Church of God churches in Britain,[97] and about the same number in U.S. cities like Chi-

---

90. Ruach Ministries, "Bishop."

91. Ibid.; also quoted on conference information that he was speaking at in 2009—see River Fellowship International, "Bishop."

92. Bishop Francis' personal assistant, e-mail message to author, Septem- ber 10, 2009.

93. Jesus House Church, "About Us."

94. "The House of Praise Mission Family was started in 1992 with only four adults. It was started under the name Agape Assemblies but was later brought under the umbrella of the Redeemed Christian Church of God. Since then, we have seen the birth of over 10 churches..." House of Praise, "About Us."

95. A summary of their fundamental beliefs and the Church's history can be accessed via Redeemed Christian Church of God, "Redeemed."

96. House of Praise, "About Us."

97. The research and policy officer for the Redeemed Christian Church of God at

cago, Dallas, and Tallahassee, Fla. Adeboye says he has sent missionaries to China and such Islamic countries as Pakistan and Malaysia. His aspirations are outsize. He wants to save souls, and he wants to do so by planting churches the way Starbucks used to build coffee shops: everywhere.[98]

As the *Newsweek* article highlights, the majority of its members are in Africa, but it has established itself as a growing church network in Britain. As a movement they are committed to embracing all five ministries mentioned in Ephesians 4:11–13, but their church structures do not as yet have a position solely for the apostle, although there are moves in Nigeria to create one. The founder Pastor Adeboye is very much viewed as having an apostolic grace, although in reference to him he is not titled as an apostle.[99]

In summary, within these independent Charismatic churches/networks the doctrine of charismatic apostolates differs from one to another. Therefore, we find emphasis on recognizing and affirming the gift of apostle publicly within groups such as Newfrontiers International (NFI) and Kingdom Faith (KF); whereas there is a softer doctrine focusing on the function within networks such as Ichthus and Vineyard, where little attention, if any, is given to naming. In relation to all of the black-majority mega-churches looked at there is a recognition of the charismatic apostolate, but the usual manner of addressing the "apostolic leader" is using titles such as "pastor."

Conclusion

As in the USA, there is within the British Charismatic sector of the church a widespread embracing of the charismatic apostolate in various guises. There are distinct differences between the American and British church scene: in Britain there is an established church whereas in the USA there is not and the independent church sector is much larger proportionately in the USA. Nevertheless, many patterns that have emerged there are evident here; for example, Wagner has identified several traits of "apostolic

---

the European Central Office, Babatunde Adedibu, had different figures which if correct highlight the extraordinary growth of this denomination. He e-mailed the following on October 12, 2009: "The churches currently have over four hundred and eighty parishes in United Kingdom. The church currently has over 12,000 parishes globally and is present in six continents."

98. Miller, "Adeboye."

99. Babatunde Adedibu, telephone conversation with author, September 10, 2009.

Apostles Today: Britain

networks" which appear on both sides of the Atlantic: apostolic networks are translocal, based on relationships and have one overall leader.[100] Similarly, his description of churches that are part of the New Apostolic Reformation can be identified in the USA and the UK.[101] Many things that are popular in America find their way over to Britain,[102] and to a limited extent vice versa (Alpha being one of the most successful UK Christian exports). Yet the fascination with the charismatic apostolate is a trend that is found on both sides of the Atlantic, and apostolic networks have become a feature in both contexts. It is noteworthy that in all my correspondences and interviews with people in the USA and Britain no one was unfamiliar with the idea of a modern charismatic apostolate.

The impact of the New Apostolic Reformation is minimal in comparison to the USA, and the independent Charismatic churches and networks do not appear to have the same appeal here as they do in the USA, although they are still collectively a significant feature of the British church scene. The British historic Pentecostal denominations have not reneged on their initial convictions concerning the charismatic apostolate. As a result of the influx and growth of the Black Pentecostal churches there is another substantial witness to the charismatic apostolate. Charismatic churches of all denominations that tie into either American Renewal hotspots and ministries, or UK radical House Churches and other UK independent church networks, have clearly been influenced by the apostolic agenda; yet even beyond Pentecostal Charismatic Movement-influenced churches there are noteworthy developments outside that stream that are advocating similar forms of ministry but using different terminology. Of particular interest is the Fresh Expressions movement with its advocacy of pioneer ministers within the older British churches; although there are Charismatics involved in Fresh Expressions they are not all so linked. As in the USA the type of apostle being advocated often differs from group to group as undergirding theologies and ecclesiologies inevitably affect the form of charismatic apostolate deemed acceptable in differing circles.

The religious landscape has so changed that there is a greater openness to the charismatic apostolate, and it is not uncommon to hear talk of charismatic apostles and apostolic ministry by renowned Renewalists

---

100. Wagner, *Churchquake*, 126–29.

101. See Wagner, "The New Apostolic Reformation" in Wagner, ed., *New Apostolic Churches*, chap. 1, for his generic markers of churches that are part of this movement.

102. For a helpful contrast of receptivity between the North America and Britain see Martin, *Pentecostalism*, 28–70.

who are still deeply committed to older churches.[103] Undoubtedly there are tensions with older structures that inhibit the kind of church planting activity that many advocates of the charismatic apostolate see as the hallmark of that ministry, nevertheless, there is an optimism amongst many denominational Charismatics that increasingly space is being made for this type of ministry and perception of it is more positive. Inevitably the type of charismatic apostolate will in practice differ according to the context and the individuality of the leader,[104] nevertheless, popular theologies undergirding them are being read, listened to, and incorporated in the USA and UK. It is often these views rather than esteemed academics that are influencing churches. Therefore, it is important that we are aware of what is being advocated, so in our next chapter we will consider some influential Christian teachers' understanding of the charismatic apostolate today.

---

103. My correspondences/interviews with the following committed Anglicans revealed this: Rev Barry Kissell, Rev Bruce Collins, Rt. Rev David Pytches, and Rev Bob Hopkins; similarly, within Baptist circles as my correspondences/interviews with Nigel Wright and Rob White have shown.

104. Ian Stackhouse highlighted how, in his experience of new church apostles, the doctrine of apostleship and shape of it flowed from the influential leader's own doctrinal framework. Ian Stackhouse, interview with author, August 5, 2008.

3

Popular Charismatic Teachers on Apostles

Introduction

THE SUBJECT OF MODERN-DAY apostles has been in the consciousness of the Pentecostal movement since its inception,[1] but unlike other spiritual gifts associated with that movement such as glossolalia, it has not gained such a wide profile in popular Christian books until relatively recently. However in the last twenty years there has been an explosion of literature on the subject.[2] Many popular Christian leaders/writers who advocate modern-day apostles have extensive international itineraries and have made full use of technological developments ranging from the widespread use of radio, tape cassettes, CDs, DVDs, internet downloads, as well as the ease of book printing and translating, and as a result have their theology heard across the world. They are arguably shaping much Christian discipleship and ecclesiology both in the West, and in places where Christian growth is happening in an unprecedented manner—examples being China, Latin America, and Africa. The Pentecostal/Charismatic churches of the future may not be shaped by renowned ecclesiologists such as Küng,

---

1. For an overview of how the earliest British Pentecostals and the resulting denominations understood the ministry gift of apostle see Kay, *Pentecostals*, 221–27.

2. For example, see the recommended reading on apostles on Peter Wagner's bookstore, known as "Arsenal Books"; there are over thirty books on the apostolic (as accessed on September 20, 2011, the majority of which have been written since the 1990s).

Rahner, or Zizioulas, but by popular Bible teachers such as Ulf Ekman or Rick Joyner. Five such men who appear to be impacting churches on a wide scale through their teaching are Derek Prince, Terry Virgo, Peter Wagner, Mike Breen, and Kenneth Hagin.

Although very different in character and theology there are similarities between them. All of them are/were[3] Protestant, Evangelical, and Charismatic, believing that all the ministries and gifts described in Romans 12, 1 Corinthians 12, and Ephesians 4 are given by God today. Although Charismatic in terms of theological conviction, they are also Charismatic in a Weberian sense—they have "charisma," "a certain quality of an individual personality, by virtue of which he is set apart from ordinary men and treated as endowed with supernatural, superhuman, or at least specifically exceptional powers or qualities."[4]

In this chapter I will be introducing these men and giving an overview of their understanding of "apostles" as well as considering who or what might have shaped their thinking and highlighting the unique features of their own viewpoints. I have chosen these five to focus on for a variety of reasons. First of all due to their popularity and influence—they all have a wide sphere of influence, not necessarily amongst the same group, but in the case of all them they are taken note of within Charismatic circles far beyond the local church they are or were involved in. At present Prince and Wagner's influence would appear to exceed Breen, Virgo, and Hagin's—David Bundy, the Pentecostal historian who travels extensively on behalf of Fuller Theological Seminary, told me in 2007 that on his travels it is the books of Prince and Wagner that he constantly comes across. Nevertheless, the others have an international and wide readership too; as the "father" of the Word of Faith movement Hagin's books are revered in those circles; Virgo's influence has spread due to the success of his Newfrontiers International network and his willingness to contribute in wider ecumenical conferences; Breen has been for many years influential in the New Wine network and his teaching has been more readily incorporated in "mainstream" churches,[5] his fame has grown since his move to the USA

---

3. Kenneth Hagin and Derek Prince are dead, although their respective ministries are still very much alive.

4. Weber, *Theory*, 358.

5. St Thomas Crooke's is held up as an exemplary missional church in Cray et al., *Mission-Shaped Church*, and the model of ministry initiated there by Breen has gained an international hearing through the work of Michael Frost and the Australian Alan Hirsch in their book, *Shaping*.

in 2004;⁶ Second, they each have written or taught in detail about apostolic ministry. Third, they each represent slightly different "streams" within the Pentecostal/Charismatic Movement. Fourth, because although sharing many features in common, they bring distinctive interpretations of the charismatic apostolate. Needless to say, I could have chosen others to look at too.⁷

Derek Prince—"Acts 13: The Missing Link Apostles"

Derek Prince was born in 1915 in India, the only child of British parents. He was baptized and confirmed within the Anglican Church. He was a scholar at Eton and became a fellow at Cambridge. He served with the army in World War II and whilst posted in Scarborough was "born again." Soon after this he was introduced to a Pentecostal group with whom he experienced the "baptism in the Spirit." He started and pastored a church in England, then set up a teacher training college in Kenya, after which he emigrated with his wife Lydia first to Canada in 1961 and then to the USA in 1963 where he began travelling and teaching widely. During the 70s Prince became, with four others, part of an influential group known as the Fort Lauderdale Five, who initiated the heavy Shepherding movement. This was a movement that emphasized the need for discipling, and for each Christian to have someone who was their discipler who was to be looked to for spiritual protection and counsel; abuse was widespread, as was condemnation of the movement. In time Prince was to disassociate with this teaching and although rejecting outright certain tenets of the movement, Prince remained convinced that at its beginning it was a genuine move of the Spirit which got hijacked by the "flesh" and became perverted.⁸ Prince's image was tarnished by it,⁹ yet he managed to regain

---

6. Breen's LifeShapes material has been published in the USA and beyond since his joining up with influential author and pastor Walt Kallestad, and he is in demand as a speaker introducing churches to this visually orientated form of discipleship. He has been given a wider platform due to his teaching at Fuller as well.

7. For example, Ulf Ekman or Rick Joyner.

8. McAlpine, *Post-Charismatic?*, 187.

9. David Bundy told me that in some ways Prince never recovered the popularity that he had in the USA as a result of that movement; however, it is clear that he did regain many people's confidence even within the USA from the church platforms he was being given, and from the endorsements of his teaching and character by other prominent ministers. See Mansfield, *Derek Prince*, 283–84, and quotes from Lyndon Bowring and Colin Dye on the back cover.

people's confidence in his ability to teach the Scriptures. In 1981 he moved, with his second wife Ruth to Jerusalem where he lived the rest of his life.[10]

Prince's ministry has spread across the world via his daily radio program, Keys to Successful Living, which according to Derek Prince Ministries UK (DPMUK) broadcasts to "half the population of the world in various languages,"[11] as well as through his books, tapes, videos and DVDs. The UK office claims that he is "the author of over 50 books, over 450 audio and 150 video teaching cassettes, many of which have been translated and published in more than 80 languages."[12] There are thirteen Derek Prince ministry offices around the world, alongside a further thirty four outreach posts;[13] their overarching purpose is to propagate his teaching in audio, visual and written form thereby fulfilling the motto of the organization to "reach the unreached and teach the untaught." Since his death in 2003, the UK office claims that Derek Prince Ministries has continued to grow with various books being published and new offices opening.[14] Therefore, his views on apostolic ministry will gain a large hearing; and due to the stature that he has within Charismatic circles, it is also probable that we will see his teaching outworked within many Pentecostal/Charismatic churches too.

Derek Prince Ministries have recently published, *Rediscovering God's Church* by Derek Prince, which includes substantial sections on the ministry of apostles;[15] he has also included an appendix in a booklet called *Sound Judgment*,[16] on "How to recognize apostles"; although Prince has other taped material on apostles[17] which did not make it into these books, there is little to add from them. Prince believed we needed apostles today, and alluding to Ephesians 4:11–13 asked, "How can the church come into

---

10. Information about his life has been taken from Mansfield, *Derek Prince*, and "Derek Prince Ministries UK."

11. See Derek Prince Ministries UK, "About."

12. Ibid.

13. Information gleaned from "Derek Prince Ministries," a website that provides links with all the offices and outreach centers.

14. DPM-UK, e-mail message to author, September 17, 2007.

15. He deals with apostles in chaps. 13–17.

16. Prince, *Judgement*, 99–105.

17. The following tapes and CDs are available from Derek Prince Ministries: "Apostles and Shepherds (4104 and 4105)"; "Apostolic Teams (AT1)"; "Mobile Ministries: Apostles (5003)." He also talks about the subject in a wider discussion on gifts and calling in a tape series called *Finding Your Place*, done in 1986—no longer available from Derek Prince Ministries.

maturity without all of the five main ministries, including the apostle?" He believed that God was restoring the church to its God-given glory, and was challenging her to "submit to the clearly defined and stated pattern of God in Scripture."[18] This process involves the restoration of all the Ephesians 4 ministry gifts—those being: apostles, prophets, evangelists, pastors, and teachers—and a rediscovery of the church as revealed in Scripture; he hopes that his writing on the church and its ministries will help "remove layers of assumptions, traditions, and erroneous teaching to lay a pure foundation."[19] Prince believed he had witnessed a restoration of apostolic ministry, but thought it was in its infant stage. He also held that true apostles would not emerge in Western nations as there is "too much ego and colonial mentality still present," therefore his eyes were "on the emerging church in Asia and other areas experiencing the harvest."[20] (The harvest Prince refers to appears to be a spiritual season in which large numbers of people become Christian.) He was convinced that this emergence will happen in an "organic New Testament" manner rather than through the traditional methods employed by most denominations.[21]

Prince divides the New Testament apostles into pre-ascension apostles and post-ascension apostles. The pre-ascension apostles are Jesus and the Twelve (the Twelve initially included Judas but due to his apostasy and death Matthias took his ministry to make up twelve again). The post-ascension apostles are Paul, Barnabas, the four brothers of the Lord (James, Joses, Simon and Judas), Titus, two nameless apostles, Epaphroditus, Silas and Timothy.[22] However, Prince believed that there are characteristics shared by both groups that are intrinsic to the calling and ministry of an apostle. Both were called by God, and possess great authority which derives from Him. Both are sent out on a mission, and are missionary-like; both groups work in teams rather than as individuals. Nevertheless, there are inevitably some features of the apostolic ministry that are linked to the organization of the church post-ascension. For example, post-ascension, the church is led by mobile apostolic teams and static, local presbyteries—together, they are the "two basic forms of leadership in the church."[23]

18. Prince, *Judgement*, 152.
19. Prince, *Rediscovering*, 164.
20. This conviction is shared by New Apostolic Reformation leaders in Africa and Asia—see Ross, "Apostolic Reformation," 13.
21. Prince, *Rediscovering*, 242.
22. Ibid., 205–19.
23. Ibid., 164.

Also post-ascension, the apostolic ministry,[24] like the prophet, teacher and evangelist, can function anywhere in the universal church. Furthermore, along with presbyters, apostles post ascension are under no human authority, but are governed by Jesus through the ministry of the Spirit.[25] Prince identified two main functions of a post-ascension apostle: "(1) to establish properly ordered churches, and (2) to bring order to churches that already exist."[26]

From his survey of the book of Acts and the New Testament epistles, Prince argues that presbyters and apostles should inter-relate in the following way: the "apostolic ministry emerges first in a region. . . . The apostles ordain elders to conserve the fruit of their work, and from these groups of elders new apostles ultimately emerge. This is a cycle that can continue endlessly."[27] He claims the wisdom of this in that it all occurs within the framework of both mission and church life and has at its heart "intimate association, interdependence and long-term relationships."[28] This principle is seen in the calling of Paul and Barnabas at Antioch, and possibly in Timothy's life as well.[29] All three were proven ministers prior to being set apart and sent out by the local leadership for the apostolic ministry God was calling them to. He claims that this is an inspired pattern and therefore we cannot improve on it.

Prince insists that no leader or apostle can make somebody else an apostle; the church can "recognize and set its official approval upon a ministry," however, "the ministry originates with God."[30] He rejects apostolic succession on the basis that no apostle from Jerusalem came and ordained Paul or Barnabas into apostolic ministry. The "principle of apostolic succession is actually set aside in the New Testament" and in "its place is the principle of spiritual birth born out of fellowship in the local church"; he concludes that "elders send out apostles, and apostles appoint elders" and that apostles "are answerable to the churches and elderships that send them forth, yet they will be the ones to establish further groups of elders."[31]

---

24. Prince does not refer to the *office* of apostle, instead he writes about the apostle's *ministry*.

25. Ibid., 184.

26. Ibid., 224.

27. Ibid., 194.

28. Ibid.

29. Ibid., 193.

30. Ibid., 220.

31. Ibid., 201.

An apostle's relationship with a congregation they have planted should be father-like, not domineering or controlling; Paul's appealing to his congregations with truth rather than reprimanding them for accepting preachers without his permission is an example of this.[32] Although in principle the apostle has a God-given authority over these churches, they should emulate Paul and the other apostles who "never claimed authority over single churches."[33] Even though they will not necessarily be a part of the church they have started and established, they can continue to relate to it and provide guidance and correction when it is needed. Although the apostles' relationship is obviously different with churches not founded by them, because of their ministry they automatically have authority over those churches too and if visiting would be the most senior minister there; they also can and did write to churches which they had not founded, so Paul writes to the Roman church, and Peter writes to Galatia, but the spirit in which they do all these things is as servants not as lords.[34] However, local congregations under the direction of their elders must discern whether someone is a genuine apostle or not.[35]

Due to the extraordinary authority bestowed on apostles,[36] there are a number of safeguards Prince has identified from the New Testament model to stop them becoming despotic: first, God's design of placing presbyters and apostles into teams;[37] second, the fact that apostolic teams function on a temporary basis rather than permanently gets rid of problems that arise from trying to make things lasting, when all that was needed was a temporary mission.[38] There is the further safeguard of interdependence between the apostles and presbyters,[39] as apostles will remain accountable to both the churches and elderships that sent them out;[40] in fact, if "an apostle ever goes astray, the local church is entitled to withdraw its endorsement of his apostolic ministry."[41]

32. Ibid., 188–89.
33. Ibid., 187.
34. Ibid.
35. Ibid., 226–27.
36. Prince states that an apostle does "have authority over local churches . . . brought into being directly by his ministry" and "over all churches, as the Holy Spirit directs." Ibid., 225.
37. Ibid., 178–79.
38. Ibid., 179.
39. Ibid., 179–80.
40. Ibid., 201.
41. Ibid., 235.

Prince has noted seven marks of a true apostle: "(1) a heart for "regions beyond" [that is, the missionary desire to take the gospel to places where it has not been before]; (2) the ability to fulfil all the special tasks of an apostle . . . ; (3) the establishment of churches that reflect the apostle's heart; (4) a desire for team ministry; (5) accountability toward the sending church; (6) signs and wonders; and (7) perseverance."[42]

Elsewhere, he also notes that a true apostle's doctrine "should in all main points harmonize with the total revelation of the New Testament" and that his life will be marked by holiness. "The primary fruit of the apostolic ministry is the local church" and the apostle will be the one who not only lays the foundation but is the "architect" and therefore can understand and "supervise every stage in the building process."[43] Of particular interest is his view on how a church would look if founded by a true apostle: multi-ethnic, missions-minded, with an emphasis on prayer and a heart for the poor.[44] He describes the true apostle using 1 Corinthians 3:10 as a "master builder"[45] and of possessing a "father's heart" toward the churches he has planted.[46] A true apostle will bear apostolic fruit; any ministry claiming to be apostolic that does not do this is viewed with suspicion by Prince.[47] This does not mean that they will all bear the same amount of fruit, as Prince sees Paul's reference to "eminent" apostles, and his description of Junia and Andronicus as being "of note among the apostles" as an indication that there are different levels of apostleship.[48]

Being a Pentecostal, Prince would have undoubtedly been influenced by mainstream Pentecostal interpretations of the apostle's ministry. Yet, it is probable that he has been influenced by some Latter Rain teaching[49] with his belief in a coming restoration of the apostolic ministry[50] as part

---

42. Ibid., 229.
43. Prince, *Judgement*, 104.
44. Prince, *Rediscovering*, 232.
45. Ibid., 231.
46. Ibid., 241.
47. Ibid.
48. Ibid., 227.
49. According to Rob McAlpine it was through Ern Baxter that the Latter Rain emphases came through to the Fort Lauderdale Five. See McAlpine, *Post-Charismatic?*, 174. This Latter Rain movement with its origins in Canada in 1948 emphasized a number of different doctrines particularly Restorationism, the five-fold ministry, laying on of hands, and prophecy. Ibid., 61.
50. According to David Moore it was Prince who whilst working with the Fort Lauderdale Five "emphasised the roles of apostles and prophets as present day ministries."

of God's end-time plan of restoring the church to its God-given glory. Prince, like all the other leaders in the Shepherding movement, was deeply impacted by Watchman Nee's writings, and features of Nee's teaching reappears in Prince's, although there remain significant differences too.[51] His image of the elders and the apostles working hand-in-hand in equal measure is distinctive to Prince, and his focus on the apostolic ministry pre-ascension to help unpack the apostle's ministry today is also noticeable when comparing with other current popular writers. His own strong conviction about women's ministry explains why he did not see women as being able to be apostles.

Peter Wagner—"Ephesians 2:20: Authoritative Multi-type Apostles"

C. Peter Wagner is a prolific author and influential figure in Charismatic circles. Once an Evangelical missionary in South America, he rose to prominence through his work at Fuller Theological Seminary, where he was mentored by Donald McGavran. He was instrumental in bringing John Wimber to Fuller, and along with him emphasized the need for signs and wonders for church growth. It was in relation to church growth principles that Wagner became controversial; particularly when he started advocating strategic spiritual warfare against territorial spirits as being key to cities being transformed and brought back to God. During the 1990s Wagner became convinced that God was restoring apostles to the church during that decade. Alongside this came the belief that God was calling him as an apostle. At present, he has severed his links with Fuller and now is the chancellor of Wagner Leadership Institute and President of Global Harvest Ministries. He was the presiding apostle over nearly 500 apostles in the International Coalition of Apostles, an organization designed to provide accountability between apostles. He is now the presiding Apostle

---

Moore, *Shepherding*, 55, quoted in McAlpine, *Post-Charismatic?*, 166.

51. Nee never embraced Pentecostalism, nor did he believe in a separate ministry of the teacher (in essence he believed in a four-fold ministry); however, his view of one church in one city was embraced by Prince—see McAlpine, *Post-Charismatic?*, 166.

Emeritus.[52] Since the late 1990s he has written extensively on apostles[53] and apostolic churches.[54]

Wagner believes that God never stopped giving apostles to the church; however, it is only as the result of four notable movements (The African Independent Churches, the Chinese House Churches, the Latin American Grassroots Churches, and the USA Independent Charismatic Movement) in the last century[55] that apostles are now emerging as a recognizable office. According to Wagner, 2001 was a pivotal year as numerous apostles were exercising their ministry and being officially recognized on a wide scale—therefore, that is when the church entered into a "second Apostolic age"; Wagner believes the first apostolic age consisted of the 200 years which followed after the end of the last of the New Testament apostles' ministry had finished.[56] Furthermore, he envisages that when the apostles are in place and the rest of the church rightly related to them, there will be a sustainable revival. In an interview Wagner put it like this: "one of the hindrances to God's sending the revival we've been praying for has been that the government of the church has not been properly in place. . . . Once the government comes into place then . . . the great outpouring of the Holy Spirit that we would call the worldwide revival."[57]

Wagner defines an apostle as "a Christian leader gifted, taught, commissioned, and sent by God with the authority to establish the foundational government of the church within an assigned sphere and/or spheres of ministry by hearing what the Spirit is saying to the churches and by setting things in order accordingly for the expansion of the kingdom of God."[58]

This is a definition that has been agreed to by the International Coalition of Apostles, which, due to being made up of nearly 500 apostles, many of whom oversee churches worldwide, carries weight and influence in

---

52. The International Coalition of Apostles was founded in 1999 and now has nearly 500 members worldwide who are officially recognized apostles in the light of their gifting and character. Apostle John Kelly "asked C. Peter Wagner to assume overall leadership of International Coalition of Apostles as Presiding Apostle"; however, in 2010, Peter Wagner asked John Kelly to be the presiding Apostle, and Wagner has become the presiding Apostle Emeritus. For history of movement and quotation see International Coalition of Apostles, "History."

53. Wagner, *Apostles and Prophets*; Wagner, *City*; Wagner, *Spheres*; Wagner, *Apostles Today*.

54. Wagner, *New Apostolic Churches*; Wagner, *Churchquake*; Wagner, *Changing*.

55. Wagner, *Apostles Today*, 8–9.

56. Ibid., 6–10. See also chap. 1 of Wagner, *Changing*.

57. Anonymous, "Joining Forces," 32.

58. Wagner, *Apostles Today*, 143.

numerous Christian networks. Wagner does not explicitly explain what he means by the "foundational government" that apostles establish; it most likely refers to his belief that the church is properly established only when done so according to Ephesians 2:20—that is, on the foundation laid by apostles and prophets. In arguing that apostles have this foundational governmental role, Wagner believes that they have "exceptional authority";[59] not only are they the initiators of things, but they are governors as well, they exercise a rule; hence they are able to set things in order. In essence they are the ones who offer leadership and direction to churches so as to align them with God's purposes.

Like a missionary, apostles are called and sent out; however they are different to them on the basis of spiritual authority; whereas a missionary is gifted to minister across cultures in whichever spiritual gift they have been given, an apostle has "extraordinary" spiritual authority "to assume and exercise general leadership"[60] in the area to which they have been called. However, the apostle's authority and gifting is limited to their assigned sphere, and "Once apostles get outside of their sphere, they have no more authority than any other member of the body of Christ."[61] The sphere of authority is vital to Wagner's understanding of the apostolic office and can either be ecclesiastical, geographical or functional. The ecclesiastical sphere relates to authority over churches and "possibly derivative ministries";[62] the geographical or territorial sphere relates to certain locations or people groups; the functional sphere relates to individuals or groups with the same ministry/gifting.[63]

For Wagner, the church is only now realizing that her foundation should be built upon apostles and prophets. He argues that in practice the church has been built as though pastors and teachers were the foundation; therefore he urges his readers to consider how much more fruitful it will be when we align ourselves with God's way of biblical government as explained in Ephesians 2:20.[64] Wagner does not like to refer to the fivefold "ministry" as he believes this confuses the fact that they are meant to equip the saints to do the work of ministry; as a result he refers to them

59. Ibid., 22.
60. Wagner, *Churchquake*, 105–6; quotes from 105.
61. Wagner, "Understanding."
62. Wagner, "Foundation."
63. Ibid.
64. "The household of God is built on the foundation of the apostles and prophets, Jesus Christ himself being the chief cornerstone."

PART ONE—Where We Are

as "'foundational' or 'governmental' or 'equipping' offices."[65] On the basis of 1 Corinthians 12:4–6,[66] Wagner asserts that although many are gifted as apostles their "activities" and therefore the type of apostle they are can differ. He has categorized apostles into four main categories: 1) *Foundational*—apostles who pioneer something new; 2) *Reformational*—apostles who reclaim truths or churches that have been lost in some way.[67] 3) *Vertical* apostles, who "lead networks of churches or ministries or individuals who look to the apostle for spiritual 'covering'"[68] (or "protection"); and 4) *Horizontal* apostles who "serve peer-level leaders in helping them to connect with each other for different purposes."[69]

There are four types of vertical apostles: First, ecclesiastical apostles, who oversee a set of churches or church-related ministries or networks. Second, apostolic team members; they exercise apostolic ministry alongside but under the main apostle's leadership. Third, functional apostles; they oversee "a certain type of specialized ministry," such as women's ministry or deliverance ministries. Finally, congregational apostles; they pastor churches and grow them beyond 700 or 800 people.[70] Horizontal apostles' "anointing" (or God-given gifting) "is in bringing together peers of one kind or another to accomplish certain purposes better than they could separately";[71] a biblical example is James who called the council of Jerusalem and gave an authoritative decree.[72] There are several types: First, convening apostles; these are those who first "call together peer-level Christian leaders who minister in a defined field on a regular basis" and second, "have the ability to form relational organizations for specific purposes as God directs";[73] this is how Wagner sees his own call and he gives several examples of groups he has convened (Apostolic Council for Educational Accountability; Apostolic Council of Prophetic Elders; International Society of Deliverance Ministers; International Coalition of

---

65. Wagner, *Apostles Today*, 11.

66. "Now there are diversities of gifts, but the same Spirit. There are differences of ministries, but the same Lord. And there are diversities of activities, but it is the same God who works all in all."

67. Wagner, *Apostles Today*, 88–89.

68. Ibid., 77.

69. Ibid., 79.

70. Ibid., 90–95.

71. Ibid., 96

72. Ibid., 79–81.

73. Ibid., 96.

Popular Charismatic Teachers on Apostles

Apostles; Eagle's Vision Apostolic Team).[74] Ambassadorial apostles are itinerant and are gifted through their meetings with apostolic peers to "catalyze and nurture apostolic movements on a broad scale."[75] Mobilizing apostles are itinerant too but will draw leaders together to "focus on a specific cause or project."[76] Finally, the territorial apostle, whose sphere of influence is place-related either to a nation, a state, a region, a city or even an area within a city—he sees biblical justification for this concept in Peter and Paul's calling to be apostles to the Jews and Gentiles respectively.[77]

Wagner believes it is possible to function in more than one type of office and accepts Bill Hamon's idea of "hyphenated apostles" so you could be an apostle-teacher; likewise one can be both a vertical and horizontal apostle. One's apostolic sphere can either be in the "nuclear church" (connected with traditional church meetings) or within the "workplace"; Wagner refers to the workplace as "extended church."[78] Workplace apostles are identified[79] owing to their level of wealth, the respect given to them due to their work accomplishments, their influence, their risk taking, their "accumulated skills,"[80] their level of experience and a passion to see kingdom values "permeate society on every level."[81]

As to how apostles relate to local leadership of the church, to pastors/elders, will depend on what kind of apostleship he/she has been called to. For workplace apostles, and those who are leading ministries, they will duly submit to the pastors in their local church. However, if you are an apostle over a church, you would have authority over the pastors/elders and would be seen as the final port of call. Wagner recognizes that it is a real problem determining who a leading apostle should be accountable to and considers different suggestions—notably that of Barney Coombes who believes the apostle should be accountable to God, to peers, and to the local church that sent the apostle out.[82] Wagner believes that peer-level accountability is key to the survival of the New Apostolic Reformation[83]

---

74. Ibid., 96–97.
75. Ibid., 98.
76. Ibid.
77. Ibid., 99.
78. See ibid., 110.
79. The following characteristics are taken from ibid., 115–17.
80. Ibid., 116.
81. Ibid., 117.
82. Wagner, *Churchquake*, 122.
83. Ibid., 122–23.

and has therefore brought leading apostles together to form accountable relationships.[84]

The image of fathering and mothering used by Paul is taken up by Wagner as an apt description of how an ecclesiastical apostle should relate to congregations he has started and established. In this role as a spiritual parent the apostle is to provide "protection, . . . role modelling, . . . correction (accountability) and . . . empowerment."[85] How they relate to other churches which they have not personally planted will be connected to their sphere of authority. They might, for example, start one main church, but in the end have authority over all the other churches that have affiliated with him/her and his/her church; however, if it is not within their God-given sphere they have no authority over them.

Wagner differentiates between the gift of apostleship and the office of apostle: the gift is given by grace alone, but the office is attained "as a result of works that have demonstrated faithfulness in stewardship of the gift."[86] The fruit of the gift becomes evident to others, and usually apostles and prophets will commission them by the laying on of hands.[87] All apostles will have a certain sphere assigned them by God[88] and must possess the following traits: "*extraordinary character . . . humility . . . leadership . . . authority . . . integrity . . . wisdom*"[89] and prayerfulness. Alongside these, all apostles will receive revelation and hear what the Spirit is saying to the churches, cast vision in accordance with this revelation, initiate works or projects, impart spiritual gifts, enable the building of projects/works, govern by setting things in order, teach the Word of God, send others out, finish projects, "lead the church in spiritual warfare,"[90] raise up new generations of leaders, equip the saints for the work of the ministry; whereas only some apostles will have seen Jesus, perform signs and wonders, expose heresy, plant new churches, impose church discipline, minister cross-culturally, take territory from the enemy and convert it to the kingdom.[91] Peter Wagner has radically broadened out what constitutes an apostle. Wagner credits Bill Hamon—who is committed to the theology that came

---

84. Wagner, *Apostles and Prophets*, 67–70.
85. Wagner, *Churchquake*, 120.
86. Wagner, *Apostles Today*, 144.
87. Ibid.
88. Ibid.
89. Ibid., 145.
90. Ibid., 29.
91. Ibid., 146–47.

through the 1948 Latter Rain movement concerning the full restoration of the five-fold ministry especially Apostles and Prophets—of profoundly impacting him. Hamon is a prolific American minister and author, who founded and heads Christian International Ministries Network which provides "covering" for numerous churches and ministers. He has written in detail on the Latter Rain Revival and made a convincing case for the influence that it had on the Charismatic Movement; he argues that many of the features that appeared in that movement were initially "recovered" in the 1948 revival.[92] Hamon likens his working relationship with Wagner in propagating "the Apostolic movement" to how "Martin Luther and John Calvin worked together in propagating the Protestant Movement."[93] Wagner has built upon Hamon's Restorationist and Latter Rain perspective and utilized Roger Mitchell's[94] categories.

Wagner's friendship with Wimber and the Kansas City Prophets rubbed off on him, and in his book *Apostles and Prophets*, he details numerous prophetic encounters with the "prophets" which he saw as genuine;[95] their particular Restorationist eschatology and (Latter Rain) predictions of a super breed of apostles re-emerging in the church and his role in it were taken to heart by Wagner.[96] It was due to Wimber that he started to take the prophetic seriously.[97] Wagner has given new terminology to thinking about apostles and has interacted with a wide spectrum of opinions. Wagner's vision of workplace apostles is uncommon—no longer are apostles identified due to their founding churches, or even church-related ministries, but through their entrepreneurship in business settings. The weight he places upon Ephesians 2:20 in regards to the apostle's ministry is very controversial, and is on a par with the Apostolic's as well as the Mormon's insistence that it is a key verse in determining true church order.[98]

92. See Hamon, *Eternal*, chaps. 24–25.

93. Ibid., 280.

94. Roger Mitchell has been involved in numerous Pioneer-connected church plants in England and is recognized by Wagner and others as an apostle.

95. E.g., Wagner, *Apostles and Prophets*, 108–9, 126–27.

96. Wagner describes an experience he had with Mike Bickle and Jim Goll in which they prophesied that Wagner would follow in John's footsteps and "call forth the apostolic community." Ibid., 127. For a look at some of the "Prophets" controversial revelations about the end-time generation and ministry, see Gruen, "Documentation."

97. Wagner, *Apostles and Prophets*, 85; and now he will even move his finances in relation to a trusted prophetic voice. See ibid., 103.

98. This is not to suggest that Wagner has been influenced by the Mormons! Nor that he is a heretic not holding to the main tenets of the orthodox Christian faith, I think it is quite clear that he does. Nevertheless, the similarities between the Mormon

Part One—Where We Are

Mike Breen—"Luke 10 Apostles"

Mike Breen became a Christian at sixteen and immediately felt called to be a missional leader;[99] having trained at Oak Hill, he was ordained, and rose to prominence as a Church of England minister in Brixton, and then as rector and team leader of St Thomas Crooke's Church in Sheffield. In 2003 he helped set up a religious order called The Order of Mission (TOM), of which he is the leader; in 2004 he joined the staff of the Community Church of Joy in Arizona, a church with a claimed membership of over 12,000 people, and started teaching at Fuller Seminary. He is a regular conference speaker in the USA and the UK, and his discipleship teaching tool, LifeShapes, is becoming popular on both sides of the Atlantic. He has lately set up Three Dimension Ministries online which claims to be "a movement of churches learning how to thrive in the future."[100] Alongside this he was made the General Director of the European Church Planting Network (ECPN) which has "the stated goal of seeing 500 new churches planted by the end of 2011."[101] Breen has contributed *The Apostle's Notebook*[102] to Barry Kissel's ministry guide series; he also discusses the apostle's ministry in his books co-written with Walt Kallestad.[103]

In *The Apostle's Notebook*, Breen considers the following three arguments to why apostles are emerging today: First, the end-time harvest (the belief that just prior to Christ's return there will be a massive ingathering of people into God's kingdom) requires end-time apostles; second, a church that has been restored by God requires a restored five-fold ministry; third, accelerating cultural change demands a fresh impetus in mission. Breen, although unconvinced by the first category, doesn't dismiss the second and clearly endorses the third. He writes positively about the New Apostolic Reformation, and is convinced that God "is allowing the decline of mainstream Christianity to follow the social and cultural changes in the West, while at the same time birthing a new church movement committed to apostolic mission."[104]

---

doctrine on apostles and prophets with Wagner's vision of these authoritative ministries that bring revelation from God is striking.

99. Jones, "Giving Shape."

100. Quotation from 3DM, "About."

101. Leadership Network, "Church Planting."

102. Breen, *Notebook*.

103. Breen and Kallestad, *Life*; Breen and Kallestad, *Workbook*; Breen and Kallestad, *Church*.

104. Breen, *Notebook*, 27.

Popular Charismatic Teachers on Apostles

For Breen, apostolic principles for mission along with apostles to implement and exemplify them are vital for the church's task today. He grounds his belief in the reality of modern day apostles on Ephesians 4:11–13 and argues that because Ephesians was a letter written for the church universal there is a universal application to the teaching on how the body functions and on what gifts people receive. From this he argues, contrary to the mainstream Charismatic interpretation, that each Christian is given a "base" ministry (this is the ministry that God has designed you to fulfill and which is in accordance with your gifts and aptitude) either as an apostle, prophet, evangelist, pastor, or teacher. Therefore, for the church to reach maturity all these ministries must function healthily together. This does not mean that if your base ministry is apostle that that is the only ministry you will ever function in; in fact, you will experience phases when you operate in another type of ministry. Furthermore, the more mature one gets the more able one is to cope with being in a "phase ministry," and thereby become more rounded. He rejects the idea it is only the apostle who can function in all five roles (this is a belief particularly prominent in Pentecostal circles, but is also espoused by Charismatic leaders like Ulf Ekman) and argues that this is potentially what all believers can do, whilst still retaining a base ministry.[105]

Breen uses a number of words/phrases to describe an apostle: one who is "sent out"; a visionary; a pioneer.[106] He sees Jesus as the perfect embodiment of the apostolic ministry; he, like all later apostles, needed to be prepared for this ministry, which involved living life in obscurity, an impartation of the Holy Spirit and the testing of his call. "All these contributed to releasing the authority and power that Jesus needed to do the work"[107] to which he was called. Breen believes we can see four main characteristics of Jesus' apostolic ministry: pioneering; planting; bridging and building; all of which can be seen in some of the early church's apostolic ministries, and therefore should be a feature of apostolic ministry today.

Breen looks at Jesus' ministry in Capernaum and shows how he pioneered by "claiming lives as new territory for the kingdom of God (*examples being the calling of the disciples*);[108] proclaiming the gospel to any who would hear; acting decisively with enemy counterattacks (*examples*

---

105. Ibid., chap. 8.
106. Breen and Kallestad, *Life*, 144–45.
107. Breen, *Notebook*, 50.
108. Ibid., 43–44.

Part One—Where We Are

being his encounters with evil spirits);[109] operating in divine authority and power; establishing a bridgehead (*at Peter's house*)[110] from which he could work."[111]

Peter and Paul's pioneering is seen in their involvement in proclaiming the gospel and bringing people into God's kingdom. Undergirding this apostolic ability is the need to have been through suffering and trials like Paul, for according to Breen it is out of weakness and submission that there comes power and authority to pioneer "a new frontier."[112] He thinks that these features are always true based on his consideration of Scripture, church history, and modern day examples.

He posits that there is an overlap between pioneering and planting, and that the essence of apostolic planting consists in establishing a new community. "As an apostolic planter, Jesus: recognized the right time to plant; identified the people who could open doors to other relationships; prioritized relationship over popularity; focused his energy and gifts into a small, gathered group; imparted a pattern of community life that could grow and multiply all by itself."[113]

He divides up Jesus' strategy into four principles: time, team, target and task;[114] Breen argues that this strategy is not only the one that Jesus himself modeled but which he gave to his disciples when (the time) he sent them out in twos (the team) on mission to proclaim and demonstrate the kingdom of God (the task), and stay with those who received them (the target—these people are known as people of peace).[115] Breen shows how these same principles are seen in Paul's ministry in Macedonia and how a local church was established as a result. He argues that these principles should be practiced today by those involved in mission, along with a reliance on the Holy Spirit to reveal what is God's timing, who the team should be, who are the targets and to grant God's manifest power in word and deed in accordance with the task of proclaiming God's kingdom.[116]

Using the examples of how Jesus taught in Galilee and Jerusalem and how he reached out in Samaria, Breen argues that we see Jesus bridging

---

109. Ibid., 44.
110. Ibid., 45.
111. Ibid.
112. Ibid., 71.
113. Ibid., 46.
114. Ibid., 83–87.
115. Ibid.
116. Ibid., chap. 4.

Popular Charismatic Teachers on Apostles

by: recognizing "the different needs of different cultures"; communicating "appropriately according to cultural needs"; using "his pioneering and planting gifts to establish a cross-cultural bridgehead"; addressing "cultural prejudices among his disciples so that their eyes would be opened to the new bridging opportunity."[117] According to Breen, Paul exemplifies this apostolic manner of building in Athens where he: "recognized the needs of the Athenian culture; communicated appropriately; pioneered and planted a cross-cultural bridgehead" (Breen defines this as "establishing new churches among different cultures");[118] and "addressed cultural prejudices in his hearers."[119]

As an apostolic "builder," Jesus established basic structures which could be easily repeated by his followers. Breen believes these can be seen by the way Jesus instituted the following into the basic structures of the new community: "teamwork; shared life; common resources; repeatable teaching; strategies for mission."[120] The apostles Peter and Paul explore building as a metaphor for the church in their writings, and drawing on their imagery and upon Paul's vision of the church as the Body of Christ Breen argues that the apostle's role is integral in ensuring that the building of the Christian community is done with biblical values and vision; these he identifies as grace (the values), and the kingdom of God (the vision). Alongside the vision and values a vocabulary is needed to convey Christian discipleship. This led Breen to develop the LifeShapes material, which involve the use of familiar shapes to help recall the teaching of Jesus.[121]

Breen does not dictate to how an apostle should relate to other members of the Body, however, his general principle is that all relationships within the body should be characterized by grace. In none of his writing does he speak of the apostle in lofty terms as one to whom others by virtue of his ministry should submit; this is borne out in Breen's practice where one of the principles established at St Thomas' was having low control but high accountability.[122] His emphasis on relationship and accountability would also militate against a dictatorial type of apostle. Nevertheless, because in Breen's scheme the apostle has a vital role to "define the structures

---

117. Ibid., 48.
118. Ibid., 113.
119. Ibid., 115.
120. Ibid., 49.
121. Ibid., chap. 6.
122. See St Thomas' Church, "Our Core Values."

PART ONE—Where We Are

and strategies and to lead the spearhead of mission,"[123] it would be imperative that the Christian community heeded him/her for the sake of the church's mission.

Breen describes how an apostle ought to function in regards to Jesus' teaching and example, but he does not make a list of marks to discern whether one is a true apostle or not. Nevertheless, his teaching presupposes that if someone shows the characteristics of Jesus' and the early apostles' apostolic ministry that would be an indicator that they were an apostle. He also believes that apostles tend to have "a definite moment when they meet God and hear his call."[124] Breen also believes one can discern whether you are an apostle or not through recognizing the kind of person God has shaped you to be, for example if you are a visionary pioneer with missional desires that would be an indication that your base ministry is as an apostle. To help people identify their base ministry he has developed a questionnaire.[125] Apostolic characteristics can be seen in "Business entrepreneurs" as they are "another example of this kind of person—someone eager to conquer the next business frontier, only to move onto some new endeavour after that."[126] The size or sphere of your ministry is not however, an indicator of whether one is an apostle or not.[127] To become mature as an apostle will involve the duress of operating in all the other four ministries and the willingness to return to them when needed; yet, this is incumbent upon all Christians to reach maturity not just apostles.[128]

From his own admission Breen was influenced by "a reformed Evangelical expository preaching ministry";[129] Breen was later influenced by the Pentecostal Charismatic Movement including the prophetic.[130] In spite of these influences his interpretation of Ephesians 4 does seem to be unique. Out of all the authors his view is the only one that arguably does away with a clergy/laity distinction, which the normal Charismatic/Pentecostal understanding of the five-fold ministry gives rise to. His detailed attention to Jesus' ministry as the exemplary apostle is uncommon as is his contention that the basis of apostolic mission is found in Jesus'

---

123. Breen, *Notebook*, 218.
124. Ibid., 189.
125. You can see the questionnaire in Breen, *Notebook*, 162–71.
126. Breen and Kallestad, *Life*, 144–45.
127. Breen, *Notebook*, 158.
128. Ibid., 192.
129. Ibid., 174.
130. Ibid., 178.

directives to the Twelve and the Seventy, rather than a mandate of the Spirit post-Pentecost. Nevertheless, he does stand upon the shoulders of other Charismatic/Pentecostal teachers by recognizing five ministries, rather than four, and seeing them as perpetual gifts to the church. He has read widely, being familiar with Wagner's work on the New Apostolic Reformation,[131] and the teaching of Watchman Nee.[132] His work with Bob and Mary Hopkins[133] has also been significant. His approach is quite broad brush, in that aside from a detailed discussion of Ephesians 4:11–13 he does not enter into the tricky exegetical issues surrounding Ephesians 2:20 or 1 Corinthians 12:28—in fact his whole theology of an ongoing apostleship is built squarely upon Ephesians 4:11–13.

Terry Virgo—"1 Corinthians 3:10: Master-teacher Apostles"

Terry Virgo was the overall leader of the Newfrontiers network of churches until 2011, when he handed over to a group of men who were well established in NFI. He still travels and preaches worldwide and is involved at King's Church in Kingston.[134] Virgo was born in Brighton in 1940. His conversion to Christianity occurred when he was sixteen, and several years later he was "baptized in the Spirit." He became very involved in the Charismatic Movement, began ministry as a Pastor of a small church at Seaford. In time he became associated with the radical House Church leaders. Walker categorizes the movement into two groups—those who are more "conservative," were classed as R1, and those that were more "liberal"—R2. When the movement split Virgo aligned himself with R1.[135] As his reputation and experience of ministry grew, some Charismatics in the Hove area asked him to come and oversee them. He duly did, and out of this the Brighton and Hove Christian Fellowship was started. Unlike many of his contemporaries in the radical House Church, due to the influence

---

131. Ibid., 27.

132. Ibid., 75.

133. Bob Hopkins and his wife Mary set up Anglican Church Planting Initiatives in 1992 and have worked alongside Breen at Sheffield. Bob Hopkins was on the working group for *Mission-Shaped Church* as a consulting editor.

134 From http://newfrontierstogether.org, accessed Dec 1, 2013.

135. For a full discussion of the difference between the two groups as well as the events that led to the split see Walker, *Restoring*, chaps. 1–4.

Part One—Where We Are

of Martyn Lloyd-Jones and others, Terry became convinced of Reformed theology.[136]

The church in Hove became a Charismatic center of influence, and it was from there that "Coastlands" began, which would evolve into Newfrontiers International (NFI). This network has now expanded across the UK and into other countries. Virgo's commitment to church planting and missions has imprinted itself upon these churches. Virgo's influence has spread beyond his network due to his appearance at various conferences such as Spring Harvest and Holy Trinity Brompton's Focus (HTB), as well as his own hugely popular Newfrontiers International-run Stoneleigh Bible Weeks and latterly the *Together on a Mission* events. He is a bestselling author and many of his books have been well received not only within Charismatic circles, but also in more Conservative Evangelical ones due to his commitment to Reformed theology and complementarian views on men and women. This has opened up opportunities for him to work with non-Charismatic conservative groups such as UCCF (Universities and Colleges Christian Fellowship). Virgo has written on apostles in a number of books[137] as well as in magazine articles.[138]

Virgo is adamant that apostles are a vital gift given by the ascended Christ to his church and that Ephesians 4:12–13 makes it clear that they will be given to the church "until" it reaches maturity. Therefore it is essential that churches both recognize apostles and receive their ministry. Unlike many popular writers on apostles, Virgo is keen to interact with credible New Testament scholarship and scholars. He draws upon the seminal work of J. B. Lightfoot to both argue that the apostles in the New Testament consisted of more than the Twelve and Paul, and to understand what a New Testament apostle is.[139] Based upon the meaning of the Greek word for "apostle" (ἀπόστολος), Terry Virgo argues that the apostle is a "sent one"; this "sentness" is seen in the primary New Testament apostle, Jesus, who often talked of himself as having been sent by the Father.[140] Virgo believes there are three types of apostle mentioned in the New Testament. The first type is Jesus; the second, the Twelve; the third consist of all the others mentioned. He argues the uniqueness of the Twelve on the basis that they were the core group chosen by Jesus as the foundation

---

136. Virgo, *Paths*.
137. E.g., Virgo, *Restoration*; Virgo, *Future*.
138. E.g., Virgo, "Local Churches under Apostolic Authority."
139. Virgo, *Restoration*, 129–30.
140. Ibid., 129.

of the New Israel. He is unsure where to place Paul due to the amount of revelation that he was given and the unique ministry that he seemed to have; nevertheless, he thinks that Paul's apostleship was not so unique, as Luke happily classes him alongside Barnabas making no differentiation between their apostolic ministries; therefore, he feels that Paul's apostleship is linked to the ascended Christ like all the other apostles mentioned in the New Testament—aside from Jesus and the Twelve.[141] Like others, he sees a case for viewing James as an apostle, as well as Andronicus and Junias.[142]

Although unsure whether to categorize Paul as unique or not, he clearly sees his ministry as a model for what apostolic ministry consists of. As a result he looks to Paul's description of his own ministry as key in discovering what apostolic ministry looks like. Therefore, he argues that a key function of an apostle is as "a master builder and foundation layer" (1 Cor 3:10). He has "a stewardship from God . . . to proclaim the unfathomable riches of Christ and bring people to an assured understanding of what it is to be in Christ and have Christ in them." He brings the "authoritative word" that sets churches "free from legalism, super-spirituality and other dangers."[143]

The ascension gift of apostle therefore has a unique role in laying the foundations of churches. That can take the form of the starting of a new church and ensuring that it is built upon apostolic doctrine; or of sending apostles to a church that has been started by a non-apostle and establishing correct foundations so that it in turn could thrive as a community.[144] It is in this regard that Paul calls himself a master-builder, and according to Virgo this building is done through teaching authoritative apostolic doctrine, for it is this that will enable the community to both grow and keep them from being infected from demonic doctrines such as legalism.[145] The apostle is "essentially a travelling man" who "is able to bring an objectivity in his appraisal of a local church's present condition."[146] The fruit of his travels will be to bring a sense of unity amongst God's churches in different locations. His authority is based on both his calling and gifting from God as well as his "working relationship . . . with any particular

141. Ibid., 129–31, and Virgo, "Local Churches under Apostolic Authority."
142. Virgo, *Restoration*, 130.
143. Ibid., 132.
144. Virgo, "Local Churches under Apostolic Authority."
145. Virgo, *Restoration*, 132.
146. Ibid., 133.

PART ONE—Where We Are

church or individual."[147] The outworking of this for Paul was a "fatherly relationship" with churches he had founded such as in Corinth, Galatia, and Thessalonica.[148] This is seen in Paul's desire to recognize and appoint local leaders gifted by the Spirit. His connection with churches that he has not founded is very different, as can be seen in Paul's relationship with the church in Rome.[149] The apostle is keen to expand the boundaries of the kingdom, and will be looking, like Paul was, to preach Christ where he has not been preached and to start churches in unchartered areas.[150] The apostle is called by God alone, and is enabled to fulfill his calling by grace alone. Apostles emerge like "evangelists and prophets, by the sovereign choice and anointing of God. Thus there is no apostolic succession, nor is there one stable producing all this thoroughbred stock."[151] A characteristic of the apostle will be a burden for the churches rather than just a church; likewise they will not work as individuals but in teams.[152]

Virgo recognizes that one cannot just transplant the biblical scene to today, as for example, in Britain there are already numerous churches that are established; therefore, he asks the question whether there might still be need for apostles here. His answer is "yes," because there is a need to plant new churches "that are healthy, powerful communities built firmly on the word of God and relevant to modern society." He believes such churches with apostolic oversight are being planted and that even older churches can look to "apostolic ministry to help them through barriers."[153] One part of the contemporary apostle's role "is to bring the plumb-line to church life to see if it matches biblical revelation." However, "he cannot impose his authority in other churches. . . . He will, however, happily respond to invitations from church elders who reach out for his help."[154] Yet in both cases, it is important to recognize the God given authority that the apostle has, and Virgo is adamant that where there is anointed leadership or apostles, they should be heeded as there is no democracy in such circumstances.[155]

---

147. Ibid., 134.
148. Ibid., 133.
149. Ibid., 134.
150. Ibid., 134–36.
151. Ibid., 136.
152. Ibid., 139.
153. Ibid., 137.
154. Ibid., 138.
155. Ibid., 135.

Nevertheless, he is clear that Christians have a responsibility to discern whether an apostle is from God or not.[156]

What is evident from Virgo's writings is the prominence of teaching correct grace-filled doctrine as an indispensable part of the apostle's ministry. The stress is on this, more than church planting or itinerant ministry—both of which are facets of the apostolic call according to Virgo. I imagine that this emphasis comes from teachers, such as Martyn Lloyd-Jones, who focused on biblical teaching and correct doctrines of "grace." From his autobiography it is clear that there are a host of books/people who have influenced him and he particularly mentions famed Evangelicals who helped establish him in Reformed doctrines: for example, Martyn Lloyd-Jones, J. I. Packer, A. W. Pink, John Stott, C. H. Spurgeon.[157] His association with the other house church leaders undoubtedly rubbed off on him—therefore, we likely see traces of Arthur Wallis, David Lillie, and Bryn Jones upon his thinking—particularly in their desire to recover New Testament church life. He also writes concerning the impact of Watchman Nee on his own views and how they as a church in Hove embraced some of his teachings.[158]

Kenneth Hagin—"Ephesians 4:11–13: Ascension Gift, Non-foundational Apostles"

Kenneth Erwin Hagin was born in 1917 in Texas, raised Methodist, born again at fifteen, after which he became Baptist and then Pentecostal. He pastored five Assemblies of God churches before becoming an itinerant Bible teacher and evangelist. He was a frequent speaker at Full Gospel Business Men's Fellowship events and was part of the voice of Healing revival in the 1940s and 1950s. He started the Kenneth E. Hagin Evangelistic Association in 1963 which began to encompass all sorts of media outreaches and ministries including book publishing, a television and radio program, a monthly magazine, a correspondence Bible school, and a prayer and healing center. In 1974 he started RHEMA Bible Training Center USA which has expanded internationally with centers in fourteen countries. Since his death in 2003, Kenneth Hagin Ministries continues

---

156. Ibid., 138.
157. Ibid., 50.
158. Virgo, *Paths*, 102.

under the leadership of Hagin's son, Kenneth Hagin Jr.[159] Controversy has surrounded his teaching on the atonement, faith, and his insistence that health and wealth are part of the Christian's inheritance in Christ. He has been charged with plagiarism, too.[160] In spite of this, his preaching and writing has impacted many and continues to do so. Hagin has produced a study guide on the five-fold ministry,[161] devoted a chapter to apostles in his book *Understanding the Anointing*, and gone into detail on the subject in *He Gave Gifts unto Men*.

Hagin reasons from Ephesians 4:11–13 that Christ will continue to give apostles, prophets, evangelists, pastors, and teachers to the church until it reaches maturity; furthermore, there is nothing in the passage to suggest that any of these gifts have been withdrawn; therefore, they have been present throughout the church's history.[162] Nevertheless, there are only certain types of apostle that Christ is still giving. Like former leading Pentecostalists Donald Gee and Gordon Lindsay, Hagin refers to an apostle as a ministry gift and as an office. To understand this ministry/office he looks at the meaning of the Greek word for apostle and concludes that it means "a sent one." This meaning is reflected in the ministry of the New Testament apostles, the perfect example being Jesus, who were all sent out on a mission with a message.[163] Hagin argues that the New Testament differentiates between "ranks or classes of apostles." This was elucidated to him during a "visitation from the Lord" in 1987 when Jesus said to him, "There are four classes or ranks of apostles. And within these different classes or ranks, apostles can have different degrees or measures of anointing."[164] Using this framework Hagin divides up apostles into four groups: First, Jesus as the Apostle; second, the Twelve apostles of the Lamb; third, "other foundational apostles"; fourth, "non-foundational apostles."[165]

---

159. For biographical information see Riss, "Hagin," 687. See also the biographical information on Hagin at Kenneth Hagin Ministries, "Founder's Memorial."

160. The similarity of wording between some of his and E. W. Kenyon's writings is beyond dispute, and as a result the charge of plagiarism is hard to refute. See Tillin, "Plagiarism," for the comparison.

161. Hagin, *Ministry*.

162. Hagin, *Gifts*, 1–3.

163. Hagin, *Understanding*, 87.

164. Hagin, *Gifts*, 8.

165. Ibid., 8ff.

Jesus' apostleship is in a league of its own, as he was given "the Spirit without measure."[166] The twelve apostles of the Lamb, or twelve disciples, are also unique in that according to Revelation 21:14 their apostleship laid the foundation of the New Jerusalem; furthermore, according to Acts 1:15–22 to be one of the Twelve, one had to have been with Jesus since John's baptism and be an eyewitness of his resurrection. Nevertheless, there is another unique group of apostles, like Paul, who alongside some prophets received infallible revelation alongside the Twelve which made up New Testament doctrine—they are mentioned along with prophets in Ephesians 2:20: "God used them to help lay down New Testament doctrine (Eph 2:20)" and "some of them wrote various Books of the Bible."[167] The unique office that the Twelve and the other "foundational apostles" operated in is unrepeatable. Once they had laid the foundation of New Testament doctrine, there was no need for Christ to give that peculiar ministry to others in the church. Hagin's Jesus said to him, "There are *no* foundational apostles and *no* foundational prophets today."[168] However, there are other apostles mentioned in the New Testament who were not "foundational" ones, and there are aspects of the apostolic ministry given to Paul that the church at large needs and Christ is still giving.

Hagin believes that Jesus spoke to him at length on this subject because Jesus knew that certain errors were about to reappear in the Body of Christ. Since that visit Hagin has identified three erroneous ideas that have arisen about apostles: the idea "that in order to have proper New Testament church government, the fivefold ministry must operate in every local church and make up the *government* of each local church";[169] the idea that apostles should govern every other ministry gift in the local church; finally, that "modern-day apostles and prophets are supposed to be laying down New Testament doctrine and foundation"[170]—as a result, if you do not have an apostle governing and a prophet guiding your church, you do not have a "correct New Testament foundation."[171] Hagin believes that apostles today cannot stand in the same office and anointing as Paul and the Twelve because the foundation of the church, which he understands as being the gospel, has already been laid, Jesus Christ being the chief cor-

---

166. Ibid., 9, quoting John 3:34.
167. Ibid., 13.
168. Ibid., 16.
169. Ibid., 17.
170. Ibid.
171. Ibid., 7–8; quote from 18.

nerstone. If there were such apostles today it would mean that the New Testament was not closed, as they could add to it. He also rejects as a misunderstanding and misapplication of 1 Corinthians 12:28 and Ephesians 4:11 the idea that the apostle is over all other ministry gifts. This is because if the gifts in these passages are listed in order of authority it would contradict the insistence elsewhere that the pastor/bishop has the highest authority; whereas read as a hierarchical list, Ephesians 4:11 implies that the evangelist has authority over the pastor; and according to 1 Corinthians 12:28, the minister of helps has authority over that "office."[172]

Hagin suggests that a better way to understand the order is to see it as a description of the development of ministries that occurred in the early church. To begin with there were apostles, then prophets, and so on. Those who think each ministry gift has to be manifested in every local church have, according to Hagin, failed to distinguish those gifts that are given to the universal church from those that are manifested in the local church. He is also suspicious of people broadcasting themselves as apostles, and warns away from titles and encourages others to make their conclusion based on the type of fruit produced in their lives and ministry.[173]

Having established that the only types of apostolic ministry possible today are non-foundational ones he discusses what they are like. First, are those like Epaphroditus, who are sent with a message either for the local or universal church. However, Hagin thinks that the more usual type of apostle is one who founds and "establishes churches and pioneers new works."[174] He sees Paul exemplifying this ministry in the way he started and established Gentile churches. The apostle has the gifting to evangelize and then nurture and pastor believers.[175] The office of the apostle "seems to embrace all other ministry gifts."[176] The reason for this is that they have the ability to "establish churches."[177] Hagin believes that God would not require one thing to qualify for one ministry gift office and expect different for another, therefore to become an apostle one must meet the conditions of 1 Timothy 3:1–8 and have good character; conduct him/herself well; be able to teach sound doctrine; not be a lover of money; be a mature Christian and have a good report from outsiders.[178] The call to ministry is

172. Ibid., 20.
173. Ibid., 24–26.
174. Ibid, 30. Also see Hagin, *Ministry*, 42.
175. Hagin, *Gifts*, 30.
176. Hagin, *Understanding*, 88–89.
177. Ibid., 89.
178. Hagin, *Gifts*, 57–70.

from God and men can only affirm and recognize a calling and gifting.[179] God will bring someone into the office of apostle if he has called you to it, and you have been faithful in the gifts he has given you before.[180] Pastors can stand in the apostolic office to a limited degree, like James did, if they have been sent by the Spirit with a message (the gospel) to build a church in a certain place.[181] Within that calling, one also needs to be aware of who one is called to—so Paul is called as an apostle to the Gentiles.[182]

Hagin considers the apostles' relationship to the Christian community and is adamant that the local pastor is the chief authority in the local church; in practice that means that any itinerant ministry, including apostles and prophets, must submit to his/her ministry.[183] In his capacity as an apostle he can obviously help and encourage local pastors but not usurp their authority. Whilst getting churches started and established the apostle assumed authority until churches became established and had their own pastors.[184] He/she can come and encourage local congregations having been allowed to do so by the pastors of that place. Nevertheless, Hagin would see that as a sideline ministry as a true apostle desires to go and pioneer new churches where others haven't been. Furthermore, Hagin thought that the New Testament apostles never exercised authority over any other churches than the ones they established.[185]

An apostle is identified by the fruit of his ministry. He will be marked by the character requirements as seen in 1 Timothy 3:1–8, will be attested to by signs, wonders, and mighty deeds; he will plant and establish "new works in the Lord on a sound biblical foundation";[186] he will have had "a deep personal encounter with the Lord and ongoing," "beyond the ordinary," "spiritually strong relationship with Him and His Word."[187] They will have been "first and foremost a preacher or a teacher of the Word."[188] He/she will also be prepared, like Paul was, to submit his revelations and

---

179. Ibid., 4–5.
180. Ibid., 173.
181. Ibid. 33–35.
182. Ibid., 56.
183. Ibid., 55, 259.
184. Ibid., 34.
185. Hagin, *Ministry*, 37.
186. Hagin, *Gifts*, 48.
187. Hagin, *Ministry*, 34.
188. Hagin, *Gifts*, 45.

ministry to those more mature in the faith.[189] As a contrast a "false apostle tears up works with division, strife, and wrong teaching" and will counterfeit "the genuine office out of impure motives for reasons of personal gain."[190]

It is well known that much of E. W. Kenyon's thinking impacted Kenneth Hagin; however, Kenyon's focus was not on the gifts and ministries of the Spirit so his influence in this area of Hagin's thinking would appear to be minimal if existent at all. Kenneth Hagin's theology on apostles is rooted in the mainstream Pentecostal tradition—he himself having been an Assemblies of God pastor. He acknowledges his respect for both Gee and Lindsay, and sees himself doing the same thing for this generation as they did for theirs. It is clear that their views are very similar to his own—the "Jesus" who appeared to him did not add much to what these men had written about before. Although familiar with the Latter Rain movement and clearly advocating some of its main features—that is, the glory of the Latter Day Church—Hagin was wary of the leap made by some in that movement that demanded that apostles be linked to every local church.

Conclusion

As one can see from this survey of prominent Charismatic leaders' views on apostles there are competing versions of what an apostle is. Nevertheless, there are nine features that they are all united upon:

1. The church needs apostles.
2. God is still giving apostles post the apostolic era.
3. No specified number of apostles.
4. This is scripturally legitimated.
5. Ephesians 4:11–13 is the key text and source of the underlying theology that drives this emphasis.
6. There is enough in Scripture to paint a picture of how an apostle functions.
7. They exercise spiritual authority based upon an empowering by the Spirit rather than delegated authority via church hierarchy.
8. All modern apostles are "under" Scripture and not authors of it.

---

189. Ibid., 52–53.
190. Ibid., 49.

9. Paul is a model apostle par excellence and his gift is evidenced through his spiritual fatherhood of initiating and nurturing churches.

Although all our authors understand genuine apostles as having spiritual authority, the amount of authority and sphere of the apostles' authority differs widely. Much of this is directly related to the verses that they apply to modern day apostles. If one sees 1 Corinthians 12:28 and Ephesians 2:20 as pertinent to apostles' ministry today, there is a tendency to have a higher view of the authority they can wield, and their importance to the local and universal church. It is helpful to classify the types of apostles so as not to confuse the different theories, so the following is my attempt to do so in the order of the amount of authority it is possible for a Charismatic apostle to have. It is a general picture and not exact, and, as there is much crossover amongst popular descriptions, the lines are blurred.

Apostle Type 1—The "hierarchical/supreme apostles" advocated by Wagner, Virgo, and Prince. Their primary Scripture for justifying an ongoing charismatic apostolate is Ephesians 4:11–13. These are more prominent in New Apostolic Reformation (NAR) churches and Apostolic Networks, and are part of the DNA of the Apostolic Church's view of apostles. Many of them look to the following Scriptures to assert the supremacy of the apostle in all church matters: 1 Corinthians 12:28 and Ephesians 2:20. Their authority can be exercised in relation to those that they have founded and even amongst those they have not (if so invited). Their authority is capable of being on a par with the apostolic authority seen in the Twelve and Paul in their dealings with the church—not in relation to their capacity to issue Scripture. Those who advocate this form of apostleship will tend to promote the following idea: a church that has not been founded by this type of apostle, or directly linked to such a figure will be lacking—and ultimately will not be able to reach the maturity Christ wants for that community of Christians.

Apostle Type 2—This is a "non-foundational apostle" who is under the authority of the local pastor. Advocates of this position are Hagin, Gee, Lindsay, Synan; it would be the default position of most Assemblies of God (exception being Assemblies of God Australia) and Elim churches. Their primary Scripture for justifying an ongoing charismatic apostolate is Ephesians 4:11–13. Current apostles are still part of the five-fold elite and therefore clearly separated from the non-five-fold "laity," but they are to be subservient to the presbyter/elder/pastor of a church that they are ministering in.

Part One—Where We Are

Apostle Type 3—This is the "non-select" form, in that, along with the other four ministry gifts they are not reserved for a select group; every member of the church is either an apostle, prophet, pastor, teacher, or evangelist. Breen, Frost, Hirsch, and Hopkins advocate this view. The primary Scripture for justifying an ongoing charismatic apostolate is Ephesians 4:11–13. The apostle is an equal partner with the other ministries; there are times when his/her leadership gifts should be heeded by others for the sake of mission but there is no assertion that the apostle is the "top dog" due to his gifting.

How new are these ideas? Can we locate similar views in the church's history? To that we now turn as we take a whistle-stop tour looking at those documents, men and movements that have espoused similar sentiments throughout the church's two-thousand-year history.

Part Two

How We Got Here

4

Post-biblical History of Charismatic Apostles

Introduction

"There is nothing new under the sun"; is this the same in regards to the modern Charismatic fascination with present day apostles? Has the church seen it all before? What I aim to do in this chapter is provide an overview of different traditions and teaching about charismatic apostles in the church's history, and pinpoint movements and characters that have given this ministry special prominence. Although my pre-Reformation evidence is not Anglo- and Western-centered, the post-Reformation evidence is drawn much more from that area because the main missionary movements increasingly tended to come from the West. This is unsurprising as that is where the economic balance of power was, with the rise and expansion of the British Empire and the subsequent ascendancy of the USA as a super power. Therefore, prominent religious movements within the West have tended to impact both the Anglo as well as the non-Anglo world rather than vice versa. There are some notable exceptions though—particularly the impact of the Chinaman Watchman Nee. Inevitably, I have not considered every movement or individual possible; but as much as necessary to give a sufficiently comprehensive picture. It is beyond the scope of this study to provide an in-depth account of how each individual considered used the term in every one of their writings/sermons—therefore, I plan to draw out those particular aspects of their work which are pertinent to this discussion. In the course of this overview I will also, where appropriate, highlight influential interpretations of biblical passages that are now used to justify an ongoing charismatic apostolate. I will divide up this post-biblical history into three eras: 1. End of the first century to the fifth century. 2. Sixth century to the Reformation. 3. The sixteenth century to the end of the twentieth century (circa 1990). As will become apparent certain eras have more relevant information than others.

The End of the First Century to the Fifth Century: The Didache to Jerome

Faced with the New Testament text alone without the centuries of tradition to view it through, it is clear that the word "apostle" was linked to other individuals aside from the Twelve and Paul—for example, Barnabas (see Acts 14:4). Furthermore, some scholars—such as James Dunn and Walter Schmithals—believe that the ascription of the title "apostle" to the Twelve, while clearly present in the New Testament, particularly in Acts, was not part of the earliest Christian traditions.[1] Even if we can agree with the overwhelming majority of scholars that there were more than thirteen apostles mentioned in the New Testament, this does not solve the question of whether there was expectancy for an ongoing Charismatic ministry of apostles after this initial period; some have argued that there is evidence for this; others dispute this. A document which might provide evidence of an ongoing charismatic apostolate is the Didache. Scholars are divided over when this was written—dates proposed have been from AD50 to AD165.[2] Yet, whenever exactly it was written, it came to be held in high esteem by the church,[3] and provides a vital insight into the self-understanding of how ministries were to function within the church of its day. In this regard, the Didache includes a chapter on teachers, apostles and prophets: "But concerning the apostles and prophets, act according to the decree of the Gospel. Let every apostle who comes to you be received as the Lord. But he shall not remain more than one day; or two days, if

---

1. See Dunn, *Unity*, 107, and Schmithals, *Office*, 67–68. Schmithals argues that it is this tradition that is prevalent in many of the early Christian writings, not just New Testament ones, whose authors, in his opinion, did not know of the Twelve as apostles. See ibid., 241–44.

2. Burkhard, *Apostolicity*, 17, n. 45.

3. It is true that the church never included it in the canon; however, according to Eusebius it was not regarded as heretical; furthermore Athanasius "recommended it for reading by recent converts." Sullivan, *Apostles to Bishops*, 81.

there's a need. But if he remains three days, he is a false prophet. And when the apostle goes away, let him take nothing but bread until he lodges. If he asks for money, he is a false prophet . . ."[4]

Although there appears to be a distinction between apostles and prophets,[5] there is a clear overlap between them. The author writes of an apostle who is deemed a "false *prophet*," rather than a false *apostle*, if he "asks for money"—this reflects the Matthean account where Jesus speaks about the reception of the apostles and yet similarly speaks of reception of prophets (see Matt 10:40–41). What is undeniable though is that when the Didache was written there is a presupposition that itinerant teachers, apostles/(and?)prophets are still roaming around the church. Furthermore, there is no linking of these ministries to historical succession in determining whether they are of the Lord or not; rather there is an appeal to what they teach and their manner of life. Whether the "apostles" being referred to are second generation (or later) Christians cannot be determined; if we assume an early date for the Didache the "apostles" *might* refer to some of the original apostles mentioned in the New Testament.[6] However, if we go with the later date, we would be forced to consider that the church of this time was happy with the concept of an ongoing charismatic apostolate[7] still ministering in the church. Nevertheless, this ancient account raises more questions than it answers: are apostles and prophets interchangeable? What exactly did they do when they came to a Christian community—did they straighten it out? Provide authoritative teaching? Or was their ministry the same as the prophet's which is described? What is clear is that there were charismatically empowered itinerant ministers called apostles who were to be treated with reverence if discerned to be genuine. They are to be welcomed as "the Lord" himself, in accordance with the teaching Jesus gave to the Twelve in Matthew 10:40.

---

4. Anonymous, *Didache*.

5. Michael Green contends that the individuals being referred to in this section are not called apostles. (Michael Green, e-mail message to author, September 8, 2009.) I understand the reasoning behind this as prophets and apostles are interchangeable in this section of the Didache, although I do think there is evidence of a distinction as well.

6. This is the view of Ben H. Sweet; he writes in 1998: "This clearly indicates that at least some of the apostles were still living when the Didache was written." See Sweet, "Didache."

7. For many scholars this is not a problem—Ferdinand Hahn has argued that the New Testament has examples of "wandering Charismatic apostles," which, according to Burkhard, would be an apt description of these "apostles" mentioned in the Didache. Burkhard, *Apostolicity*, 17, n. 46.

Dr John McKay argues that these apostolic prophetic figures were seen as more authoritative than the static ministries at this time; he further postulates that this high accord given to these Charismatic figures diminishes as history progresses, and more authority was invested in the historical succession.[8] This argument has great merit and is indeed a reasonable inference from the evidence. If this reading is correct, we have early examples of a highly authoritative charismatic apostolate, akin in this regard with Apostle Type 1s, but sharing the usual missionary features of Apostle Type 2s with a submissive attitude toward the local community they are visiting. However, whether the Didachean situation was meant to be the norm for churches through the ages is a different matter.

Colin Kruse has identified other documents amongst the Apostolic Fathers which refer to the ministry of apostles; these include: the Epistle to Barnabas, the Epistle of St Clement, as well as Ignatius' letters, Polycarp's letter to the Philippians, 2 Clement, the Shepherd of Hermas and the writings of Irenaeus.[9] The Epistle to Barnabas mentions Christ's "own apostles" who were called to preach the gospel;[10] it is not clear whether he is referring to the Twelve or not; Kruse thinks they might well refer to other apostles;[11] but the evidence is too thin to be dogmatic about. The fact that he is recounting salvation history would make it likely that he is referring to a fixed body of apostles who were recognized by all and who were no longer being added to. Obviously the writer is not giving a complete picture of his conception of Christian ministries; nevertheless, it is hard to argue from this that he saw an ongoing apostolate as possible. The emphasis is on a past group who occupied a unique place in God's economy; the author gives no hint that they could or would be replicated.

The Epistle of Clement to the Corinthians mentions "Christ's apostles" a number of times, their main function being to proclaim the gospel and to appoint bishops and deacons; Clement believed the apostles were sent by Christ and had foreknowledge of the controversy which would surround the office of the bishop, and therefore they laid out a pattern to ensure that their apostolic ministry would continue and be handed down through reputable men at the consent of the whole church.[12] Clement does not identify who these apostles are, although he mentions Peter and

---

8. McKay, *Movements*, chap. 8.
9. Kruse, "Apostle," 80–82.
10. *Epistle of Barnabas*, in Schaff, *The Ante-Nicene Fathers 1*, 186.
11. Kruse, "Apostle," 80.
12. *1 Clement*, in Schaff, *The Ante-Nicene Fathers 1*, 28.

Post-biblical History of Charismatic Apostles

Paul as exemplary apostles—he further differentiates them from Apollos whom he calls a "man whom they (*the apostles*) had approved."[13] Clement gives the impression that the apostles were unique and had completed their divinely ordained task of establishing churches with bishops and deacons:

> Christ therefore was sent forth by God, and the apostles by Christ. Both these appointments, then, were made in an orderly way, according to the will of God. Having therefore received their orders, and being fully assured by the resurrection of our Lord Jesus Christ, and established in the word of God, with full assurance of the Holy Ghost, they went forth proclaiming that the kingdom of God was at hand. And thus preaching through countries and cities, they appointed the first-fruits [of their labours], having first proved them by the Spirit to be bishops and deacons of those who should afterwards believe. Nor was this any new thing, since indeed many ages before it was written concerning bishops and deacons. For thus saith the Scripture in a certain place, "I will appoint their bishops in righteousness, and their deacons in faith."[14]

These apostles are those who were "fully assured by the resurrection," which correlates with a common reading of the Pauline[15] and, to a certain extent Lukan,[16] idea that apostles had to have witnessed the resurrected Christ. Clement does not mention any other sort of apostle, but there may have been no need to do so as he was not discussing different ministries the Spirit was placing in the church. Nevertheless, it is clear that Clement gives a unique place to the apostles who had been "assured" of the resurrection of Christ, which would imply that they like Peter and Paul had witnessed it in some way.

Within the Epistles of Ignatius,[17] there is no mention of itinerant charismatic apostles functioning in his day. The focus is on bishops and presbyters and their importance to the church. He differentiates between

---

13. Ibid., 31.

14. Ibid., 28.

15. See 1 Corinthians 15:7–8 and 9:1, although see biblical discussion in chap. 5 as there are alternative ways to understand these verses.

16. Luke identifies this as a qualification to be one of the Twelve; nevertheless, he also refers to Barnabas as an apostle (see Acts 14:4), and there is no biblical evidence that he witnessed the resurrected Christ.

17. Short, Middle and Long letters—see Sullivan's discussion of authenticity. Sullivan, *Apostles to Bishops*, 105ff.

Part Two—How We Got Here

these two ministries, viewing the bishop above the presbyters: he writes, "your bishop presides in the place of God, and your presbyters in the place of the assembly of the apostles."[18] Ignatius writes of the bishop in very exalted terms: for example, "we should look upon the bishop even as we would upon the Lord Himself";[19] nevertheless, he does not equate the bishop with the apostles. He writes about the "college of apostles" who were the recipients of the true doctrine of Christ which they have passed onto the faithful;[20] the memory of them provides an example for the faithful to know how to respond appropriately to the bishop and presbyters.[21] The apostles are in a league of their own, and his present ministry and writing does not compare to theirs: "I do not, as Peter and Paul, issue commandments unto you. They were apostles; I am but a condemned man: they were free."[22] It is possible he sees Timothy as an apostle alongside Paul and John as he writes of the Christians at Ephesus being connected with "the apostles . . . with Paul, and John, and Timothy the most faithful."[23] The manner in which he writes about the "apostles" makes it clear that he does not believe any are alive at the time of writing—therefore, it is safe to assume that Ignatius saw the apostles as having had a once for all ministry that had passed away.

The Bishop of Smyrna, Polycarp, mentions the apostles in his letter to the Philippians: "I exhort you all, therefore, to yield obedience to the word of righteousness, and to exercise all patience, such as ye have seen [set] before your eyes, not only in the case of the blessed Ignatius, and Zosimus, and Rufus, but also in others among yourselves, and in Paul himself, and the rest of the apostles."[24]

Polycarp is referring to a recognized group called the apostles, which include Paul amongst them, who were exemplary Christians. Grammatically, one could posit that Polycarp saw Ignatius, Zosimus and Rufus as apostles but the fact that Ignatius wrote that he himself was not an apostle makes it unlikely that Polycarp heralded him as one—it therefore

---

18. See Ignatius, *Epistle to the Magnesians*, in Schaff, *The Ante-Nicene Fathers 1*, 90.

19. Ignatius, *Epistle to the Ephesians*, in Schaff, *The Ante-Nicene Fathers 1*, 75.

20. Several times Ignatius refers to the doctrine of the Lord and the apostles. See ibid., 94.

21. Ibid., 94–95.

22. Ignatius, *The Epistle to the Romans*, in Schaff, *The Ante-Nicene Fathers 1*, 108.

23. Ignatius, *Ephesians*, 80.

24. Polycarp, *The Epistle of Polycarp to the Philippians*, in Schaff, *The Ante-Nicene Fathers 1*, 54.

Post-biblical History of Charismatic Apostles

seems unlikely that Polycarp believed in a continuation of a charismatic apostolate.

The brief mention of the apostles by the writer of 2 Clement draws attention to their authoritative teaching and places their authority alongside that of the then accepted Scriptures: "the Books and the Apostles teach that the church is not of the present, but from the beginning."[25] The apostles are presented as a fixed group, the recipients of authoritative revelation; there is no indication that they are still around at the time of writing.

The Shepherd of Hermas[26] implies that there were a number of apostles[27] still alive and ministering at the time of his vision: "Those square white stones which fitted exactly into each other, are apostles, bishops, teachers, and deacons, who have lived in godly purity, and have acted as bishops and teachers and deacons chastely and reverently to the elect of God. Some of them have fallen asleep, and some still remain alive."[28]

Intriguingly the apostles do not appear to be part of the first generation of believers. Hermas makes a distinction between them in the following passage: "And the stones, sir," I said, "which were taken out of the pit and fitted into the building: what are they?" "The first," he said, "the ten, viz, that were placed as a foundation, are the first generation, and the twenty-five the second generation, of righteous men; and the thirty-five are the prophets of God and His ministers; and the forty are the apostles and teachers of the preaching of the Son of God."[29]

Hermas does not seem to be equating them with the Twelve and Paul. These apostles were noteworthy in their holiness,[30] and operated as bishops, teachers, and deacons,[31] which likely means they exercised oversight (bishops-overseers), taught the Word of God (teachers), and acted as servants (deacons). Due to the nature of Hermas' visions, it is hard to de-

---

25. 2 Clement, www.earlychristianwritings.com, chap. 14.

26. Hermas was "a lay member of the Roman church who claimed to have had visions and received instructions from heavenly messengers." Ibid., 132. *The Shepherd of Hermas* was greatly lauded in the early church: "Clement and Origen, considered the book divinely inspired, and St. Athanasius recommended its usefulness for catechesis." Ibid., 133.

27. He twice writes about forty apostles and teachers (see chaps. 15 and 16)—in both cases it appears to be symbolic, but it is noteworthy that it is far more than twelve.

28. Hermas, *Shepherd*, chap. 5.

29. Ibid., chap. 15.

30. Concerning them he writes that they "have acted . . . chastely and reverently to the elect of God." Ibid., chap. 5.

31. Ibid., chap. 5.

cipher exactly what he is communicating in regards to who these apostles were; but the fact that they are not first-generation believers lends further weight to the idea of later charismatic apostles still being recognized within certain parts of the church. Kevin Giles argues that Hermas is indeed referring to itinerant Spirit-empowered apostles still active in his day.[32] Very little can be gleaned from these slightly oblique references to apostles, however, they clearly are viewed with reverence, but not necessarily as the authority figures; therefore, we may have apostles more akin to type 2–3 apostles rather than Apostle Type 1s.

In the apocryphal work, The Acts of Thecla, Thecla is described in the last chapter as being a "martyr and apostle of God."[33] Although she is so described in the text, it became commonplace to see her in the Orthodox Church as "equal to the apostles" rather than an "apostle." Nevertheless, the fact that it does call her an apostle, gives us an early example of using the title "apostle" to describe exceptional Christians who exhibit the power of God and missionary zeal in a manner similar to some of the recognized New Testament apostles.

Irenaeus mentions apostles in Asia who appointed Polycarp bishop in Smyrna[34]—who they were he does not say; aside from this (noting that this may not be an exception) his explicit references to apostles are confined to the New Testament ones and are a fixed group—definitely the Twelve, but possibly the Seventy, too. [35] He sees valid bishops as successors of the apostles,[36] whilst recognizing a difference between them.[37] Even though he is at home with Charismatic phenomena,[38] he does not envisage apostles

---

32. Giles, "Apostles Before," 251.

33. Anonymous, *Thecla*, chap. 11.

34. Irenaeus, *Against Heresies*, Book III, in Schaff, *The Ante-Nicene Fathers 1*, 598.

35. See his discussion in *Against Heresies*, Book II, in Schaff, *The Ante-Nicene Fathers 1*, 558–59.

36. Irenaeus refutes the heretics by arguing the importance of a historical succession of bishops which trace their ordination "lineage" back to the apostles. He writes, "It is within the power of all, therefore, in every Church, who may wish to see the truth, to contemplate clearly the tradition of the apostles manifested throughout the whole world; and we are in a position to reckon up those who were by the apostles instituted bishops in the Churches, and [to demonstrate] the succession of these men to our own times; those who neither taught nor knew of anything like what these [heretics] rave about." Irenaeus, *Against Heresies*, Book III, 596.

37. The apostles have a unique role—they were the original recipients of the faith from the Lord himself; whereas, the bishops received the tradition second hand. For a fuller discussion of Irenaeus' concept of apostolicity and tradition, see Burkhard, *Apostolicity*, 49–57.

38. For example: "For some do certainly and truly drive out devils, so that those

still functioning in his day—Irenaeus' emphasis is on the tradition that the New Testament apostles passed on, and the historic episcopacy that they instituted. Tertullian similarly makes much of apostolic succession. In a fight against heretics he appeals to unbroken Episcopal succession as a guarantor of the truthfulness of the teaching they hold:

> Let them produce the original records of their churches; let them unfold the roll of their bishops, running down in due succession from the beginning in such a manner that [their] bishop shall be able to show for his ordainer and predecessor some one of the apostles or of apostolic men—a man, moreover, who continued steadfast with the apostles. For this is the manner in which the apostolic churches transmit their registers: as the church of Smyrna, which records that Polycarp was placed therein by John; as also the church of Rome, which makes Clement to have been ordained in like manner by Peter. In exactly the same way the other churches likewise exhibit (their several worthies), whom, as having been appointed to their episcopal places by apostles, they regard as transmitters of the apostolic seed.[39]

What is clear both from this excerpt and elsewhere within Tertullian's writings is that the Latin scholar viewed the apostles as a unique group who had received the true faith from God and had duly passed on that heritage to faithful men whom they appointed as bishops. The bishops were important to Tertullian not so much due to their office but the fact that they have been entrusted with "the apostolic seed." His views may have changed on charismatic apostles due to his later embracing of Montanism—yet possibly not, as there is no evidence that that movement spoke of charismatic apostles, rather the focus was on prophets instead. What he did advocate in his Montanist days was that what mattered was not bishops, but rather the working of the Spirit which he believed was evident within Montanism rather than the official church of the bishops: "Then show me, apostolic Sir, prophetic evidences, so that I may recognize your divine endowment. . . . Accordingly, the Church will indeed forgive sins; but it will be the

---

who have thus been cleansed from evil spirits frequently both believe [in Christ], and join themselves to the Church. Others have foreknowledge of things to come: they see visions, and utter prophetic expressions. Others still, heal the sick by laying their hands upon them, and they are made whole. Yea, moreover, as I have said, the dead even have been raised up, and remained among us for many years." Irenaeus, *Against Heresies*, Book III, 588.

39. Tertullian, *Prescription*, chap. 32.

Church of the Spirit that will do so by means of a spiritual man, not the Church that consists of a number of bishops."[40]

Eusebius of Caesarea begins his ecclesiastical history with reference to the "holy apostles" and the "lines of succession" from them.[41] He does not limit the number to the Twelve; commenting on 1 Corinthians 15:7 he writes, "in addition to these there had been, on the pattern of the Twelve, a large number of apostles such as Paul himself, he adds: 'Later He was seen by all the apostles.'"[42] Nevertheless, for Eusebius these "holy apostles" are connected to the earliest days of the church. This view that apostles were a first-century ministry never to be repeated due to their unique place in salvation history becomes the dominant one as church history progresses. As a result the commentary given by esteemed church leaders on pertinent verses in Paul tend toward a cessationist perspective. For example, Chrysostom although seeing a much wider band of apostles[43] than the Twelve and Paul, believed that Paul was the last of them. He comments on 1 Corinthians 15:7: "The apostles mentioned here would include the seventy and others beside the Twelve."[44] Similarly, Marius Victorinus: "The apostles beheld [God incarnate]; the prophets received the Spirit. These are the saints mentioned above: those who saw and those who were inhabited by the Spirit. Hence the teachings of the apostles and prophets are indeed the teachings of Christ, which proclaim the foundation of all eternal hope."[45]

Ambrosiaster sees Paul as the last of the apostles on the basis of 1 Corinthians 15:9. He states, "Paul is least because he was the last in time, not because he was inferior in any way to the others."[46]

Augustine (354-430) divides up the apostles into two groups, those who became apostles during Jesus' earthly ministry and the latter—the last of whom was Paul—who were chosen after his resurrection. He states in his commentary on Galatians:

---

40. Tertullian, *On Modesty* 21, quoted in McKay, *Movements*, 129.

41. Eusebius, *History*, 31.

42. Ibid., 65.

43. Chrysostom views the seventy and Junia as apostles. See his comments on 1 Corinthians 15:7 in Bray, ed., *1–2 Corinthians*, 151; and on Romans 16:7 in Bray, ed., *Romans*, 372.

44. Ibid.

45. In Edwards, ed., *Galatians, Ephesians, Philippians*, 143.

46. In Bray, ed., *1–2 Corinthians*, 152.

the earlier apostles, who were sent not from human beings but by God through a human being—that is, through Jesus Christ while he was still mortal—were truthful. And the *last* apostle, who was sent by Jesus Christ now wholly God after his resurrection, is also truthful.... The earlier apostles are those sent by Christ while he was still in part a human being, that is, mortal; the last is the apostle Paul, sent by Christ now wholly God, that is, immortal in every respect.... The authority of Paul's witness should therefore be regarded as equal to theirs, since the glorification of the Lord compensated for any lack of honour attributable to the lateness of his commission.[47]

Professor Thomas F. Martin,[48] reflecting on Augustine's position on apostles wrote the following to me: "I think it is safe to say that Augustine restricts the term "apostle" to those specifically chosen by Christ—thus Paul, for Augustine, is the 13th Apostle (see, e.g., *en. ps.* 90, sermon 1, 9)—but the counting stops there. This is certainly influenced by events preceding him—e.g., Montanism's Charismatic theology but also his own experience with the Manichaeans as Mani claimed to be Apostolus Iesu Christi—a title Augustine derided. Also Augustine turns repeatedly to the notion of apostolic succession—against both Manichaean and Donatist theological assertions."[49]

This theme of apostolic succession recurs in a number of his writings.[50] Augustine would have shunned any attempt to argue for a charismatic apostolate after the calling of Paul.

Many esteemed early church leaders and theologians commented on Ephesians 4:11–13—a passage that is pertinent to this discussion. From a brief survey of their views it is clear that the majority of them do not see an ongoing charismatic apostolate as being the implication of these verses. They either view these gifts as a past phenomenon relating to the original apostles (for example, Chrysostom[51] and Theodoret[52]),

---

47. Plumer, *Augustine's Commentary*, 127, 129, emphasis mine.

48. Professor Martin is the Director of the Augustinian Institute and on staff at Villanova University in the Department of Theology/Religious Studies.

49. Thomas F. Martin, e-mail message to author, October 23, 2008.

50. The Augustinian scholar, Professor Frederick Van Fleteren, helpfully e-mailed to me a number of places in Augustine's writings which refer to apostolic succession: "Letter 232, *de utilitate credendi* 17:35," and *Contra Faustum* 11:2, 5; 13:5; 28:2, 5.Frederick Van Fleteren, e-mail message to author, October 12, 2008.

51. In. Edwards, ed., *Galatians, Ephesians, Philippians*, 165.

52. Ibid., 167.

or as possibly continuous via the office of bishop, although still making a distinction between them (for example, Ambrosiaster).[53] Nevertheless, there is a remarkable exception in Jerome who appeared to believe[54] that apostles were still being given to the church in his time; in his commentary on these verses he states, "I also think that in the churches today just as prophet and evangelist, as well as pastor and teacher, are found so also an apostle can be found in whom both the signs and proofs of the office of apostle are fulfilled."[55]

Jerome sees the ministry as a charismatic one manifesting signs that accord with its office which he does not (in this instance)[56] tie to the bishop.

With the exception of Jerome, it seems that by the fifth century it was a nigh-on universal tradition that charismatic apostles were limited to those described in the New Testament. The majority see the Twelve and Paul as definite apostles, and on occasion other New Testament figures such as the seventy or Junia(s). The spotlight is on the ministries that the New Testament apostles put in place—bishops/presbyters and deacons; and a widening view that the bishop (presbyter?)[57] was in some way a successor to the apostle.[58] The movement toward this had begun much earlier. Diarmaid MacCulloch argues that the author of the Didache is addressing the apparent tension between the mobile ministry, which includes itinerant apostles/prophets/teachers, and the local one; the Didachist was contending that the local ministry was as authoritative as the mobile. This tension continues and is only resolved when the mobile ministry disappears from the mainstream church, an event which was sealed by the defeat of Montanism.[59] MacCulloch does not adjudicate on whether this was bad or not and suggests that "this was inevitable as the church began to settle down round local centers which had their own traditions and their own way of life." Furthermore, "the need to show a settled continuity of Christian

---

53. Ibid., 166.

54. I am indebted to Flegg for highlighting that the Catholic Apostolics referred back to Jerome for support to the idea of Christ still giving apostles to his church. See Flegg, *Gathered*, 119.

55. Heine, *Commentaries*, 175.

56. Jerome is a firm proponent of apostolic succession and refers to bishops as "successors of the apostles"—see Jerome, "Epistle 146".

57. Many scholars argue that even in this period there is no real distinction made between presbyters and bishops in terms of succession. See Burkhard, *Apostolicity*, 56.

58. See ibid., 49–64.

59. MacCulloch, *Christian History*, 53–56.

doctrine against the alternatives offered by the Gnostics was a powerful incentive to shift the balance of authority in favour of the local ministry."[60] John McKay saw it negatively as a suppression of the "Prophetic Spirit" that was taking root within the institutional church.[61]

Although spiritual authority was increasingly being tied to the clergy, there was one "orthodox" movement during these early centuries that affirmed that apostolic charisms could be given outside of the ordained ministry. Within the Eastern and Western monastic movements we encounter individuals characterized by Charismatic manifestations and spiritual authority.[62] The Celtic monastic movement has a hagiographic history highlighting Charismatic manifestations; it also had fluidity in regards to its structures.[63] Therefore, we find many of the Abbots, who were effectively the leading religious figures, as not being ordained; these people had a "spiritual fatherhood" role.[64] Within this movement, like the later Franciscans, there was a conscious embracing of pre-Pentecost apostolic methods of evangelism with an expectation of signs and wonders.[65] However, it must be noted that within the Eastern and Western movements people were not referred to as "apostles"—at least not in their lifetimes.[66]

To summarize, within the early post-biblical literature from the Didache to the Acts of Thecla some writers posit that the apostles were a fixed group who were witnesses of Christ's resurrection and were associated with the church's beginning; others speak of later apostles as Spirit-empowered itinerant missionaries[67] still present in the church. It is impor-

---

60. Ibid., 53–54.

61. McKay, *Movements*, 79–131.

62. For example, Colomba—see Cocksworth's discussion of this inspirational figure in *Holding Together*, 253–55—or Athanasius' *Life of St Antony*. There is obviously debate over how seriously we are to take what is hagiographic material, whether any of it is historical or not. Whichever way one comes down on that issue, it cannot be denied that many Christians believed that spiritual authority was not limited to those in ecclesiastical office.

63. For a helpful description of the Celtic Church see Edwards, *Christianity*, 175–77.

64. It must also be remembered that there were Abbesses too, who likewise had a "spiritual motherhood" role.

65. For a good description of their methods, see McKay, *Movements*, chap. 12.

66. Brendan Lehanne writes of how in later times "the scribes were to select the 'Twelve Apostles of Ireland,' including Columba . . ." Lehanne, *Celtic*, 104.

67. Kevin Giles has argued that this is the case in Didache 11:4–6, in Pseudo-Clement, *Hom*. 11:35, and in the *Shepherd of Hermas*, Sim. 11:15:4. See Giles, "Apostles Before," 251.

tant to note that many of these documents are pastoral letters written to churches to guide them in the faith and are pinpointing specific problems and therefore, unless a particular letter or document is addressing that issue, we will not necessarily get the mind of the church on that matter. The fact that the Didache does address it head-on makes its witness very important; likewise, that the Shepherd of Hermas sees apostles amongst the next generation of believers is also noteworthy. Yet, in relation to the other documents it is significant that there is a continual reference back to the apostles and the revelations they received; even though the writers are assuming a similar ministry, these authors do not see themselves as apostles, and defer to *the* apostles' authority. It appears likely that in certain quarters the church was still receiving and recognizing charismatic itinerant individuals as apostles with a perceived spiritual authority similar to Apostle Type 1s; alongside this, however was an increasing focus on the ministries (bishops/presbyters and deacons) that the universally recognized apostles had put in place to sustain the life of the churches. Within this early period, one could (with good reason) speculate that there is a moving away from the use of the term "apostles" to describe ministries that might have been so called before, to a more settled conviction that it referred to a fixed group who were the original recipients of the "faith" who were commissioned to minister by the risen Jesus himself. An important figure in solidifying this tradition was Irenaeus, and the events that put the itinerant charismatic apostolate on a backburner was the rejection of Montanism—however, there still remained openness to ideas associated with the charismatic apostolate which were evident within the Monastic movements.

The Sixth Century to the End of the Sixteenth Century

From the beginning of the sixth century up until the Reformation there are no real advocates for charismatic apostles—in the main, there was a settled conviction that the true successors of the apostles were the bishops, who in turn share that authority with priests; as a result both ministries have been granted apostolic authority to administer the sacraments. Nevertheless, there has always remained, particularly in the East, a belief that charismatic gifts believed to be present in the "successors of the apostles" (the ordained) were operative amongst holy non-ordained individuals.

This high view of what is charismatically possible amongst unordained Spirit-filled lay people is also evident in more controversial groups in the Western church during this period—for example, the Friends of God: "It is a telling, concrete illustration of the ruling idea of the Friends of God that a divinely instructed layman, who has attained the highest stage of mystical experience, 'speaks in the place of God' and has an apostolic authority which puts him above any priest or doctor who has only the authority of ordination or scholarship."[68]

There has been a revival of interest in Orthodox circles concerning the man who alongside St John of the Gospel and St Gregory of Nazianzus has been credited with the title, "Theologian." St Symeon (949–1022) has been of especial interest to one of the main centers of Charismatic Renewal within the Orthodox Church—based around the controversial ministry of Fr. Eusebius Stephanou.[69] For many years now he has been calling for Orthodox to delve into the writings of Symeon and discover for themselves the "baptism in the Spirit" that Symeon both experienced and called for.[70] This Charismatic emphasis evident in his writings makes St Symeon an important figure to consult on this question. He did not write specifically about charismatic apostles; however, he did assert that the spiritual gifts associated with their successors could still be demonstrated amongst Spirit-empowered laity. Symeon believed that one could experience a divine ordination apart from the hands of men. Turner writes,

> Symeon, though himself ordained, produced Ep 1 (De Confessione) as a vehement rejoinder to those who sought to attach the power to absolve simply and exclusively to the holders of ecclesiastical office as such. He had been asked whether it was lawful to confess to unordained monks, since authority to bind and loose was believed to have been granted to none but priests, and in reply, after writing at some length in favor of his "Charismatic" stance, concluded with what for him was the most important argument of all: his own father, the Studiete, had been one "who had no ordination from men."[71]

---

68. Jones, *Mystical Religion*, 263, quoted in McKay, *Movements*, 212–13.
69. See Burgess, "Stephanou," 1106–7.
70. Brotherhood of St Symeon, "Brotherhood."
71. Turner highlights how St Symeon saw a qualified spiritual father—monk—as being able to charismatically do the things usually seen as the Priest/bishop's ministry—for example, absolve sins. Turner, *St. Symeon*, 56–57.

Much of this thinking is resident in the Orthodox tradition of "staretz." Symeon's forthright "insistence that spiritual leadership can be based solely on a personal experience of the Spirit, rather than on ecclesiastical position"[72] makes him an implicit supporter of the idea of Christ himself charismatically ordaining people to apostolic ministry apart from the "hands of men."

With the Reformation, many traditions that had seemed untouchable were scrutinized. With a renewed zeal to return to the Scriptures and reform the church, it is not surprising that the subject of apostles came back on the radar. Nevertheless, it is only John Calvin (1509–64) and some associated with the Radical Reformation who conceive of apostles still being given to the church. Calvin on Ephesians 4:11 is categorical concerning the cessation of apostles: "Apostles, Evangelists, and Prophets were bestowed on the church for a limited time only."[73] Nevertheless, elsewhere he modifies his view and argues that God "still occasionally raises them up when the necessity of the time requires" and that was what God had done in his own day "to bring back the Church from the revolt of Antichrist."[74] Maybe, it was due to his shifting opinion that he decided not to comment on Paul's phrase of being "last of all" in 1 Corinthians 15:8?[75] Interestingly, he does not limit the apostles to being the Twelve and Paul, in his commentary on 1 Corinthians 15:7 he writes: "By *all the Apostles* I understand not merely the *twelve,* but also those disciples to whom Christ had assigned the office of preaching the gospel."[76]

The Radical Reformation brought with it an emphasis on the charismatic dimension of the Christian life and mission.[77] Not only was there a desire to get back to the pristine teaching of the apostles, but an expectancy that God could work amongst them in their day as he had in the days of the earliest Christian church. Often modeling themselves upon the practice of the primitive church it became incumbent upon them to follow the directives of Jesus when he "sent out" the Twelve on mission. As a result, we have examples of Anabaptist "apostles" who embarked on missionary journeys, appointing leaders along their way. Norman Cohn

72. Burgess, *Holy Spirit*, 62.
73. Calvin, *Galatians and Ephesians.*
74. Quoted in Bridge and Phypers, *Spiritual Gifts*, 38; Calvin, *Institutes*, 4.3.4.
75. Calvin, *Corinthians.*
76. Ibid.
77. Stuart Murray-Williams has highlighted the overt charismatic dimension which appeared amongst the Anabaptist movement. See his article written in 1995, "Anabaptism."

writes in this regard: "From the Netherlands Matthys sent out to the various Anabaptist communities apostles who believed that the Holy Spirit had descended upon them as upon the original Apostles at Pentecost. In each town that they visited they baptized great numbers of adults and appointed 'bishops' with the power to baptize. Then they moved on, while from the newly converted town new apostles set out on similar missions. In the first days of 1534 two apostles reached Münster, where their arrival at once produced a veritable contagion of enthusiasm."[78]

However, this particular branch of the Anabaptist movement descends into a rather strange form; Cohn continues, "The first apostles moved on but they were replaced by two more; and these—most significantly—were at first taken to be Enoch and Elijah, those prophets who according to traditional eschatology were to return to earth as the two "witnesses" against Antichrist and whose appearance was to herald the Second Coming."[79]

Positively, scholars have recognized the farsightedness of many of the Anabaptists in that they clearly perceived a much wider form of ministry than that which was the main emphasis of the mainline Reformation churches—which was the pastor/teacher ministry.[80]

It is also important to note in connection with the Anabaptists that one of their main leaders, Menno Simmons, did not believe modern charismatic apostles were still present in the church. In the context of his various works on the subject of preachers, he always refers back to the apostles and prophets of the Bible, and does not speak of either ministry as operative in his day. For example, in his *Of the Mission and or Calling of the Preachers*, he refers both to the past exemplary ministries of apostles and prophets, as well as recognizing present ministries of pastoring and teaching.[81] Stuart Murray-Williams, the Anabaptist scholar, believed that this was because Menno was reacting against the abuses of the Münster prophets; nevertheless, Murray was quite clear that the movement as a whole recognized a wider ministry than the pastor/teacher, which was more of a pioneering one.[82] Even though it is indisputable that sectors

78. Cohn, *Pursuit*, chap. 13.
79. Ibid.
80. I am grateful to George Hunston Williams for bringing this to my attention—he writes about the "missionary impulse" that was present in the movement, in contrast to the magisterial reformation churches who had no place for the prophet or apostle. See his *Radical Reformation*, 1276.
81. Simmons, *Complete Works*, Book 2, p. 21.
82. Murray-Williams, telephone conversation with author on October 3, 2008.

PART TWO—How We Got Here

within the diverse Anabaptist movement did recognize charismatic apostles, it is not clear whether this belief was rooted in Ephesians 4:11–13. Murray-Williams, who has done extensive work on the charismatic nature of the Anabaptists, was not aware in all his reading that Ephesians 4 was ever quoted; whereas 1 Corinthians 14 with its emphasis on the prophetic was quoted numerous times.[83]

Between the sixth century and the end of the Radical Reformation there is a solidification of many of the beliefs being formulated by the earlier Fathers within the Orthodox and Roman Catholic churches—namely that apostolic ministry is subsumed within the episcopal succession.[84] Nevertheless, there always remained the belief that apostolic-type gifts could appear outside the institutional hierarchy (according to Burgess more so in the East than the West).[85] This was the exception not the rule, and even within this stream I have yet to find an unambiguous affirmation that charismatic apostles are still given to the church.[86] Amongst the Magisterial Reformers there is no real difference in this regard, aside from Calvin's intriguing ruminations allowing for the possibility of modern-day apostles, which he seems to contradict elsewhere. However, the prospect definitely gains more currency within certain parts of the Radical Reformation—yet it is important to note that even within this movement there was strong disagreement on the matter. The majority view within this period would not sit easily with the belief in present day charismatic apostles; yet as before, there is room for finding some (however small) precursors within this period that supported such an idea—often it was assumed that they had a charismatic authority which put them above other historic ministries.

---

83. Murray-Williams, telephone conversation with author on October 3, 2008.

84. This is a very simplified view, as inevitably the evolution of the episcopacy in this period was very complex and not always healthy—see Bouyer, "Bishops," 25ff.

85. Stanley Burgess comments, "Through the centuries, Eastern Christians have also placed a great emphasis on the gifts of the Holy Spirit. . . . Eastern Christians also have tended to incorporate the Pauline lists in 1 Cor 12 . . . , Rom 5 . . . , Rom 12 . . . , Eph. 4 (apostles, prophets, evangelists, pastors, and teachers), and 2 Tim 1. . . ." Burgess, "Holy Spirit," 747.

86. It is possible that both East and West did start in this period to view certain individuals as "Apostles" to parts of the world (a tradition that seems well established in both communions)—usually meaning that they were missionaries to pagan countries and started churches; however, these people were not independent of the institutional church, nor claimed an authority above those within the recognized historical succession.

THE END OF THE SIXTEENTH CENTURY TO THE END OF THE TWENTIETH CENTURY (CIRCA 1990)

After the Reformation, desire was high amongst many Protestants to further reform the churches to a more biblically pure expression. Two such groups were the Puritans and the Campbellites. Alongside them were the more enthusiastic movements that were looking for a charismatic revival of spiritual power such as the Quakers and Shakers. Through these movements two impulses were coming more and more into focus one with its overt focus on Scripture (especially the Puritans and Campbellites) and the other on the Spirit (Shakers and Quakers). Both stressed the importance of a link with both the apostolic faith and the apostolic experience of the Spirit as described in the Scriptures, but not the necessity of historical succession.

It has been well documented that many of the leading Puritans had a hope, fuelled by their biblical interpretation that God would pour out his Spirit upon the church before the return of Christ.[87] Nevertheless, even though there was a hope that God would visit his church with Pentecostal power, there was no hint that they believed God would restore apostles to the church. For example, the Puritan spiritual gifts enthusiast, John Owen "sets forth exactly the standard Reformed distinction between the offices of apostle, evangelist, and prophet, which were temporary and extraordinary, ceasing with the apostolic age, and the office of presbyter, which is permanent and ordinary, and is to last till the Lord returns."[88]

Alexander Campbell (1788–1866) and the Campbellites were also eager to get back to apostolic practice and ministries, nevertheless, Campbell himself commenting on Ephesians 4:11 only appears to recognize bishops, deacons and evangelists as present in the church.[89] Furthermore, the Mormons refuted Campbell's claims to have restored primitive Christianity because amongst other things the Campbellites did not have any apostles or prophets.[90] There is also no indication in the church's official websites that they envisage modern-day apostles [91] However, there were

---

87. Murray, *Puritan*, chaps. 4–5.

88. Packer, "John Owen."

89. See his comments on Eph. 4:11 found in Campbell, *System*, chap. 25. Ironically he has been given the title of "Apostle of truth" by those who hold him in high esteem—see for example William Blake's "Campbell."

90. Harlan, "Dowie," 96.

91. E.g., see Christian Church (Disciples of Christ), "Design."

PART TWO—How We Got Here

other movements that looked for the restoration of apostolic men and authority unconnected to historic succession, for example, the Seekers.[92] The Quakers and the Shakers believed that that spiritual restoration had occurred in their day, their literature is littered with references to spiritual manifestations which replicate extraordinary apostolic gifts.[93]

The early Baptists desired to rid themselves of man-made tradition and return to the New Testament vision of church, as a result an apostolic style ministry appeared. Vinson Synan wrote about: "A little-known instance of Protestants sending out 'apostles' as missionaries amongst the Baptists in colonial America. For a time, Baptists in New England ordained 'apostles' as missionaries to such Southern colonies as Virginia, Carolina and Georgia. After some time, however, the term 'apostle' was dropped for the more traditional term 'missionary.'"[94]

A similar practice happened in the early Baptist Church in Britain, where there was a recognized office of "Messenger," which was seen to be a literal translation of "apostle"; their duties were: "the care of a number of churches, the strengthening and encouragement of elders and churches, the spread of the gospel, and the defence of doctrine. They were also, but not exclusively, involved in the ordination of other Messengers and of Elders."[95]

This office was evidently quite widespread as both "Particular and General Baptists (especially the latter) employed the office of messenger."[96] It was seen as having a Scriptural foundation and the General Baptist Thomas Grantham, himself a messenger, wrote an apologetic for the office in 1674.[97] It continued for quite some time for in 1775 the following was stated concerning it from the Lincolnshire Association, held at Coningsly, May 30, 1775:

> The messenger, who is chosen by the unanimous consent and approbation of the churches which stand in a close connection together, hath full liberty and authority, according to the gospel, to freely enquire into the state of the churches respecting both

92. McKay, *Movements*, chap. 20.
93. Ibid., chaps. 20, 23.
94. This is from an article entitled "Apostolic Practice," which was published in an Assemblies of God book in 2004 on apostolic ministry. Professor Synan e-mailed the article to me and informed me that it was the Baptist minister and scholar Gary Clarke who had told him this.
95. Dowse, "Monksthorpe."
96. Weaver, *Search*, 25.
97. Ibid.

> pastor and people, to see that the pastors do their duty in their places, and the people theirs; he is to exhort, admonish, and reprove both the one and the other, as occasion calls for. In virtue of his office, he is to watch over the several flocks committed to his care and charge—to see that good order and government be carefully and constantly kept up and maintained in the churches he is called and appointed to look after and to watch over; to labour and to keep out innovations in doctrine, worship, and discipline, and to stand up in the defence of the gospel.[98]

However, as C. Douglas Weaver explains,

> In light of the Baptist aversion of the Episcopal government of the state Anglican Church, Grantham was careful not to call the messenger a bishop. Nevertheless, the itinerant messenger was to evangelize, help start churches, ordain ministers, especially in remote areas, as well as correct deficient theology and solve disciplinary problems. The messenger, seen in the example of the Apostle Paul's evangelists, Timothy and Titus, was a divinely instituted office of the New Testament church. However, the tendency toward excessive centralized organization hampered the concept of the messenger: it bore too many similarities to an office of a bishop and lost its effectiveness.[99]

As a result, the office of Messenger which had the hallmarks of modern charismatic apostolates, disappeared.

Edward Irving (1789–1834) put the possibility of modern day charismatic apostles firmly on the map; he along with others, who would help form the Catholic Apostolic Church, on the basis of Ephesians 4:11–13 proclaimed that Christ was still giving four (pastor–teacher being one office) Charismatic ministries to the church. The Catholic Apostolic Church believed that amongst them God was restoring a limited number of apostles who would be essential to the church's maturing and perfecting. They saw the apostles "as the means of healing the divisions of the Church, of restoring her ordinances, of settling her doctrines, and of bringing out the full organization of the Fourfold Ministry, for the perfecting of the saints and for edifying the Body of Christ."[100]

Further information about the apostle's ministry is laid out in their catechism:

98. Quotation from Christian, *History*, chap. 19.
99. Weaver, *Search*, 25–26.
100. Writer unknown but representing the Catholic Apostolic Church writing in the preface in 1882 to a reprint of Woodhouse, *Substance*.

Part Two—How We Got Here

> 5. Q. What is the meaning of the word *Apostle*?
>
> A. *Apostle* is "one sent forth."
>
> 6. Q. How are apostles distinguished from all other ministers?
>
> A. Apostles are neither of men, nor by man; but by Jesus Christ, and God the Father, sent forth immediately and directly.
>
> 7. Q. How are all other ministers set in the Church?
>
> A. They are set in the Church by our Lord Jesus Christ, not immediately, but through ordination by apostles, or by those whom they have delegated for that purpose.[101]

It appears that prophetic utterances were key in this conviction being formed.[102] According to Flegg there were "ecstatic utterances" in the early 1830s which declared that God would send apostles again and these utterances were followed by petitionary prayer for "a restoration of the apostolic office."[103] The indication that these prayers were answered and the prophecies fulfilled occurred in 1832 when Cardale was called to be an apostle, through a "prophetic" word given by Henry Drummond.[104] Nevertheless, it is important to note that Irving believed that the illumination that there were still to be apostles in the church was due to the Scriptures, and in his defense of himself in 1831 and what was occurring in his church he stated, "We cried unto the Lord for apostles, prophets, evangelists, pastors and teachers, anointed with the Holy Ghost the gift of Jesus, *because we saw it written in God's word* that these are the appointed ordinances for the edifying of the body of Jesus."[105]

Ephesians 4:11–13 was the backbone of his argument that these "ordinances" were still to be expected in Christ's church.[106] N. Armstrong, one of the Catholic Apostolic Church's restored apostles, argued that

---

101. Catholic Apostolic Church, *Catechism*, 17–18.

102. Flegg notes that "there had been frequent references to the restoration of apostles during the Charismatic phenomenon which occurred in Scotland, England and (later) Bavaria in the 1820s and 1830s." Flegg, *Gathered*, 120.

103. Ibid., 58.

104. Emily Cardale, describing what happened at a prayer meeting in Irving's house on 7 November, 1832, wrote that "Mr Drummond rose from his knees and went across the room to my brother, and said, in great power, 'Convey it, convey it, for are thou not an Apostle?'" Ibid., 59.

105. Patterson, "Designing," 180, my emphasis; quoting from *The Trial of the Rev. Edward Irving, M. A. Before the London Presbytery* (London: W. Harding, 1832), 24.

106. See Irving, *Collected Writing*, Vol. 3, 526.

1 Corinthians 13:8 coupled with this text demand a continuing apostleship within the church, furthermore, he sees Ephesians 4 as explaining when this gift, alongside the others, would disappear: "When He ascended up on high, he led captivity captive, and gave gifts unto men. And he gave some, apostles; and some, prophets; and some, evangelists; and some, pastors and teachers; for the *perfecting* of the saints, for the *work* of the ministry, for the *edifying* of the body of Christ: TILL we *all* come in the unity of the faith, and of the knowledge of the Son of God, unto a *perfect* man, unto a measure of the stature of the fullness of Christ."[107]

Flegg highlights that the Catholic Apostolics did not claim that the restoration of apostles was a concept that began with them, they "were keen to point out that there had been a number of occasions in the Church's history when prophetic voices had claimed that apostles would be restored in association with a special work of the Spirit within the Church before the Parousia."[108]

Flegg notes that they referred back to the following writings and sermons to support this contention:

> the *Commentary on Ephesians* of St Jerome (c. 342–420); the *Institutes* of John Calvin (1509–64); several of the writings of Jane Leade (1623–1704); the interpretation of the Apocalypse by Isaac Newton (1642–1727); a study of the Apocalypse by Johann Albrecht Bengel (1687–1752); records of debates in De Maistre's *Soirées de St. Petersburg* (1809); works by Philip Matthew Hahn (b. 1790); *La Venida del Mesias en Gloria y Majestad* by the Jesuit, Father Emanuelo Lacunza (1731–1801), subsequently translated by Irving . . . ; a pseudonymous Roman Catholic work, Pere Lambert's *Exposition des predictions et promesses, faites a l'église pour les derniers temps de la gentilité* (1806); a sermon included in the works of the Russian Orthodox Bishop Innokenti of Cherson (preached in his Cathedral at Pentecost 1857).[109]

After Irving's death and after the separation of the Apostles in 1835, the Catholic Apostolics developed a detailed account of apostleship. A theology developed that saw within Scripture two types of apostle: that to the circumcision which was based around the Twelve, and that to the Gentiles exemplified by Paul and Barnabas. The Apostolics were convinced that God was restoring amongst them a new college of apostles to

---

107. Armstrong, *Tracts*, 16.
108. Flegg, *Gathered*, 119.
109. Ibid., 119–20.

the Gentiles. The restored apostles had a vital ministry in regards to the church's perfecting, yet they did not see themselves as being essential to the church's being in that without them there could be no valid Eucharist, or orders. However, they believed that it was only through their ministry that those ordained in other churches could come into the fullness of holy orders.[110] By the end of 1835 a completed college of apostles had been called and recognized; this was in accordance with prophetic utterances.[111] These apostles were separated for their work in the universal church through the laying on of hands by the seven "angels" (bishop) in charge of the seven churches. Although this separation involved the laying on of hands they understood this event not as an ordination for apostles were called by Jesus and the Father alone.[112]

Flegg notes that similar spiritual manifestations were appearing in Germany; of note was a "revival in the area of the Roman Catholic parish of Karlshudd, Bavaria, which began in 1827 and culminated in ecstatic utterances prophesying the restoration of apostles, prophets, evangelists, and pastors to the Church, the nearness of the Second Advent, and the restoration of the spiritual gifts of the primitive Church."[113]

The priest in charge of this parish was finally excommunicated in 1857 and began ministering "within the Catholic Apostolic Church."[114] In time the Catholic Apostolic Church developed its own understanding of ministry which incorporated these restored fourfold ministries alongside the more familiar threefold ministry of bishop (known as the "angel"), priest and deacon. Flegg unpacks how these ministries functioned and related to each other:

> the apostles were set, as ministers of the universal Church, over the traditional threefold catholic ministry of angel (bishop), priest, and deacon. There was thus a fourfold *order* (or *degree*) of ministry, outwardly similar to that which has existed in the Church Catholic from early times, except for the superimposition of the apostolic office. However, a more restricted view of the role of the episcopate was held—angels being seen as minister of particular Churches only . . . —and the diaconate was restored as a permanent office with duties more nearly approximating those indicated in the New Testament writings.

110. Ibid., 121.
111. Ibid., 65.
112. Ibid., 68–69.
113. Ibid., 57.
114. Ibid.

Superimposed upon this fourfold order was a fourfold *character* (or *function*) of ministry—representing the fourfold ministry of Christ as apostle, prophet, evangelist, and pastor—derived partly from Scripture, partly from the nature of man, and (inevitably) partly from typology.[115]

One of the apostles in the Catholic Apostolic Church contrasted the role of the former apostles and the restored apostles: "To testify of the resurrection of Jesus was the work of the Apostles at the beginning of the Christian dispensation; to preach the resurrection of the Church, and to press the Church unto it, will be the work and mark of Apostles in the time of the end: one ministry of God laid the foundation, another ministry raised up by Him brings in the consummation."[116]

The Catholic Apostolic Church believed there were unique things that the apostle was called to do: ordaining angels, priests, and deacons; "laying on of hands and sealing with chrism; confirming the orders of episcopally ordained priests; the presentation of priests before the Lord as candidates for the episcopate . . . ; the induction of angels into their particular charges and the blessing of angels for special missions; the consecration of churches, altars, fonts. . . . The apostles also made the final determination concerning words spoken in prophecy."[117]

As the apostles started dying out provision was made for a few of the duties that were reserved for them to be taken up by others.[118]

Ephesians 4:11–13 was central to both Irving and to the Catholic Apostolic Church providing evidence for the Lord's intention that apostleship continue in his church. Nevertheless, due to the Catholic Apostolic Church's understanding that the restored apostolate would only number twelve, and that these could not be replaced, the Catholic Apostolic Church diminished in size and influence unable to sustain its own worshipping life.[119] The significance of this movement is not to be minimized due to its current state. Andrew Walker believes that Irvingism coupled with

---

115. Ibid., 119.

116. Armstrong, "The Bride of the Lamb," in *Tracts*, 441.

117. Flegg, *Gathered*, 126–27.

118. See ibid., 131. However, some of the duties that the apostles allowed coadjutors to participate in were stopped when the apostles died, as it was believed that one could only be a coadjutor to a living apostle. See ibid., 91.

119. Although Larry Christenson recounts that even in the midst of decline there was a hopeful attitude based on a belief that God would in time restore a company of "70" which would be an even greater work. See his *Message*.

Brethrenism were the forerunners of the radical House Church movement.[120] Irving and the Catholic Apostolic Church were the first to give serious attention to Ephesians 4:11–13 and the implications of that upon modern church life, which has been central to later Pentecostal denominations and the radical House Church. This along with their commitment to the Charismatic gifts and ministries do make them an identifiable forerunner, but that is where the similarities end. There is a case to be made for the radical Anabaptists as more appropriate forerunners as they advocated a charismatic apostolate amongst other Charismatic gifts before Irving and aspects of their beliefs fit more readily with the theology of the radical House Church movement. For example, Irving and the Catholic Apostolic Churches were committed to infant baptism and clericalism; whereas the radical House Church movement are all credo-Baptists and due to the Brethren influence advocate a removal of the clergy/laity divide (although whether they do that is another question)—which were all core features of the radical Anabaptists. Although much of the Catholic Apostolic Church's allegorical interpretations can carry no weight with "thinking" Evangelicalism, they did provide a reasonable Protestant anti-cessationist hermeneutic and did so in consultation with the wider catholic church.

Whilst Irving and the Catholic Apostolics were making a mark on the British church scene, unusual, but in some aspects similar, events were occurring in the USA. Joseph Smith (1805–44) and his followers were heralding a restoration of apostles and prophets. Joseph Smith and the resulting Mormon movement have always insisted that their faith is a recovery of primitive Christianity. Charismatic phenomena were a hallmark of the early Mormon movement. Like the Catholic Apostolics they saw a need for a council of twelve apostles; nevertheless, unlike the Catholic Apostolic Church they believed that these apostles would be replaced by others when they died—so that there would always be an ongoing council of twelve apostles. The traditional story is that in 1835 the "three witnesses" ordained twelve apostles who were according to Smith a Quorum. Smith describes their authority and function in the following way: "The twelve travelling councilors are called to be the Twelve Apostles, or special witnesses of the name of Christ in all the world—thus differing from other officers in the church in the duties of their calling. And they form a quorum, equal in authority and power to the three presidents previously mentioned."[121]

120. Walker, *Restoring*, chap. 11.
121. This is from "revelations" Joseph Smith received in 1835 which have been

Joseph Smith himself was not one of the Twelve, he became known as the first president of the church, and specifically referred to as a prophet in the same vein as Moses.

The three "churches" that all have their spiritual roots in Smith's revelations are The Church of Jesus Christ of Latter-Day Saints, The Reorganized Church of Jesus Christ of Latter-Day Saints, and the Church of Christ. All three of them incorporate twelve apostles, and each of them views the other apostles as false ones.[122] All of them share the view that apostolic succession was broken during the "Great Apostasy" and only began to be restored through the ministry of Joseph Smith. It is important to note that although there are some interesting similarities between the Mormons and the Catholic Apostolic Church, the doctrines held by Mormonism would inevitably put it outside the bounds of Christian orthodoxy, whereas the Catholic Apostolic Church did not reject the catholic creeds. Furthermore, the means by which Joseph Smith received most of his "revelations"[123] are unlike the way in which the "prophets" in other more "orthodox" charismatic movements have. Even so, they were a significant voice arguing for modern-day charismatic apostles, and drew attention to verses that would become significant in Pentecostal/Charismatic circles.[124]

The New Apostolic Church (1863–) was an offshoot of the Catholic Apostolic Church and the next major movement advocating modern-day apostles. It was viewed as aberrant by the Catholic Apostolic Church's apostles, but continued in their footsteps. Its beginnings occurred due to a prophecy given by Heinrich Geyer who "prophetically called two angels to the apostleship during a meeting at Albury"; this prophecy was rejected by the apostolic college, however, Geyer continued with the idea inherent in that prophecy that God was continuing to call others to become apostles; a year later whilst in Germany he called a recognized elder to the apostleship. Once again this was rejected by the apostolic college and it led to the

---

collected into the authoritative work (for Mormons) known as *Doctrine and Covenants*. It is divided up into sections—the section I quote from is 107.

122. Bales, *Apostates*, 43.

123. It is well documented that he would spend a long time looking into his hat at two stones—which he believed were the Urim and Thummim—which would convey "revelations" to him. See Ankerberg and Weldon, *Cults*, 282.

124. "Prophets: The Church is built upon the foundation of Apostles and prophets, Eph. 2:19–20. Apostles and prophets are essential to the Church, Eph. 4: 11–16. Joseph Smith was called to be a seer, prophet, and Apostle, D&C 21: 1–3. We believe in prophets, A of F 1: 6." Brown, "Don't Understand."

Part Two—How We Got Here

exclusion of Geyer, Rudolf Rosochaki (the one called to the apostleship), and Friedrich Schwartz (the angel at Hamburg who recognized Geyer's prophetic call of Rosochaki), and ultimately to their excommunication. This offshoot, which traces its history back to the Catholic Apostolic Church's twelve apostles, has had numerous apostles, many of whom are still active.[125] Flegg notes that this movement became more Protestant and abandoned the more ceremonial and sacramental teaching of the Catholic Apostolic Church.[126] Flegg may be right in his assessment, however his comments may give the impression that the New Apostolic Church is not very sacramental—that is not the case; although, definitely Protestant, the New Apostolic Church has a very high view of their three Sacraments: Baptism, Sealing, and Holy Communion. They see sealing by the apostle as the way in which those baptized receive the baptism in the Spirit and are incorporated into the Body of Christ. They also give pride of place to the chief apostle who is viewed in a quasi-Catholic manner as being like Peter first amongst the apostles. The New Apostolic Church has been beset by divisions, nevertheless, it continues strong today having established bases throughout the world, and its website claims that there are as many as 11 million members worldwide.[127]

The Catholic Apostolic Church and the New Apostolic Church did not pay attention to outward manifestations when receiving the Spirit, and although prophecy played a vital role within their churches, emphasis was placed upon the inward reality of the Spirit's presence received through the sacrament of Sealing. What is particularly significant about the NAC's view of apostles is that there was no limit to how many there could be, unlike both the Catholic Apostolic Church and the Mormons. Common to all these groups was a belief in God's restoration of the apostolic ministry—this idea became very prominent amongst two individuals who would give this idea a bad name: Frank Weston Sandford and John Alexander Dowie.

---

125. According to Flegg there were, at the time when he wrote his book, "more than 270 apostles" who had "been called, some fifty or more of whom are currently working." Flegg, *Gathered*, 89. It is clear that the New Apostolic Church saw no restriction to the number of apostles that could be operating at once.

126. Ibid., 90.

127. See New Apostolic Church, "United Kingdom & Ireland." This may well be correct. According to Barrett and Johnson's research in 1970 there were 1.7 million members worldwide; by 2000 there were 9.6 million in 180 countries. See Barrett and Johnson, *Trends*, 289.

Frank Weston Sandford (1862–1948) was initially influenced by recognized Evangelical leaders such as D. L. Moody, A. B. Simpson and Hannah Whittal Smith. He also came into contact with the controversial healing minister, John Alexander Dowie. All these figures left their mark on Sandford who became more and more convinced that he was to live a life of complete abandonment to the will of God, and help restore the church to its apostolic power and purity. It was in 1893 that he started to consider the possibility of modern apostles—which according to Shirley Nelson was "a subject of great interest among Higher Life Christians"[128] and reasoned that if "early church power could be restored, that suggested the possibility of contemporary apostles, with no less authority than a Peter or a Paul." Furthermore, such a "purifying movement" that Sandford felt called to be a part of "demanded the leadership of such a person."[129] At this stage, Sandford was clear that he did not have the patience to be an "apostle." As time went on, his perception of his own ministry grew in grandeur and he believed himself to be: "Apostle; prophet; overseer of the world's evangelization; baptizer of all God's true 'sheep,' meaning all true Christians; Elijah, the 'restorer of all things' and forerunner of the Messiah's second advent; David, who is to rule the whole earth and prepare the throne for the Messiah; 'The Branch'; High Priest of the Melchisedec priesthood; the first and chief of 'the two witnesses,' with power to command fire and plague upon his enemies whenever he will."[130]

Of all the titles that he claims for himself, it is noteworthy that he like Dowie (see next section) saw himself as a charismatic apostle wielding great authority.[131]

John Alexander Dowie (1847–1907) was a notable influence on some key figures (for example, John G. Lake and F. F. Bosworth, both members of his church)[132] that became prominent in the early Pentecostal movement. Dowie established a Christian city, and endeavored to found a church upon apostolic principles and practices. The resulting church,

---

128. Nelson, *Fair*, 60.

129. Ibid.

130. Quote from one of his co-workers, Rev N. H. Harriman, who separated himself from Sandford's "Kingdom" movement and repudiated Sandford's claims. The article quoted from first appeared in the *Lewiston Saturday Journal* on September 26, 1903. See Harriman, "Inside Story."

131. In an essay by one who trained under him, Frank Murray, he recalls Sandford speaking of himself as the "chiefest apostle." See Murray, "Egotist?"

132. Lindsay, *Dowie*, 271.

Part Two—How We Got Here

named the Christian Catholic Church,[133] founded in the 1890s was shaped by Dowie's Restorationist beliefs, particularly that there was a divinely established "organization" of the church evident in the New Testament. This is pertinent to his understanding that the apostolic office was still present in the church. Harlan notes concerning Dowie,

> In his address of January 22, 1896, he sets forth the Divine organization of the church. 1 Cor. 12:28 reads: "And God has set some in the church, first apostles, secondarily prophets, thirdly teachers, after that miracles, then gifts of healings, helps, governments, diversities of tongues." He says "Now, then, what is the way of perfect wisdom as to the order of the church? What is the first office God has established?" "Answer, Apostles." "The second?" "Prophets." "The Third?" "Teachers." "Now then, did God form a church with these officers?" "He did." "Is that the order of the church of God?" "It is." "Does the church of God ever alter?" "No." "Can the church of God be acceptable to Christ if it is not organized after His own order?" "No."[134]

In answer to a question put to him by the Rev Mr Jones at the Second General Conference for Believers in 1896 on the subject of the church's organization and its acceptance of apostles and prophets, Dowie responded in the following way: "The contention of Dr. Jones is not correct. The Prophetic Office is permanent, as is also the Apostolic and Teaching office; it is as permanent as both. The words are clear in 1 Cor. 12:28. . . . There is no limitation there as to the time of the duration of the offices of either apostles or prophets or teachers. The word 'set' is 'etheto' and it means 'to build into,' as a permanent part of a permanent organization."[135]

When Dowie's Christian Catholic Church was about to start, someone had commented to him that he "bore the marks of an apostle," to which he retorted that he had not "reached a deep enough depth of true humility."[136] However, this attitude soon changed and near the end of his life he became convinced that he was the "Elijah to come," "the Restorer of all things" prophesied in Scripture as well as the "Messenger of the Covenant" and soon started to refer to himself as "the First Apostle of the

---

133. It was named Christian Catholic Apostolic Church after Dowie announced that he was the "First Apostle" in 1904, but "Apostolic" was dropped after Dowie was deposed in 1906. Harlan, "Dowie," 1.

134. Ibid., 47.

135. Quoted in Lindsay, *Dowie*, 153.

136. Ibid., 186.

Lord Jesus Christ."[137] In July 1903 according to Harlan, Dowie stated the following, "I believe that some of these times there will come such a holy; sacred and pure unction from on high that we will get to the place where I shall be able by the Holy Spirit's guidance, acting in my prophetic authority, to call out the Apostolic College, and re-establish the fundamental and perpetual order."[138]

He became convinced that he would help bring "the entire apostolate into existence."[139] Dowie, like the Catholic Apostolic Church, saw "12" as the number of apostles that God needed to restore to the church. Nevertheless, with his declaration of being the promised "Elijah," Dowie's beliefs were viewed with even more suspicion than ever before.

Like the radical Reformers before them, those who recognized charismatic apostles in this era from the Campbellites to Dowie, did so in part as a result of their eschatological convictions. This is especially pronounced in the Catholic Apostolic Church and with Sandford and Dowie respectively. The New Apostolic Church and the Mormons have put systems in place to ensure the permanent nature of apostles in their church structure; yet due to their exclusivist, and especially in the case of the Mormons, unorthodox beliefs they are not appealed to by modern charismatic apostolate advocate writers as models to be looked to. Likewise, the very liturgical nature of the New Apostolic Church, which it inherited from the Catholic Apostolic Church, makes its "modelability" very suspect for many Charismatic Evangelical churches with their suspicion of anything that is liturgical or traditional. The self-proclaimed apostles, Dowie and Sandford, are inherently tainted due to their strange conviction that they were "Elijah." The apostles that were advocated by these individuals and movements were seen as the highest order of ministry—more akin to modern-day Apostle Type 1s. All in all, although a very significant time for "apostles," this is an era that is fraught with problems that made the idea of charismatic apostles seem very unorthodox and decidedly dubious. Nevertheless, some of the impulses that caused this call for modern apostles and prophets were more "acceptable" as they were a mixture of a desire to get back to a primitive and "pure" Christianity, alongside an eschatological belief that saw the coming of Christ as being on the horizon.[140] It was during this period that a movement arose that would define

137. Ibid., 234.
138. Harlan, "Dowie," 38.
139. Lindsay, *Dowie*, 235.
140. This can be clearly seen in Sandford and Dowie's claim that they were the

aspects of the Pentecostal and Charismatic Movements and would provide further impetus for the restoration of charismatic apostles.

The emphasis of the Higher Life Movement (1858–) was sanctification by faith, nevertheless, the teachers who gathered at the Keswick convention were also interested in receiving "power from on high" and this also became a central theme at Keswick. Therefore, key figures such as Andrew Murray and A. B. Simpson propagated the message of the Spirit's power and His gifts. According to Shirley Nelson the possibility of modern apostles was "a subject of great interest among Higher Life Christians."[141] One of those figures who was indirectly impacted by this Stream was a Chinese Christian evangelist and teacher, Watchman Nee.[142] His theology of Spirit baptism fits with Keswick theology rather than the Pentecostal variety. The Little Flock movement that he started in China not only has left an indelible mark on the Christian scene in China,[143] but his writings have had a profound impact upon key figures within the Charismatic Movement and his voice continues to be heard.[144]

Watchman Nee's ecclesiological beliefs, including his view of apostles, are brought out in his book, *The Normal Christian Church Life*. Within this book he writes in detail about apostles, the reasons to why they are still an integral part of God's church and how they are to demonstrate their office. Nee sees Ephesians 4:11–13 as a key text for proving that the ascension gift

---

"Elijah to come" preparing God's people for Christ's return; likewise the Catholic Apostolic Church saw itself as participating in the "Latter Rain" of God's Spirit that would ultimately usher in the return of Christ; the New Apostolic Church to this day holds fast to the "imminent" return of Christ. Joseph Smith even prophesied the Christ would return around 1890—see Ankerberg and Weldon, *Cults*, 293.

141. Nelson, *Fair*, 60.

142. Both Andrew Murray and A. B. Simpson were highly regarded by Nee; *War on the Saints* by J. Penn-Lewis and Evan Roberts was influential on his book, *The Spiritual Man*.

143. Dennis McCallum makes a compelling case for the unique and lasting legacy of Nee on the Chinese House Church scene in "Watchman Nee."

144. Nee's influence has been very much felt by Charismatic groups on both sides of the Atlantic, where his writings were recommended by the influential publications *New Wine* in America (see for example, Holy Spirit Teaching Mission, *New Wine*, February, 1970, pp. 23, 29), and *Renewal* in Britain (I was privileged to have access to some of the earliest publications whilst helping the late Father Michael Harper—who founded *Renewal*—archive various correspondences). Terry Virgo refers to the impact of one of Nee's books on himself—see Virgo, *Paths*, 102; from reading the various exchanges between Michael Harper and David Lillie, it was clear that Nee was influential on both of them. It was Nee's book, *The Normal Christian Life* that revolutionized Colin Urquhart's life and ministry—see his opening testimony in *Spirit*, chap. 1. More recently, Garner references his work positively as well—see *Apostles Today*, 22.

of apostle must continue until Christ's return.[145] Unlike the Pentecostals who tended to see five ministries in Ephesians 4:11–13, Watchman Nee, like Irving, saw only four: pastor/teacher being one ministry.[146] According to Kinnear, around 1935 Nee's Little Flock "movement also had 'apostles' (shi-tu, an envoy). These were full-time workers with a roving commission to evangelize the unreached, to establish churches where there were none, and to build up the believers. They might move farther afield, perhaps hiring a public hall for some fresh outreach in a new situation."[147]

According to Nee in 1938 "there were 128 such 'apostles' out in full-time service."[148] Although, as I will argue, the Fort Lauderdale Five were influenced by Nee, they were more at home in the Pentecostal stream. Nevertheless, other groups who have created a stir in America and further afield were inspired by Nee's writings and ecclesiology—particularly his anti-institutionalism and his "organic" vision of the church—figures such as Stephen Kaung, Witness Lee, Gene Edwards and Frank Viola.

With the advent of the Pentecostal movement beginning at Charles Parham's Bible School, a renewed interest in the empowering and enabling work of the Spirit came to the fore. The Pentecostals very early on saw themselves in a similar way to some of the Catholic Apostolics,[149] as recipients of the Latter Rain—this is the belief that in the very last days God would again pour out his Spirit upon all flesh as on the day of Pentecost—characterized by the empowering of the Spirit with the various gifts and ministries that he brings. Donald Gee in a book recounting the history of the Pentecostal movement in Britain, *Wind and Flame*, stated that "the Pentecostal movement as a whole believes that Divine grace has distributed the gifts of Ephesians iv. 11 freely throughout the whole Body of Christ . . ."[150]

As seen in chapter 2 and 3, there was widespread agreement across all the Pentecostal churches that God was giving people as apostles, prophets, evangelists, pastors, and teachers; nevertheless what constituted these ministries—particularly the apostle and the prophet—was disputed.

---

145. Nee, *Normal*, 7–13.
146. Ibid., 8.
147. Kinnear, *Tide*, 137.
148. Ibid., 138.
149. The Catholic Apostolic Church apostle, Rev N. Armstrong stated in a sermon, "The time of the latter rain is now come; the harvest is near at hand": "Exposition and Sermon; delivered at Salem Chapel, Deverell Street, Dover Road, Sunday Evening, November 11, 1832, by Rev N. Armstrong, A. B. Text is Zechariah 10.1," in *Tracts*, 2.
150. Gee, *Wind*, 105.

According to William Kay, "most Pentecostal groups did not officially recognize apostles or prophets within their ecclesiastical polity: they usually only spoke of pastors and evangelists."[151] The Apostolic Church took a different view and saw apostles as central to the local church.

Donald Gee recounts that the Apostolic Church was an offshoot of the "Apostolic Faith Church" (AFC) which had been started by W. O. Hutchinson; the Apostolic Faith Church relied heavily on prophetic utterances and the authority of the resident apostle, which due to abuses led to the formation of the Apostolic Church, headed by D. P. Williams.[152] Nevertheless, this new church was viewed with suspicion by Gee and other Pentecostals; hence Gee writes concerning them, "From the first the Apostolic Church claimed to possess a 'fuller vision' concerning church order and government.... Moreover the strong emphasis... placed upon prophetic utterances in church government is... quite rightly treated with the greatest reserve by those who conscientiously believe that the New Testament supplies no such authority for such weight...."[153]

After the Apostolic Church had established itself, its statement of belief was hammered out and in 1920 they noted eleven key beliefs one of which was that church government is "by apostles, prophets, evangelists, pastors, teachers, elders and deacons."[154] Apostles have "the constitutional right to attend any service or meeting of the church and to take a leading role"; they have a "distinctive work" of ordaining all the other ministries—in this way they bring "leadership, revelation and government of a super-local character."[155] Their 1916 constitution states:

> APOSTLE means one of the Gifts of Christ in the Ascension Ministries and is the first Office in Church government.
>
> APOSTLESHIP means the whole Council of Apostles in whom there are vested: -
>
> a. The responsibility for the clarification of doctrinal matters.

---

151. Kay, "Dynamics," 167.

152. According to Kay, Hutchinson's "influence on Williams and the young Apostolic Faith Church was considerable." His view that prophecy could be used to both guide and govern "the church, were largely, if not completely, accepted and his view of the role of the present-day ordination of apostles, prophets, pastors, evangelists and teachers became foundational to the Apostolic Faith Church's understanding of itself." Kay, *Pentecostals*, 18.

153. Ibid.

154. Quotation from Kay, *Pentecostals*, 19.

155. W. A. C. Rowe, *One Lord One Faith*, 243, quoted by Kay, *Pentecostals*, 225.

Post-biblical History of Charismatic Apostles

b. The sole power to call, ordain and locate ministers.

c. The authority to control administrative affairs at General Council under the control of the Overseas Department in the United Kingdom), Regional, Area, District and Local levels.

d. The right to apply discipline as detailed in the relevant sections of this Constitution.

e. The right to attend and chair any business meeting or church service within the sphere of their jurisdiction.

The term Apostleship also means an Apostle or a number of Apostles serving in a Region, Area or District.[156]

These definitions remain central to the Apostolic Church's understanding of church Government, and although relatively small in the UK, its missionaries have gone far and wide and the Apostolic Church now has a large membership in Australia[157] and Africa.[158]

The controversial Latter Rain revival of 1948 that began amongst a spiritually hungry group of Christian leaders and students in Saskatchewan, Canada brought apostles and prophets back to the fore within Pentecostalism in the USA and beyond.[159] Prophetic utterances and impartation of spiritual gifts were a hallmark of this "outpouring" with prophecies emphasizing the five-fold ministry and God's intent on restoring them to the church. Bill Hamon records, "This movement strongly taught Ephesians 4:11–13, emphasizing that all five ministries must continue to function in their ministry of perfecting the saints until the Church reaches the 'unity of the faith and of the knowledge of the Son of God...'"[160]

The overall emphasis of the Latter Rain movement was a conviction that God was restoring the church to make her fit to be Christ's glorious bride;[161] therefore all five of the perfecting ministries were being restored. The particular beliefs that came out regarding apostles and prophets was critiqued and denounced by the Assemblies of God USA in 1949 who saw

---

156. Apostolic Church UK, "Constitution," 169.
157. Anderson, *Introduction*, 142.
158. Ibid., 121.
159. See Hamon, *Eternal*, chap. 24; Jackson, *Quest*, 183–87; Riss, "Latter Rain," 830–33. For a critical history of the movement see Graves, "Anointing."
160. Hamon, *Eternal*, 235.
161. Jackson, *Quest*, 184.

PART TWO—How We Got Here

it as aberrant[162] rejecting as erroneous the idea that the church is built on the foundation of present-day apostles and prophets.

With the emergence of the Charismatic Movement in the 1960s a renewed interest in the charismatic gifts also gave rise to an interest in the charismatic ministries. The radical House Church movement[163] which emerged in Britain during the 1960s heralded the restoration of the apostle's ministry, alongside the other four ministries, as vital to the health and perfecting of the Body.[164] Across the Atlantic, similar ideas were being proposed by the Fort Lauderdale Five.[165] In the first *New Wine* magazine (June 1969), which advocated and included the teaching of the Fort Lauderdale Four/Five, it is significant to note that the Scripture verses that end the editorial are Ephesians 4:11–13.[166] It is also notable that Nee's books on the church (*The Normal Christian Church life*; *The Body of Christ*) were often advertised in the *New Wine* magazine.[167] According to Moore, the fivefold ministry was a vital part of the teaching of the Fort Lauderdale Five; he points out that Prince was teaching about the present-day ministries of apostles and prophets in 1973;[168] and that that movement "emphasized the restoration of the fivefold ministries of apostles, prophets, evangelists, shepherds and teachers";[169] and that they "believed that, in their day, God was restoring the ecclesiological dimensions of New Testament life. This restoration focused on the five-fold office gifts of biblical government with special emphasis on the role of shepherd and on covenant relationships."[170]

---

162. The following features of the "revival" were denounced by the Assemblies of God: "(1) it relied too heavily upon present-day apostles and prophets (i.e., a self-appointed Charismatic leadership); (2) it practiced the confessing and pronouncing of forgiveness by one member upon another; (3) it advocated the practice of bestowing spiritual gifts by the laying-on-of-hands; and (4) it distorted Scripture so as to arrive at conclusions not generally accepted by members of the Assemblies." Buttner, "Latter Rain," 84.

163. For an in-depth study of this movement, see Walker's *Restoring*.

164. For apologetics for modern-day apostles and theories on how the ministry should be outworked today see the collection of articles by radical House Church leaders in Matthew, ed., *Apostles Today*.

165. Initially there were just four of them in covenant relationship: Charles Simpson, Bob Mumford, Derek Prince, and Don Basham; in time Ern Baxter was to join them.

166. See "Holy Spirit Teaching Mission," *New Wine*, June 1969, 2.

167. See for example "Holy Spirit Teaching Mission," *New Wine*, February 1970, 23, 29.

168. See Moore, *Shepherding*, 55.

169. Ibid., 72.

170. Ibid., 82–83.

Although they were very influential, the Shepherding movement that came from their stable was very divisive and denounced by prominent Charismatic leaders.[171]

The influence of both the Latter Rain movement and Watchman Nee on the Fort Lauderdale Five is clearly discernible. Although the Shepherding movement incorporated many of Watchman Nee's teaching, particularly in regards to spiritual authority,[172] it went with the Pentecostal and Latter Rain view that there were five ministries written about in Ephesians 4:11, rather than four. The Latter Rain's emphases might well have come through Ern Baxter[173] who had worked with the controversial William Branham who was seen by some as the forerunner and inspiration for the Latter Rain Revival, and who in turn promoted it.[174] There was considerable overlap between Fort Lauderdale Four/Five and the radical House Church; Arthur Wallis' writings were connected to both movements,[175] and there was interaction between leaders from both sides;[176] the only official discipling amongst these leaders I am aware of occurred between Bob Mumford and Barney Coombs.[177] Nevertheless, there were distinct differences between these movements.

The focus amongst the Fort Lauderdale Four/Five was much more on shepherds and discipleship and less on apostles and prophets, whereas in Britain the radical House Church emphasized apostles and prophets more. The influence of the Shepherding movement was felt on the UK side of the Atlantic among certain groups within the wider House Church movement which imbibed and used much of the shepherding language and practices. This overall difference in emphasis is likely to be because many of the key leaders in the radical House Church movement in Britain saw themselves as apostles, whereas the leaders of the Fort Lauderdale Four/Five believed themselves to be Spirit-filled teachers and pastors. Undoubtedly, both movements put apostles and prophets firmly on the Charismatic church's

---

171. For a detailed history of the Shepherding movement, see ibid.

172. Moore notes that Nee's book, *Spiritual Authority*, was recommended by Mumford in *New Wine* 1972. Ibid., 55.

173. This is the view of McAlpine in *Post-Charismatic?*, 174–75.

174. See DeWaay, "Roots."

175. In an early edition of *New Wine*, there is an article by Arthur Wallis. See Wallis, "Faith." Wallis himself was an influential voice promoting the ministry of apostles. For his views on the subject see his "Apostles Today?" 171–74.

176. Walker, *Restoring*, 92ff.

177. Moore, *Shepherding*, 147.

consciousness (both denominational and non-denominational churches) and provided an assortment of biblical arguments to support their beliefs.

Conclusion

Since the seventeenth century those groups that limited the number of charismatic apostles due to eschatological convictions, such as the Catholic Apostolic Church or certain streams within the Anabaptist movement, undermined their very existence when those Apostles died out. Those that allowed a continuing apostolic ministry through either having a fixed number which can be refilled each time one of the apostles dies—such as the Mormons—or which sees the possibility of an innumerable company of apostles—for example the New Apostolic Church, Nee's Little Flock, the various house church movements and those groups associated with the Pentecostal Charismatic Movement—have continued to generate new apostles. A form of ministry that had not been widely accepted and promoted by name since the church's earliest days, which prior to the Pentecostal Charismatic Movement was surrounded by controversy and often discredited, has over the last century become a replicable and respectable idea in a significant portion of the church. Whether there are differences between the modern charismatic apostolate and the ones looked at in the course of this chapter is something that I will address in the next chapter, but in spite of any differences we are in a situation today where there is a widespread embracing of an idea that had very little support in the past—why the change?

5

Shifting Perspectives

How a Minority Viewpoint Became Widespread

Introduction

As I have shown in the previous chapter the charismatic apostolate is not a new phenomenon, however, when we look at popular descriptions of the charismatic apostolate today we see both old ideas resurrected and innovative ones. In this chapter I look at the similarities and differences between older conceptions of the charismatic apostolate with the popular forms looked at in chapter 3, and then posit reasons to why what was a minority view has now become so widespread. Although modern conceptions of the charismatic apostolate differ from one another there are certain features that tend to be shared by all of them:

1. The church needs apostles.
2. God is still giving apostles post the apostolic era.
3. No specified number of apostles.
4. This is scripturally legitimated.
5. Ephesians 4:11–13 is the key text and source of the underlying theology that drives this emphasis.
6. There is enough in Scripture to paint a picture of how an apostle functions.

7. They exercise spiritual authority based upon an empowering by the Spirit rather than delegated authority via church hierarchy.

8. All modern apostles are "under" Scripture and not authors of it.

9. Paul is a model apostle par excellence and his gift is evidenced through his spiritual fatherhood of initiating and nurturing churches.

Many of these ideas are not new: the contention that God can and does still give apostles to his church in the post-apostolic era has resurfaced at different times in the church's history.[1] Furthermore, the idea that the church needs them is inherent in all of the conceptions of the charismatic apostolate of previous eras—simply put, God would not give apostles if the church did not need them. Those who advocated the charismatic apostolate appealed to Scripture whether that be the Anabaptists, Irvingites, or the Pentecostal groups. Calvin, however, relied on the historical situation to justify his belief, rather than Scripture, which he saw as invalidating that claim.[2] Ephesians 4:11–13 has been the main text of Scripture justifying an ongoing charismatic apostolate: it was given special primacy during Irving's ministry, was central to the Catholic Apostolic Church, appealed to by Nee, Pentecostal churches, Latter Rain advocates, Edwards and even used by Jerome many centuries before.[3] 1 Corinthians 12:28 and Ephesians 2:20 have not had the same weight put upon them; although in certain circles they have been vital—the Mormons, Dowie, the Apostolic Church, and now Peter Wagner and others involved in the New Apostolic Reformation have proof-texted their convictions with these verses.[4]

The belief within Protestant Charismatic circles of the non-importance of historical succession in regards to an apostle's call and ministry fits with prior Protestant convictions; similarly, the recognition of spiritual authority and power being mediated via the Spirit rather than a historical chain has a rich history within the Protestant Church and the Orthodox Church.[5] The Roman Catholic Church has more tightly limited "apostolic charisms" to those in Episcopal succession; but even here it has been widened since Vatican II which made it clear that the various charisms of the Spirit were not distributed to the clergy alone but to all God's people.[6]

---

1. See chap. 4.
2. See chap. 4.
3. See chap. 4.
4. See chaps. 3–4.
5. See chaps. 1–4.
6. See Vatican II, *Lumen Gentium*, particularly chap. 2.

The Catholic Apostolic Church, the Mormons, and Dowie all put a quota on how many apostles could be operating.[7] Yet the New Apostolic Church, Watchman Nee, the Pentecostals, and their offshoots have not—that conviction has continued to this day and is the main view propounded by Charismatics.[8] All these groups saw Scripture as providing enough to demonstrate what an apostle's ministry should look like, and were clear that all apostles are under the rule of Scripture. In practice this can appear blurred amongst movements both past and present that equate pronouncements made by an apostle as the "voice of God." Paul as an exemplary apostle is not new, the Catholic Apostolics majored on his ministry as a pattern,[9] as did Nee,[10] and the Pentecostals have long viewed him as a model to be emulated.[11]

The broadness of what constitutes apostolic ministry is new and is particularly exemplified in the writings of Wagner with his innovative categories of apostolic ministry and his conviction that apostleship is not limited to the workings of local churches, but can extend into the "workplace."[12] Aside from these new facets, much of what is being passed off as new are ideas that have been around for a long time. The most notable change is the widespread acceptance of the possibility of charismatic apostles (see chaps. 1–2); Rob Warner describes the current situation aptly when he writes,

> Some have resisted strenuously the suggestion that all five of the ministries (Ephesians 4:11 ministries) are still available today, let alone advisable or even necessary for the well-being of the Church. Here too the consensus seems to be shifting. Increasing numbers of Evangelicals have come to accept in recent years the continued apostolic ministry of the secondary kind. . . . There are continued ministries of vision and direction, leadership and teaching that involve oversight of a number of local churches. . . . Today it is by no means only the new churches that are talking about the need for apostles. Anglican and Baptist leaders have also been suggesting that their bishops and super-intendents

---

7. See chap. 4.
8. See chaps. 1–3.
9. See chap. 4.
10. See Nee, *Normal*.
11. For example, Hagin; see chap. 3.
12. See chap. 3.

need to be released from administrative tasks in order to fulfil an apostolic function. . . .[13]

The shift is evident but why has it occurred? From personal interaction with people who have embraced this new "paradigm," as well as general awareness through my research I have become convinced that there are a number of factors that has led to this sea change. In this chapter I will consider those factors.

Reasons for the Shift

The recognition by the Academy of the importance of the Pentecostal Charismatic Movement can be shown by the recent decision by the Center for Religion and Civic Culture at the University of Southern California to "award five centers and 16 individual scholars and their teams a total of $3.5 million for research." Kimon Sargeant, the vice president of human services for the foundation said the following in relation to this funding: "The researchers selected for the Pentecostal and Charismatic Research Initiative have a unique opportunity to help scholars and the broader public understand how this movement inspired by powerful worship and religious experience is changing the cultural, social and religious landscape around the world."[14]

Basing it on the statistical work of Barrett and Johnson, Allan Anderson made the following comment in 2004: "If these figures are not wild guesses, they indicate that in less than a hundred years, Pentecostal, Charismatic and associated movements have become the largest numerical force in world Christianity after the Roman Catholic Church and represent a quarter of all Christians."[15]

With its essential evangelistic DNA, Pentecostal/Charismatic Christians are at the forefront of missionary endeavors; and it has been the Pentecostals in particular who have used the airwaves and satellite television to great effect, even to the point of dominating religious broadcasting.[16] The availability and propagation of Pentecostal/Charismatic teaching is huge and spans the globe. As a result Christians of other persuasions are being forced to take note. Anyone desiring to see churches grow as well

13. Warner, *Alive*, 182.
14. Lowe, "Researchers."
15. Anderson, *Introduction*, 1.
16. Harrell Jr, "Healers."

as promote spiritually vibrant Christianity cannot avoid asking pertinent questions about the validity of the Pentecostal Charismatic Movement. Therefore, it is unsurprising that people with those desires, particularly Evangelicals, wanted to investigate it.

The testimony of those involved in the Pentecostal Charismatic Movement is that through the experience of the Spirit they were enabled to bridge the gap between the early Christians' experience and their own. The world that they now inhabited through their Pentecostal experience was remarkably similar to the one they read about within the NT; it was in the words of John McKay a "shared experience."[17] Once experientially in the "world of the New Testament," one would naturally begin to expect similar styles of ministry modeled by those first Charismatics. No longer could much of the New Testament be relegated to a bygone era, but those neglected sections became relevant to how the church was the church. Many of those outside this movement have derided it and argued that the adherents are clearly deluded and what they perceive as shared experience is clearly not.[18] Nevertheless, for others a significant bridge has been forged that makes imitating the initial apostles more plausible in theory at least—but for some it has been more than theory.

Seeing effective Pentecostalism and Charismatic ministries in action has played a part in helping change people's minds on the possibility of a charismatic apostolate.[19] The Reverend Barry Kissell, formerly on staff at St Andrew's Chorleywood now with St Mary's Battersea Rise, claimed not to have had a dramatic change of thinking on the matter, nor recall any books that contributed to his acceptance of a charismatic apostolate, only pinpointing events in the early 1970s that convinced him that this ministry was still valid when he "started to see anointed people functioning in the ways indicated by Paul."[20] The former Bishop of Chile, founder of New Wine and ex-vicar of St Andrew's Chorleywood, David Pytches was a cessationist prior to going to Chile; however, whilst there he came across spiritual gifts amongst the Pentecostals which convinced him that

17. McKay, "Veil," 26.

18. For a classic, irenic appraisal of the Pentecostal Charismatic Movement that argues that Pentecostal claims that their supernatural gifts are the same as the first Christians is misguided, see Packer, *Keep in Step*, chap. 6.

19. Barry Kissell for example claimed to never have had a change of mind, unlike others he was not tied to a particular theological interpretation. Barry Kissell, e-mail message to author, December 11, 2008.

20. By this he was referring to Ephesians 4:11–13. Barry Kissell, e-mail message to author, December 11, 2008.

PART TWO—How We Got Here

God had not withdrawn any of his charisms, including the gift of apostle.[21] Once the cessationist hermeneutic was removed he saw no biblical reason to counter the idea. The Reverend Bruce Collins, an Anglican leader of the international wing of New Wine,[22] was deeply immersed in Conservative Evangelicalism, and by default took on their cessationist hermeneutic. Much of that changed when he encountered John Wimber in the 1980s: "I guess I came to be aware that the Lord was still giving apostles to his church through the influence of John Wimber in the early 1980s. I came to this conviction through seeing his ministry and seeing/reading about the ministries of other leaders who were being used by the Lord to pioneer new expressions of church, church planting etc."[23]

Peter Wagner similarly moved from a cessationist perspective in the 1970s when, whilst researching church growth, he saw a correlation between growth and "the supernatural ministry of the Holy Spirit," particularly when he studied the remarkable expansion of the Pentecostal churches in Latin America.[24]

The positive examples within the Pentecostal Charismatic Movement were making a case for the charismatic apostolate by example which in turn drew attention to their hermeneutic. Similarly, personal experiences of mainstream Christians being "filled" with or "baptized" in the Spirit led many to embrace a Pentecostal/Charismatic hermeneutic with its conviction that all the charisms of 1 Corinthians 12–14 were still being given.[25] Pentecostalism from its very beginnings attracted other Christians, as well as repelled them, yet with the advent of the Charismatic Movement an influx of people who were prepared to treasure elements of tradition as well as biblical and theological scholarship gave the Charismatics a semblance of intellectual weight that Pentecostalism did not have.[26] Today there are

21. Pytches, *Leadership*, 23.

22. On the New Wine website Collins is described in the following ways: "*Bruce Collins* is a member of the New Wine's leadership team as a prophetic pioneer. He is also on the International Oversight Group, having pioneered and overseen the development of the overseas work until February 2010. Additionally he co-leads the work in New Wine Cymru (Wales). For 12 years he was the team rector of the Roxeth team ministry in Harrow. Now based in Wales, he works full-time for New Wine." New Wine, "Our Leadership."

23. Bruce Collins, e-mail message to author, January 4, 2009.

24. Out of this research he wrote Wagner, *Look Out!*

25. Peter Hocken has collected numerous testimonies of influential mainline Christians coming into "baptism in the Spirit" and the effects on them. See Hocken, *One Lord*, chap. 1.

26. Charismatic Roman Catholic scholars such as Simon Tugwell and George

a host of Pentecostal and Charismatic theologians and biblical scholars,[27] and their anticessationist stance has increasingly been vindicated within biblical studies.[28] The testimony of Dr Michael Eaton, a reputable theologian[29]/biblical scholar[30] and church leader[31] is telling in this regard:

> I changed my mind about apostleship. . . . Like many Bible-believing Christians I had been taught that apostles were a one-generation affair, that apostles had to be eye-witnesses of the resurrection, that they had to be commissioned by the literal, physical and bodily-present Lord Jesus Christ and that by definition no one today could be an apostle. They were the unique one-generation-only foundation of the church. Their work was to lay down the infallible teaching upon which the church was built, and to write—in conjunction with a few other non-apostolic figures—the New Testament. Only certain extremist Pentecostals and peculiar groups like the Mormons and the Irvingites taught that apostles continued in the churches. . . . All of this I was taught and taught myself until about eleven years ago. . . . What made me change my mind? It was the Bible.[32]

Eaton goes on to explain how this new perspective came through a Charismatic minister pointing out to him that in Ephesians 4:11, the gifts mentioned are those given by Christ post-ascension, and therefore did not refer to the Twelve or any other apostles who were so called prior to Christ's ascension. Eaton proceeds to give a number of exegetical reasons to why he believes apostles are still given to the church, as well as practical reasons to why they are still needed.[33]

This recognition that there is a substantial biblical case for the charismatic apostolate and other charismatic gifts and ministries has enabled

---

Montague brought scholarly reflections to bear on the Pentecostal Charismatic Movement, as did Tom Smail by promoting theological reflection amongst Charismatics by editing *Theological Renewal* between 1975–83 and several theological books—"Smail," 1074.

27. E.g., James Dunn, Gordon Fee, Max Turner, and William Menzies.

28. The work of NT scholar James Dunn has been particularly important in this regard.

29. R. T. Kendall refers to him as "A world-class scholar and writer . . . tomorrow's theologian." See back cover of Eaton, *Enjoying*.

30. He is the author of a Tyndale commentary on Hosea.

31. Eaton was a curate in the Church of England, then became a Baptist pastor in South Africa, and presently leads the Chrisco Fellowship of Churches in Kenya.

32. Ibid., 74.

33. Ibid., chap. 12.

Pentecostals and Charismatics to be embraced by Evangelical initiatives and organizations. For example, many Pentecostals and Charismatics are established members of the Evangelical Alliance;[34] a plethora of Charismatic leaders who are five-fold ministry advocates have been actively involved in ecumenical conferences and initiatives in Britain such as Spring Harvest[35] and the National Evangelical Anglican Congress.[36] Pentecostals and Charismatics now have a level of respectability within the British scene that enables them to assert their vantage point confidently knowing that it will not be dismissed so easily anymore.[37]

Wider theological and ecclesial trends[38] have also combined to legitimize attention on gifts and ministries: there has been and continues to be talk about the mobilization of the laity, and a recognition of the vital role each person plays within the Body of Christ.[39] This focus on every member ministry brought the attention of churches to the gifts and ministries that Christ has bestowed on his people by the Spirit as mentioned in the "gift" passages within the New Testament. A notable development occurred at Vatican II where there was a renewed emphasis on the church as the people of God with an affirmation that the charisms of the Spirit are distributed to all God's people not just the ordained.[40] The concept of spiritual gifts and the need to discover, affirm and exercise them has taken on a life of its own and been popular in Evangelical/Charismatic churches, and as I have shown in a previous chapter,[41] the prolific ones are advocating a charismatic apostolate.

Another gift that has received much attention in light of the Pentecostal Charismatic Movement has been prophecy. This medium of revelation has been instrumental in calling for apostles as well as recognizing them and has played a prominent role in this regard in older movements, for example, in Mormonism, amongst the Catholic Apostolic Church and

34. A cursory look at members shows this: see Evangelical Alliance UK, "Search."

35. E.g., Terry Virgo and Roger Forster.

36. E.g., Mark Stibbe.

37. Of former heads of the Evangelical Alliance UK, Clive Calver, and Joel Edwards were Charismatic and Pentecostal respectively; the present head of the EA, Steve Clifford, is also Charismatic.

38. Which may well have been directly influenced by or at least spurred on by the Pentecostal Charismatic Movement.

39. As a Church of England minister I hear these ideas being discussed and aimed for.

40. See Vatican II, *Lumen Gentium*, particularly chap. 2.

41. Chap. 2.

the Apostolics; and it has done so throughout the Pentecostal Charismatic Movement. For example it was a feature in the Latter Rain revival; the Shepherding movement; the radical House Church; Kansas City Prophets; Baptist Mainstream, amongst others.[42] This trend continues within Charismatic circles,[43] and has found an official place amongst groups that have incorporated a "prophetic presbytery."[44] According to Bill Hamon, "during the forty-three years of my ministry I have prophesied to more than two thousand individuals that they were called to be apostles or were apostles."[45] The weight given to these types of prophecy differ widely amongst Christians; nevertheless, even for those who are not prone to take them seriously, there have been other trends afoot which have made the idea of the charismatic apostolate more compelling.

Missiology as a discipline has taken off[46] and *missio Dei* has become common terminology in church leadership circles; as Bosch explains, "During the past half a century or so there has been a subtle but nevertheless decisive shift toward understanding mission as God's mission. . . . Mission is thereby seen as a movement from God to the world; the church is viewed as an instrument for that mission. There is church because there is mission, not vice versa. To participate in mission is to participate in the movement of God's love toward people, since God is a fountain of sending love."[47]

Missiology is no longer a minor subset of theology; it is at the heart of it. These seismic shifts in relation to the place of mission have had a profound effect upon both our understanding of God and the nature of the church. It appears uncontested amongst theologians that God is a missionary God, and that he calls the church into his mission. This in turn has brought "apostolicity" to the forefront. Coinciding with this reappraisal of

---

42. See chap. 4.

43. Colin Urquhart owned and affirmed his own calling as an Apostle after an international "prophet" singled him out. (Colin Urquhart, interview with author, May 13, 2009). Peter Wagner also tells of both his and Trevor Newport's three-year period of grappling with their vocation until submitting to the prophetic revelation that was calling them both apostles. Wagner, *Apostles Today*, 68–69.

44. An informed defense of the prophetic presbytery can be found in Blomgren, *Prophetic*. It is a form of ministry particularly embraced by groups who accepted the Latter Rain movement, as it was a key feature of that "Revival."

45. Hamon, *Apostles*, 120–21.

46. Based on J. Verkuyl's research, Craig Van Gelder notes that "The formal discipline of missiology emerged within seminary education in the late nineteenth century." Gelder, *Essence*, 33.

47. Bosch, *Transforming*, 389–90.

mission has been an ecumenical drive that has opened up Christian communities to one another in a more conciliatory manner. The World Council of Churches has been instrumental in encouraging these ecumenical impulses and undoubtedly one of the most significant papers to have come from the World Council of Churches has been *Baptism, Eucharist and Ministry*. This document, although still affirming historic succession, promoted the ecclesial validity of other church ministries. *Baptism, Eucharist and Ministry* reflected a growing consensus that the concept of the apostolicity of the church must be considered much wider than historic succession. This shift has been described well in the Church of England Ely Diocesan Missionary booklet,

> Until recently, the language of apostolicity has been used to discriminate between churches which have maintained a ministry in direct succession to the first Apostles and those (especially Free and Reformed Churches) which have not. We are now urged to think of the church's apostolic nature as "continuity in the permanent characteristics of the Church of the apostles: witness to the apostolic faith, proclamation and fresh interpretation of the Gospel, celebration of baptism and the eucharist, the transmission of ministerial responsibilities, communion in prayer, love, joy and suffering, service to the sick and the needy, unity among the local churches and sharing the gifts which the Lord has given to each."[48]

A change of emphasis can also be seen amongst prominent theologians. For example, the then Anglican Archbishop of Canterbury, Rowan Williams in an address to the 3rd Global South to South Encounter Ain al Sukhna, Egypt in Oct 2005 on the subject, *One Holy Catholic and Apostolic Church*, made the following statement:

> And while we can and rightly do concern ourselves with apostolic integrity in terms of continuity and recognizability in the church, we ought not to lose sight of the fact that the language of "sending," the apostolic language of scripture, is first of all about God's mission in Jesus, or indeed we could say God's mission as Jesus. And the forms, once again of apostolic continuity, especially the forms of apostolic ministry are to be seen in that context: they serve the mission of God which is in Christ Jesus.[49]

---

48. Diocese of Ely, "Good Gifts," 13. The quote at the end is from World Council of Churches, *Baptism*.

49. Williams, "One, Holy."

Williams draws attention to "God's mission in Jesus," that is the heart of "apostolicity," the various forms are subservient and directed by that. God's mission is the emphasis of apostolicity—the weight is no longer placed upon "apostolic succession," and when it is, many theologians are not content with traditional definitions of it. For example, the controversial Catholic Theologian, Hans Küng, redefines the term "apostolic succession" to describe not office bearers but rather the church: "As a result of the continuing apostolic mission there is, in the apostolic ministry, an apostolic succession: an apostolic succession of obedience. *Who* then are the followers of the apostles? . . . There can be only one basic answer: the Church. The whole Church, not just a few individuals, is the follower of the apostles."[50]

Together these developments and changing emphases on a catholic level have provided fresh impetus for the older churches to recognize apostolic-type ministries outside the historic churches, and also to encourage and affirm apostolic-type ministry within their own communions.[51] The fact that all of these differing theological aspects have converged has allowed for older traditions, both Evangelical and none, to re-evaluate the possibility of a charismatic apostolate in a more positive light—rather than automatically react negatively. There is still suspicion of newer ("schismatic"?) groups who appear to magnify this ministry and appear to use the appellation as a form of power/control.[52] At the same time the church in Britain has becoming increasingly aware that it needs to change to facilitate mission. No-one is under any illusion about the demise of the older churches in Britain, and the West generally.[53] According to the Tearfund survey conducted in 2007: "Two thirds of UK adults (33.2m) have no connection with church at present (nor with another religion) These people are evenly divided between those who have been in the past but have since left and those who have never been in their lives. This secular majority presents a major challenge to churches. Most of them

---

50. Küng, *Church*, 355.

51. E.g., Anglican pioneer ministers.

52. With good reasons! I was once present at a large Christian conference where an "Apostle" was calling for people to ensure that they were linked up to an anointed "Apostle," irrespective of their denominational allegiances.

53. Some of the figures quoted by Wagner concerning denominational decline in America included: "The Episcopal Church . . . dropped from 3.4 million in 1968 to 2.5 million in 1994. . . . United Methodists decreased from 11.0 million to 8.6 million; Presbyterian Church (USA) from 4.2 million to 3.7 million . . ." Wagner, *Churchquake*, 11.

(29.3m)—are unreceptive and closed to church: church going is simply not on their agenda."[54]

Ekklesia, the religion and society think-tank, has recently highlighted a new academic study from the National Centre for Social Research (NatCen) which shows the decline of mainstream, institutional religion, and quotes Professor Voas, an analyst on the data: "The results suggest that institutional religion in Britain now has a half-life of one generation, to borrow the terminology of radioactive decay."[55] With such evidence before the church, the demand for effective mission has become heightened.

Bob Hopkins felt that the church in Britain has been forced to revisit the charismatic apostolate because of the church's decline and fall in finances.[56] This appears plausible, particularly as there has been a growing awareness that we are living in a post-Christian society, and that the ossified models of mission that many churches operate with are not working today.[57] Understandably, there has been a fresh appreciation and demand for a ministry that is "pioneering" in shape and a desire to see individuals operating in ways that apostles, such as Paul and Barnabas, modeled in setting up churches. This type of thinking is well established in foreign missions, particularly due to the influential writings of Roland Allen,[58] and is now finding a place in the UK despite the presence of an established church. The General Synod-approved document, *Mission-Shaped Church*, has been widely read and makes a compelling case for Fresh Expressions and pioneer leaders in light of cultural changes and our missionary calling as church.

This missionary impulse has reshaped theological discussion on the church and has filtered down to the way communities are doing church. Ecclesiological discussions are highlighting that "Ecclesiology," like the church, "is not static," and as a result "changing contexts require the church to address new issues in understanding its life and ministry."[59] The Church of England's drive to initiate fresh expressions and train pioneer ministers is an outworking of this appreciation of the need to change structures for the sake of mission. There is awareness that many of the forms of church

---

54. See the "Executive Summary" in Ashworth and Farthing, *Churchgoing*.

55. Ekklesia, "News Brief."

56. Bob Hopkins, interview with author, January 11, 2010.

57. The following books/reports have made this point in differing ways: Cray et al., *Mission-Shaped Church*; Frost and Hirsch, *Shaping*; Murray-Williams, *Christendom*; Gibbs, *Church Next*; Gibbs, *Leadership Next*.

58. See particularly Allen, *Methods*, and Allen, *Spontaneous*.

59. Gelder, *Essence*, 42.

Shifting Perspectives

have been assumed due to cultural accretions rather than dominically mandated so do not have to be slavishly adhered to.

Bob Hopkins thought that one of the reasons why the churches in Britain were looking afresh at pioneering/apostolic ministers was the prominence in our culture given to entrepreneurs, innovators and pioneers.[60] I think this is debatable as Western societies often have heralded innovators, pioneers and entrepreneurs and this has not led to a widespread embracing of a charismatic apostolate in the past, but I am willing to admit that thrown in with the other factors it may contribute to it, too. Yet his acknowledgment of the place of culture in influencing the church is surely correct. It is inevitable that culture has shaped and does shape the church and hallmarks of postmodernity such as pragmatism and relativism will rub off on Christian churches. Therefore, there will be interest in modes of mission that are working (pragmatism) and due to globalization we are increasingly aware of stories from other parts of the world that are doing mission well, oftentimes actively promoting charismatic apostolates. At the same time there is a willingness to engage with a variety of perspectives (effects of relativism?) rather than assume that inherited traditions are infallible. As a result it is likely that our culture has contributed in redirecting the church to reconsider the charismatic apostolate, and the combination of other factors looked at have made it more appealing than ever before.[61]

CONCLUSION

As this chapter has shown there are a whole host of factors that have led to a re-examination and acceptance of this type of ministry on a broader scale within Britain. The place given to the experience of and examples provided by the Pentecostal Charismatic Movement is a key factor. The widespread Charismatic experience of the Spirit outside the confines of official church ministrations (that is, baptism, confirmation/chrismation, ordination) has drawn church leaders and theologians to affirm and recognize a rich biblical narrative that spoke of a God who was not bound

60. Bob Hopkins, interview with author, January 11, 2010.

61. It is important to remember that the charismatic apostolate has been convincing prior to postmodernity, too! Irving and the Catholic Apostolics predate postmodernity, and depending when you date its inception one could argue that many of the Independent Pentecostal Indigenous churches in Africa are from a modernistic era, too.

by institutions, but free to blow as and when he wills within and without those very structures. Although Pentecostals and Charismatics have not always been a good advertisement for the Holy Spirit—moral failings are as rife in this sector as in any other Christian branch—high-profile theological appraisals of the Pentecostal Charismatic Movement have led a growing number of older Christian churches to affirm the work of the Spirit amongst newer Pentecostal and Charismatic Christians.[62] At the same time there has been a widespread reaffirmation of the centrality of mission by the church catholic, an awareness of the missionary challenges and the need for the Holy Spirit to empower the church. Into that mix, the Pentecostal Charismatic Movement appears to offer a pragmatic, experiential dynamism to answer the challenge.

The Pentecostal Charismatic Movement has been the seedbed out of which the practice of identifying people's charisms has taken root as well as being the main protagonist and propagator of a Scriptural interpretation that allows for a charismatic apostolate, both of which have been widely circulated via globalization and modern technology. The renewed commitment of Christians to ecumenism has inevitably given the Pentecostal Charismatic Movement an opportunity to spread their ideas to other Christians who are more "open" to Christian brothers/sisters of other persuasions; it has also been instrumental in furthering ecumenism as it has brought together Catholics, Protestant and Orthodox into a "shared experience" that has provided a basis for genuine communion.[63] The thrust in all sectors of the church toward more missional-minded communities has contributed to the rise, identification and categorizing of more "missional/apostolic" type leaders amongst Charismatic and non-Charismatics. It is likely that in certain circles, there are less noble characteristics that push for recognition of this ministry, such as prestige, power, self-justification, self-appointment and selfish ambition; furthermore, the individualistic nature of charismatic experience can often work against the church rather than for it—maybe this is one reason the Pentecostal Charismatic Movement has not slowed down the Protestant trait of ever more denominations and has arguably accelerated it in parts of the world.[64]

---

62. A good example of this is the Roman Catholic Church's official endorsements of the Catholic Charismatic Renewal.

63. The International Charismatic Consultation on World Evangelization is an example of this.

64. The emergence of the New Apostolic Reformation networks is an example of this.

Therefore there are spiritual and theological trends that have enabled the charismatic apostolate to become widespread; at the same time there are societal and sociological trends that have similarly enabled it to become much more attractive as well. Even though a shift has occurred and the idea of the charismatic apostolate has been embraced on a large scale by individuals and churches, there are influential theologians and church leaders who are concerned about the biblical legitimacy of the charismatic apostolate, and what can be viably advocated from Scripture. This important debate will be the subject of the next chapter.

Part Three

What We Should Make of It

6

Biblical Counter-arguments and Legitimations for an Ongoing Charismatic Apostolate

INTRODUCTION

AS WE HAVE SEEN in the course of this study there are whole Evangelical denominations and networks that are looking to Scripture to justify their belief that charismatic apostolates are integral to churches today. Yet there are other equally committed Evangelicals who see this move as unbiblical and therefore mistaken. The "battleground" centers on the exegesis of key verses, particularly in 1 Corinthians and in Ephesians. In this chapter therefore, we will be focusing on those, taking a good note of what the individual verses or "parts" are saying; in the following chapter we will consider the message of the "whole" much more.

PART 1: BIBLICAL COUNTER-ARGUMENTS

> It is best . . . to see the apostolic office, in the sense of an authoritative ministry in the Church, as being intended only for the early days of the Church.[1] *Michael Harper*

How one approaches Scripture will determine what it is possible to hold doctrinally. Those who have been influenced by the liberal tradition that

---

1. Harper, *People*, 223.

has its roots within German critical studies will expect to see errors and contradictions within the Scriptural text. Nevertheless, for those within the Conservative Evangelical/Charismatic wing of the church their understanding of the nature of Scripture would prevent them from seeing such faults. A view that holds sway over many within this wing of the church is one that holds that the biblical text is inerrant; and where there are seeming contradictions this is either due to the fact that we are interpreting it wrongly, or we do not have the original manuscripts. This particular belief appears to have its origins with the Princeton scholars such as Charles Hodge.[2] Not all Evangelical/Charismatics hold this view; in fact many distance themselves from "inerrancy" language—but would still want to affirm the "God-breathed" nature of all of Scripture and therefore be very hesitant in seeing any errors, especially doctrinal or ethical ones, propounded by the texts. Wayne Grudem and J. I. Packer are committed to inerrancy language, whereas John Stott and Michael Green are not. The debate over an ongoing charismatic apostolate is located most prominently within the Evangelical/Charismatic section of the church; therefore, I will in the main[3] be drawing upon well regarded scholars/biblical expositors within this tradition, which is my own, to help consider whether the recognized canon of Scripture promotes the majority view within the Pentecostal Charismatic Movement that charismatic apostles will continue to be given until the Parousia of Christ. Similarly, I will consider whether some of the key verses used to promote the modern charismatic apostolate, as highlighted in chapter 3, and its supposed shape, can stand exegetical scrutiny.

Amongst those who reject the idea that there are still apostles who operate in Charismatic authority and manifestations are eminent Protestant teachers who claim the Scriptures as their sole authority, and believe that that book correctly interpreted does not allow for this ministry today. Two such men, who wield great influence within the Evangelical "world," are Wayne Grudem and John Stott. It is fair to say that neither Stott or Grudem are classed in the same category as Raymond Brown and Tom Wright when thinking of great biblical scholars—nevertheless, they both engage with scholarship at the highest level, and their works are looked

---

2. For an in-depth look at Hodge's view on Scripture see Battle, "Hodge," 28–41.

3. I say in the "main," as I will look to other scholars who represent different traditions as well—for example, Schnackenberg and Schmithals (German historical scholarship), and Burkhard (Roman Catholic)—who offer valuable insight into the text; however, the majority of scholars will inhabit the Evangelical and/or Charismatic worldview (e.g., Wright, Bruce, Dunn).

to by reputable Evangelicals across the denominational spectrum when considering interpretations of particular Scriptures. In introducing their arguments it is important that we recognize who they are as this will inevitably shape their approach to the topic.

Wayne Grudem is a Baptist, a Professor of Theology at Phoenix Seminary in Arizona, and a well-regarded Christian author. "He has served as the president of the Council on Biblical Manhood and Womanhood, as President of the Evangelical Theological Society (1999), and as a member of the Translation Oversight Committee for the English Standard Version of the Bible. . . . Dr. Grudem has written more than 100 articles for both popular and academic journals."[4]

His magnum opus, *Systematic Theology*, has become a standard textbook in both Evangelical and Charismatic settings.[5] He treads an interesting path, in that his theology is Conservative and Reformed as well as being Charismatic. He was very influential in Vineyard circles, and was supportive of John Wimber.[6] He is one of few theologians who has a good name amongst leading Conservative Evangelicals, due to his uncompromising stance on the inerrancy and primacy of Scripture, and leading Charismatics because of his insistence that the manifestations of the Spirit which were central to the Pentecostal movement are to be expected in the ongoing life of the church. He has also made many friends (and enemies) due to his outspoken complementarian views on men and women.[7] His works are popular on both sides of the Atlantic, and his influence is felt in the UK Evangelical scene as well as in the USA.

The recently deceased John Stott has been an influential figure both in Britain and abroad. He was born in 1921 in London, educated at Rugby school, then Trinity College Cambridge, after which he trained for the Anglican ministry at Ridley Hall; he became curate at All Souls, Langham Place in 1945, the rector in 1950, and rector emeritus in 1975. His influence within the Anglican Church was notable through the opportunity he

---

4. Phoenix Seminary, "Grudem."

5. One only has to see the endorsements given to it by J. I Packer and Terry Virgo on the back cover to recognize this. I have even heard Terry Virgo recommend this book to Christians at a large Charismatic gathering. It was also used as a teaching aid at a large Conservative Evangelical Church that I worshipped at.

6. For information on some of the ways in which Grudem publicly defended Wimber and the Vineyard and aided them theologically, see Jackson, *Quest*, 157–65, 212.

7. This is the idea that men and women have God-assigned roles inherent within creation which sees men as the authoritative "head" within the marital relationship, and the only ones who can be elders and preach to men within the church assembly.

PART THREE—What We Should Make of It

gave to Evangelicals to club together and become a force within the Church of England—this was done through many of his initiatives such as the re-invention of the Eclectic Society which began as a meeting of twenty-two of his friends aiming to "raise the sights and morale of young Evangelical clergy" and became a society consisting of "over 1,000 members by the mid-1960s." This movement in turn produced the National Evangelical Anglican Congresses of 1967 and 1977, which he chaired. Alongside this he has had periods where he has been the president of influential Christian organizations: the British Scripture Union, the British Evangelical Alliance and the Universities and Colleges Christian Fellowship (UCCF). In 1982 he set up the London Institute for Contemporary Christianity which aims to equip Christians to integrate their Christian faith into modern life and to penetrate the secular world.

His international ministry began when Michael Baughen took over as vicar of All Souls giving him the opportunity to travel widely. He spoke on numerous occasions at "the triennial Urban Student Mission Convention arranged by InterVarsity Christian Fellowship" and led "some 50 university missions between 1952 and 1977 in Britain, North America, Australia, New Zealand, Africa and Asia"; he was also "vice president of the International Fellowship of Evangelical Student . . . from 1995 to 2003."[8] He was the "chair of the committees that drafted the Lausanne Covenant (1974) and the Manila Manifesto (1989)."[9] His numerous books have been translated into different languages; and through these, and the work of Langham Partnership International,[10] his voice has been influencing Christians in both the Western world and the developing one. According to David Brooks in the New York Times, if Evangelicals were to elect a pope they would likely choose John Stott.[11] It was when Stott was rector at All Souls that the Charismatic Movement started to emerge in the UK; and this movement began gaining momentum within his own church after the then curate, Michael Harper, had a Charismatic experience. Nevertheless, John Stott was critical of the movement's exegesis and maintained his Conservative Evangelical Reformed emphases.

In my research I have not found any of the more renowned, scholarly biblical commentaries interacting with the mainstream Charismatic

---

8. See his biography at Langham Partnership, "Stott."

9. From an introduction to Tim Stafford's interview with John Stott; see Stafford, "Evangelism."

10. For information about this organization that grew out of Stott's ministry see Langham Partnership, "History."

11. Referred to in Stafford, "Evangelism."

interpretation of Ephesians 4:11–13 advocating apostles today. This may be because they do not give any scholarly weight to their interpretation, or that they are not familiar with it; nevertheless it is to Stott and Grudem's credit that they do so in light of its prominence in Charismatic circles. Neither author has written a book on the subject, and what they have done is not very substantial, but there is enough to grasp clearly what they believe Scripture teaches on the matter and why they contest modern Charismatic beliefs on apostles. Wayne Grudem addresses it in a chapter on church Government in his *Systematic Theology*;[12] John Stott does so in his commentary on Ephesians.[13] Their respective cases are not based upon a clear scriptural injunction as there is no biblical statement saying "apostles are no longer given," but rather upon reasoned deduction from what they perceive as the sweep of the New Testament revelation concerning God's *oikonomia*. Nevertheless, they build their arguments on certain texts that appear pivotal to their conclusions. To follow their reasoning it is therefore helpful to have those verses before us. These are they:

> For I handed on to you as of first importance what I in turn had received: that Christ died for our sins in accordance with the scriptures, and that he was buried, and that he was raised on the third day in accordance with the scriptures, and that he appeared to Cephas, then to the twelve. Then he appeared to more than five hundred brothers and sisters at one time, most of whom are still alive, though some have died. Then he appeared to James, then to all the apostles. Last of all, as to someone untimely born, he appeared also to me. 1 *Corinthians* 15:3–8. NRSV

> So then you are no longer strangers and aliens, but you are citizens with the saints and also members of the household of God, built upon the foundation of the apostles and prophets, with Christ Jesus himself as the cornerstone. *Ephesians* 2:19–20. NRSV

> The gifts he gave were that some would be apostles, some prophets, some evangelists, some pastors and teachers, to equip the saints for the work of ministry, for building up the body of Christ, until all of us come to the unity of the faith and of the knowledge of the Son of God, to maturity, to the measure of the full stature of Christ. *Ephesians* 4:11–13. NRSV

---

12. Grudem, *Systematic*, chap. 47.
13. Stott, *Ephesians*.

Part Three—What We Should Make of It

> And the wall of the city has twelve foundations, and on them are the twelve names of the twelve apostles of the Lamb. *Revelation 21:14*. NRSV

Grudem approaches this discussion and makes his argument on the basis of his Conservative Evangelical convictions concerning the Bible. He is a staunch defender of the inerrancy of Scripture and subscribes to the idea that in their original form the Scriptures rightly understood are without error on whatever topic they are referring to; he states, "The inerrancy of Scripture means that Scripture in the original manuscripts does not affirm anything that is contrary to fact."[14] He argues this on the basis that Scripture speaks of itself as truthful and inspired, the ultimate author being God. This circular reasoning demands that there were people who heard what God said, and transmitted it faithfully without fault to others. Grudem believes that before Christ, God enabled prophets[15] to do that; post-Christ, he did the same with the apostles.[16] If we are to understand God's mind concerning apostles, the Scriptures are the place to look as they alone contain authoritative revelation on the matter; correctly interpreted, the Scriptures will not contradict each other and none of the authors are mistaken in what they say. It is within the confines of these established parameters that Grudem exegetes and discusses the texts connected to apostleship.

Grudem raises a number of arguments against modern, authoritative charismatic apostles:

New Testament Scripture replaces apostles. First, Grudem believes that the New Testament apostles chosen by Christ had divine authority "to speak and write words which were 'words of God' in an absolute sense."[17] As a result they could "write words which became words of Scripture,"[18] on the same level as the Old Testament prophets.[19] Therefore, although fully human and frail, by a supernatural gift of the Spirit the apostles were enabled to give oracles of God. Grudem's belief that apostles could speak and

---

14. Grudem, *Systematic*, 90.

15. Although he recognizes that it was not just those who functioned in the office of a prophet who wrote words from God, ". . . others in Israel, usually those who fulfilled the office of prophet, wrote additional words from God." Ibid., 55.

16. He does believe that the Holy Spirit also enabled others who were not apostles "to write God's own words"—for example, Mark and Luke. Ibid., 63.

17. Ibid., 905–6.

18. Ibid., 906.

19. Those who have "the office of apostle in the early church are seen to claim an authority equal to that of the Old Testament prophets." Ibid., 60.

write "'words of God' in an absolute sense"[20] which could become Scripture, leads him to conclude that once Scripture was completed there was no need for apostles, and hence no more would ever be given.[21] The idea that there were still apostles would imply that the canon was still open—a view that no Evangelical would hold. As a result it is the "New Testament Scriptures" which "fulfil for the church today the absolutely authoritative teaching and governing functions which were fulfilled by the apostles themselves during the early years of the church."[22]

Their role was foundational. Grudem argues similarly on the basis of the "foundational" imagery used in Ephesians 2:20 (Grudem argues on the basis of the Greek that the "apostles and prophets" mentioned in this verse, and in Ephesians 3:5 refer to one group: "apostles who are also prophets")[23] and Revelation 21:14 to assert that the apostolic ministry is now not needed. His argument is that these Scriptures show that apostles were foundational to the church's structure—that is because they were given the authoritative teaching of Christ on which the church could be built; once they had delivered this teaching, their foundational authoritative ministry was no longer needed as it had been passed onto the saints via their messages and writings which ultimately would form the New Testament.[24]

Paul was the last apostle. "*Then he appeared to James, then to all the apostles. Last of all, as to someone untimely born, he appeared also to me.*" He understands this verse in 1 Corinthians 15 as linking apostleship to having been a witness of the resurrected Christ[25] and underlining that

---

20. Ibid., 905–6.

21. Grudem argues that to belong to the New Testament canon, just like the Old, the writing must have had God as its author. He draws upon Hebrews 1:1–2 and Revelation 22:28–19 to argue that the revelation found in the New Testament is final with no more to be given after it (ibid., 60–68). He is obviously well aware of the historical processes that led to the formation of the Christian canon, nevertheless, he sees those who were involved in making the decisions to what constituted Scripture, were recognizing the divine authorship on the basis of a number of different factors—see ibid., 62–63.

22. Ibid., 911.

23. See ibid., 1051, n. 4. Most commentaries I have consulted do not agree with this view and think two groups are in mind; nevertheless, it fits well into Grudem's overall scheme as seeing the apostles as the dispensers of authoritative revelation.

24. This is in essence the same stance that Hagin takes in regards to "foundational apostles"—see chapter 3.

25. He concurs with Lightfoot in this regard, recognizing this occurrence as constituting one of the two qualifications necessary to become an apostle: "(1) having seen Jesus after his resurrection with one's own eyes (thus being an 'eyewitness of the

PART THREE—What We Should Make of It

Paul was the last apostle—as he was the last witness to the resurrection. Grudem identifies fifteen definite apostles who must have been witnesses, alongside possessing the other qualifications, as they are clearly called apostles in the New Testament: the Twelve, Paul, James, and Barnabas. He thinks Andronicus and Junias might possibly be apostles on the basis of Romans 16:7, and Silas on the basis of 1 Thessalonians 2:6, however, he is convinced that Timothy was not.[26]

Tense of "gave" in Ephesians 4:11. He considers the key text used by advocates of modern apostles, Ephesians 4:11–13, and argues that these verses are not helpful in discerning whether Christ still gives apostles because the tense used to describe when these gifts were given (in v. 11) is aorist, therefore, referring to an event that happened once for all in the past; he concludes that the giving of these gifts occurred after Christ's ascension at Pentecost. Hence, Grudem argues that we can only understand whether these gifts are still given from what the New Testament tells us elsewhere; and because we know that Paul was the last apostle, that particular office would never be given again.[27]

For Grudem, these "biblical" reasons are conclusive enough to dismiss the contention for modern, authoritative apostolic ministry—thereby ruling out Apostle Type 1s. To give further support to his arguments, he appeals to church history, noting that no "major leader in the history of the church . . . has taken to himself the title of 'apostle' or let himself be called an apostle."[28] Grudem does recognize that the New Testament uses the word "apostle" in other ways too: "The New Testament itself has three verses in which the word *apostle* . . . is used in a broad sense, not to refer to any specific church office, but simply to mean 'messenger.'"[29] Therefore, he affirms that the term can be used today to refer to a messenger or a pioneer missionary.[30] Nevertheless, he thinks that it is an unhelpful term to describe "effective church planters or evangelists"[31] as it can be confusing to people who then read the New Testament and see the term being used to describe authoritative ministers. From his perspective if anyone

---

resurrection'), and (2) having been specifically commissioned by Christ as an apostle." Ibid., 60.

26. Ibid., 907–10.
27. Ibid., 911.
28. Ibid.
29. Ibid., 906.
30. Ibid., 911.
31. Ibid.

Biblical Counter-arguments and Legitimations

chooses to call himself an apostle today "they immediately raise the suspicion that they may be motivated by inappropriate pride and desires for self-exaltation, along with excessive ambition and a desire for much more authority in the church than any one person should rightfully have."[32] Although Grudem certainly affirms the type of ministry that is usually associated with Apostle Type 2 and Type 3 (church planting), he would repudiate the idea that they were Ephesians 4:11–13 apostles, and would denounce attempts to call them apostles.

Like Grudem, Stott has a very high view of Scripture and is committed to the idea that it is "God-breathed." According to John Stott Ministries' webpage: *"The Holy Scripture in its entirety is inspired by God's Spirit through human authors and constitutes the revelation of God's truth to humanity. It is wholly true and trustworthy in all that it affirms. Whatever the Bible, rightly interpreted, is found to teach, we are bound to believe and obey. It is our supreme authority in every matter of belief and conduct."*[33]

Nevertheless, Stott is not an advocate of "inerrancy" language to describe Scripture—and sees it as detrimental.[34] His belief in the divine inspiration of Scripture demands that charismatic gifts of such intensity were given to ensure that what was written down was exactly what the Sovereign God desired. He sees the promise given to the apostles concerning the Holy Spirit leading them into all truth as being just for them, and therefore once that revelation had been given to the apostles, and had been recorded in the writings of the New Testament, there was no more that needed to be said.[35] With this confidence in the reliability of Scripture, Stott is clear that we can turn to it and find a definitive answer concerning the ongoing presence or absence of apostles.

Although Stott does affirm that the word "apostle" is used in the New Testament not only in reference to the Apostles of Christ but also to describe all Christians (John 13:16), in that like their Master they are sent ones; he also highlights that some are referred to as "apostles of the churches" (2 Cor 8:23), which he sees as a reference to them being "sent out by a church either as missionaries or on some other errand."[36] Think-

---

32. Ibid.

33. Taken from John Stott Ministries, "Statement," emphasis original.

34. See Stott, *Evangelical*, 73–74.

35. He speaks about this in an interview for Christianity Today in 1996; see anonymous, "Basic Stott."

36. Stott, *Evangelical*, 160. Stott actually holds that Paul was both an apostle of Christ and an apostle of the church, in that he like Barnabas was sent out by the church in Antioch; see Stott, *Acts*, 229.

Part Three—What We Should Make of It

ing of apostles in this manner, Stott would have no problem in advocating modern-day apostles; however, he is fundamentally opposed to the radical House Church's conceptions of apostleship, and therefore would take issue with much of what is being advocated today for the following reasons:

The foundation has been laid. Ephesians 2:20. Like Grudem, he sees the apostles mentioned in Ephesians 2:20 as being a first-century phenomenon, "consisting of the Twelve plus Paul and James and perhaps one or two others." They were that "small and special group whom Jesus chose, called and authorized to teach in his name, and who were eyewitnesses of his resurrection. . . . What they taught they expected the church to believe and preserve, what they commanded they expected the church to obey."[37]

It was this group along with some New Testament prophets[38] who are described as the foundation of the church in Ephesians 2:20. Stott argues that because both these offices were connected with a teaching role, Ephesians 2:20's mention of them being the foundation of the church relates not to their office or person but to "their instruction."[39] These apostles and prophets[40] were instructed through the Spirit's revelation (Eph 3:5), and it is their teaching which laid the foundation for the church. According to Stott, this teaching is now found in the New Testament Scriptures, as a result they "are the church's foundation documents," which the church must remain loyal to, by neither adding to nor subtracting from them.[41]

Qualifications to be apostles of Christ now unobtainable. John Stott argues that the view of John Noble,[42] that there are apostles of Christ in

---

37. Stott, *Ephesians*, 107.

38. Stott does consider the idea that this might be a reference to the Old Testament prophets, but because they occur in the sentence after the apostles this would seem unlikely. Ibid.

39. Ibid.

40. Stott likewise rejects the idea that prophets are still given to the church today; their role, along with the apostles of Christ has been replaced by the Scriptures. He does not deny that there might be a "subsidiary gift of some kind" (ibid., 162), but in the sense that someone can still be "a vehicle of" God's "direct revelation" (ibid., 161) there is no such ministry today. He is therefore very suspicious of Charismatic claims that God is raising up prophets and prophetesses who speak God's word under the direct inspiration of the Spirit (ibid., 162).

41. Ibid., 107.

42. John Noble was, at the time when Stott wrote this commentary (in 1979), one of the leading House Church figures who published a booklet, which Stott interacts with, called *First Apostles, Last Apostles* (1975). Andrew Walker refers to him as the "senior apostle" in the Restoration 2 churches (this is the "less pure" of the two types of house churches identified by Walker which were all committed to the restoration of authoritative apostolic ministry); see Walker, *Restoring*, 61.

God's church today is misguided because Noble "misses in his exposition the vitally important truths (1) that the original apostles as eyewitnesses of the historic risen Jesus can in the nature of the case have no successors, and (2) that their authority is preserved today in the New Testament, which is the essential 'apostolic succession.'"[43]

For both Stott and Grudem the apostles described in Ephesians 2:20 provide a foundation for the whole church through the revealed doctrine they have received both from the historical Jesus (with the exception of Paul) and the direct inspiration of the Spirit. It is not a description on the right way in which every local church has to be founded, that is, through a Spirit-filled apostle and prophet who offer apostolic and prophetic direction for that particular local assembly which they (usually the apostle) have started. The only ones who can rightfully be called apostles of Christ are those who have both witnessed the risen Lord and been commissioned by him; they were the recipients of the authoritative revelation which the church was to submit to, which became embodied within the New Testament—which now "succeeds" them.

It is unclear how Stott understands Paul's words in 1 Corinthians 15:8 concerning being the "last of the apostles," as he does not use that argument at all—however, it is noticeable that all the people who he believes are "apostles of Christ" are those who were "in Christ" before Paul, which would seem to suggest that he takes a similar line. Both authors concur that the apostles described in Ephesians 2:20 are of the same type as those mentioned in 3:5 and 4:11. Grudem differs in regards to who the prophets are in 2:20 and 3:5, contending that Paul is referring to apostles who are also prophets.[44] Stott views the text as presupposing two groups and gifts not just one. Stott also has no comment to make about the tense of "gave" in Ephesians 4:11; nevertheless, he clearly believes like Grudem that the author is referring to a group of apostles who had already been given to the church, and that the verses do not imply an ongoing giving. Therefore, aside from minor differences, there is little to tell their two views apart.

Stott and Grudem are not alone amongst scholars in their cessationist understanding of the apostolic office. A. T. Lincoln, F. F. Bruce, Ernest Best, and J. D. G. Dunn all agree with the idea that the apostles and prophets referred to in Ephesians 2:20 were a unique group who were the

---

43. Stott, *Ephesians*, 161.

44. He seems to hold this position as he believes the New Testament allows and presupposes an ongoing ministry of prophets within the church.

Part Three—What We Should Make of It

foundation or who had laid it; as a result, it was not an ongoing ministry that could ever be repeated. For example, Ernest Best writes,

> In 2:20 the apostles and prophets are the foundation of the church and this suggests a group belonging to the past, or at least a group which would cease to exist once its original members were dead. . . . When we look elsewhere in the NT we find a strong tradition that a revelation of the universal nature of the gospel was made to a group approximately equivalent to the apostles (cf. Mt 28.16–20; Lk 24.47; Acts 1:8; Jn 20.21). This revelation belonged to the past in the period immediately after the resurrection.[45]

Along with Tom Wright,[46] Dunn believes that Paul saw the call to apostleship as bound up with having witnessed the resurrected Christ and being commissioned by him.[47] Furthermore, Dunn thinks that Paul "saw his commissioning as 'last of all' (1 Cor. 15.8)" and "did not think that there were any further appointments to apostolic rank after him (hence the 'before me' of Rom. 16.7)."[48] Similarly, Schmithals believes that that was Paul's conviction, although he leaves open whether he was correct or not.[49] Dunn departs from Stott and Grudem in that he does not believe Ephesians nor the Pastorals were written by Paul,[50] nevertheless, he sees them as "the school or studio of Paul" which are "still able to tell us something about what went before."[51] By looking at Ephesians 4:11 in light of 1 Corinthians 9:2, he understood the apostles as "church founders,"[52] but that these apostles are not to be replicated according to Ephesians 2:20 as they were "part of the foundation."[53]

---

45. Best, *Ephesians*, 141.

46. Wright, *Prison Letters*, 211.

47. Dunn, *Unity*, 111.

48. Dunn, *Paul*, 571, n. 30. However, in our e-mail exchange he allowed for the fact that Paul might not see himself as the very last one, but he was sure that he was one of the last. In response to my question, "Do you think that Paul believed he was the last apostle of Christ, and therefore there were no further apostles being given to the Church?", Dunn answered, "Yes, or one of the last—1 Cor. 4.9—last act on the world stage." J. D. G. Dunn, e-mail message to author, June 8, 2008.

49. See Schmithals, *Office*, 79.

50. Ibid., 13, n. 39.

51. Ibid., 13.

52. Ibid., 1174.

53. J. D. G. Dunn, e-mail message to author, June 8, 2008. Dunn's exegesis on the same passage in "Ephesians," 1171, suggests the same thing.

Biblical Counter-arguments and Legitimations

F. F. Bruce is clear that the ministry of apostle would and did disappear, he writes: "The apostles, as an order of ministry in the church, were not perpetuated beyond the apostolic age, but the various functions which they discharged did not lapse with their departure, but continued to be performed by others—notably by the evangelists and the pastors and teachers."[54]

He supports this further by the idea that if the Christian conception of apostle corresponded to the Jewish *saliah* then, like that ministry, it was only given until the work entrusted had been completed. Bruce argues therefore, that the "authority of the apostle (in the sense of 1 Cor. 15:3–9) was bound up with a special appearance and commissioning of the risen Christ, but while that authority could not be transmitted, the apostle's various activities could be continued by others."[55]

There are other possible reasons to support their cessationist position: the fact that the later Pastoral letters have no mention of apostles—rather the focus is upon presbyters and deacons; likewise, Luke does not mention any other apostles being called after Paul and Barnabas—the implication possibly being that there were not any more of them. Nevertheless, these particular arguments are not conclusive as they are both based upon silence; furthermore, the late book of Revelation is aware of "false apostles" which might imply that the church was still familiar with true apostolic ministry. The renowned Anglican scholar, J. B. Lightfoot, believed that this passage along with the mention of the false apostles in 2 Corinthians 11:13, makes it clear that there was a much wider group than the Twelve who were called apostles: ". . . only by such an extension of the office could any footing be found for the pretensions of the false apostles (2 Cor. xi. 13, Rev. ii. 2). Had the number been definitely restricted, the claims of these interlopers would have been self-condemned."[56] Watchman Nee argues similarly:

> It seems clear from this verse that the early churches expected to have other apostles apart from the original twelve, because, when the book of Revelation was written, John was the only survivor of the twelve, and by that time even Paul had already been martyred. If there were to be only twelve apostles, and John was

---

54. Bruce, *Epistles*, 346–47. Best similarly assumes that there are only three "offices" still present in the church: shepherds, teacher, and evangelists. Although he does not explicitly reject the idea of modern apostles and prophets, it just appears to be the underlying assumption in his commentary. See Best, *Ephesians*, 2, 119–20, 197–99.

55. Bruce, *Epistles*, 347, n. 68.

56. Lightfoot, *Galatians*, 97.

> the only one left, then no one would have been foolish enough to pose as an apostle, and no one foolish enough to be deceived, and where would have been the need to try them?[57]

Within Grudem and Stott's respective writing on the topic there is a lack of depth in that they have not really engaged with some of the seminal work exploring the differing concepts of apostles in the early church done by such scholars as C. K. Barrett,[58] Schmithals,[59] and Schnackenberg;[60] nevertheless, Stott and Grudem have both provided a weighty Scriptural case against an ongoing apostolic office. Even so, there are pertinent questions to be asked of both schemes which might unhinge what appear as impressively strong and persuasive arguments. The most notable of these we will consider in the next section. Stott and Grudem have allowed a very generalized form of "apostleship" more akin to "messengers of the churches," but they are united in their opposition to Apostle Type 1, and by their exegesis of Ephesians 4:11–13 undermine the central text undergirding both Apostle Type 2 and 3—although functionally, neither are opposed to pioneering, church planting ministries, and, in the case of Grudem, to charismatic signs and wonders that might accompany them.

Part 2: Biblical Legitimations

> But there is another order of apostles, chosen by the Holy Spirit, and as long as the building up of the Church goes on and the Holy Spirit's presence on earth continues, the choosing and sending forth of this order of apostles will continue too. *Watchman Nee*[61]

---

57. Nee, *Normal*, 6.

58. Barrett, *Signs*. Barrett comes to the conclusion that in the New Testament, there is "no simple, rigid definition of an apostle" (ibid. 85). He makes a formidable case for the differing traditions about apostles within the early church, coming to the conclusion that there are "at least eight . . . groups of persons, all denoted, with varying degrees of propriety, by the term 'apostle' . . . , and probably all giving it somewhat different meaning" (ibid. 71). Although one might disagree with him, surely no detailed discussion on the topic should avoid his important contribution. See especially his chapter, "Apostles in the New Testament."

59. Schmithals, like Barrett, makes much of the differing traditions present in the New Testament—see Schmithals, *Office*, 67–68, 81–82.

60. Schnackenberg, "Apostles Before," 297–303.

61. Nee, *Normal*, 5.

Biblical Counter-arguments and Legitimations

Most popular books on apostles today appeal directly to biblical texts to justify their belief in an ongoing charismatic apostolate. Nevertheless, there have been very few Charismatic scholars advocating the kind of views being put forward on a popular level. However, that is beginning to change, and there are an increasing number of reputable scholars who are giving more credence to the idea that authors of the New Testament did not envisage an end to the charismatic apostolate. One of the strongest voices supporting the idea of ongoing apostleship has been Pentecostal scholar Jon Ruthven. He is currently Professor Emeritus of Systematic Theology at Regent University School of Divinity, and was an ordained Assemblies of God minister.[62] He has written a few books, as well as numerous articles for academic journals.[63] Alongside this he is, in his own words, "involved in supporting missions by encouraging Biblical power evangelism and also in reaching out to traditional seminaries with a gospel determined by the emphasis of scripture" and is now "mentoring a DMin cohort that includes Randy Clarke, Rolland Baker (Heidi's husband), and a number of other church leaders."[64] His doctoral work was a rebuttal of Warfield's cessationist position.[65] He has developed an argument that the five-fold ministry is demanded biblically, and has done substantial work exegeting some of the key biblical texts which are used by cessationists to argue against the possibility of charismatic ministries, such as apostles, continuing today. His work is particularly important as it provides Evangelical—in that he sees Scripture as inspired and inerrant,[66] he is coming from the same starting point as Grudem and a similar one to Stott—scholarly support for much of the activity that goes under the guise of the New Apostolic Reformation. He makes the following detailed arguments in support of a modern charismatic apostolate:

Distorted Reformation lenses versus Paul's expectations of continuing charismata. Ruthven has written extensively on Ephesians 2:20,

---

62. There is far less biographical information available on Jon Ruthven in comparison to Stott and Grudem.

63. See Regent University, "Ruthven," for details.

64. Jon Ruthven, e-mail message to author, September 30, 2011. Clarke and Rolland are closely associated with the New Apostolic Reformation.

65. Ruthven, *Cessation*. It has been described by the Pentecostal scholar W. W. Menzies as "the most comprehensive assessment of the cessationist issue currently available." See Menzies, "Reformed."

66. He writes, "As one committed to the infallibility and inerrancy of Scripture, I would never seek to minimize the central significance of the Bible for faith." Ruthen, *Cessation*, 13.

PART THREE—What We Should Make of It

recognizing that that text is vital to the cessationist's position. He outlines the case that they make and argues that their thinking is clearly influenced by a Protestant anti-Catholic polemic; his thesis is that at the time of the Reformation, the Protestants moved the authority that the Catholics believed was inherent in the Pope to the New Testament documents. They and their followers "further protected the 'Papal' authority of the New Testament by denying any *additional divine revelation* based implicitly on the 'foundational' role of prophets in Eph 2:20."[67] Ruthven questions whether this is a valid biblical interpretation on the grounds that Ephesians 4:11–13 and 1 Corinthians 12:28—13:13 imply that all the divine gifts will remain present in the church until the eschaton. For Ruthven, when apostles and prophets will cease is bound up with the eschatological hope asserted in Ephesians 4:13, when the church will attain the full measure of the fullness of Christ; until then the functions that these ministries have will still be needed. Ruthven also believes that 1 Corinthians 12:28—13:13 supports the view that Paul saw the gift of apostle continuing until "perfection" comes. He argues that when Paul entreats the Corinthians to seek after the greater gifts (1 Corinthians 12:31), this must include the gift of apostleship which he has already shown as being one of the "higher" gifts.[68] As a result, he believes that this cessationist tradition has been uncritically received by modern Protestant scholars and theologians and thinks an alternative exegesis is needed.[69]

Four faults with the traditional Protestant interpretation of Ephesians 2:20. Ruthven holds that the traditional Protestant interpretation of Ephesians 2:20 is mistaken for four reasons. First, the assumption made is that the role for apostles and prophets was to "establish the parameters of church doctrine," and therefore once this was done their office was no longer needed. Ruthven thinks this is untenable because the New Testament does not explicitly state that this was their role, nor even that it was one of them.[70] Second, the traditional view sees the apostles and prophets as "the unique receivers and articulators of Christian revelation, a role that no one may subsequently share";[71] however, there is no reason why they cannot be seen as foundational in terms of being "prototypes, role models for others

---

67. Ruthven, "'Foundational,'" 5.
68. Ruthven, "Apostleship," 215.
69. Ibid., 215ff.
70. Ibid., 216.
71. Ibid., 217.

to follow."⁷² He argues this on the basis that apostles are to be continually given until the church reaches maturity (Eph 4:11–13), and the fact that the same revelatory experience that the apostles and prophets had through the Spirit, by which they comprehended the reconciliation that took place between Jew and Gentile in Christ, is given to the saints too.⁷³

Elsewhere, he attacks the underlying assumption that the New Testament apostles and prophets are "repositories of unwritten Scripture" as "a caricature."⁷⁴ He points out that the New Testament itself was written more by those who were not apostles than those who were.⁷⁵ Likewise, although prophecy is related to inspiring Scripture ten times in the New Testament, there are 153 other types of prophetic utterance mentioned. Furthermore, he argues that the New Testament gives a variety of different functions to New Testament prophecy: "Indeed, the *specific functions* of NT prophecy are explicitly written: to praise and glorify God (Acts 2:14), for edification, exhortation and consolation (1 Cor 14:3, *cf.* Acts 15:32) and the equipping of believers toward ultimate spiritual goals (Eph 4:12–13). One hypothetical case of prophecy offered by Paul (1 Cor 14:24–25) shows prophecy revealing the secrets of the heart to lead toward repentance."⁷⁶

His review of how Acts describes New Testament prophecy also militates against the cessationist contention that prophets were given prophecy to establish foundational, canonical doctrine.⁷⁷

Third, Ruthven argues that the traditional Protestant interpretation of Ephesians 2:20 which binds the apostles and prophets to the historical, initial foundation of the church, must as a consequence see Christ as the cornerstone being relegated to that era too; however, the text in Ephesians sees Christ's role as the cornerstone as being dynamic and ongoing in that the whole building is related to him and being built into him—therefore, the cessationist interpretation does not add up. As a result, Ruthven argues that the "foundation metaphor probably echoes the tradition of Jesus about Peter's revelation/confession"⁷⁸ in Matthew 16:18, where the rock on which the church is built is the revelation by the Spirit and confession of

---

72. Ibid.
73. Ibid., 216–17.
74. Ruthven, "'Foundational,'" 11.
75. He estimates it as 49 percent by apostles and 51 percent by non-apostles; he also notes that the most prolific author amongst the apostles was Paul, who was not one of the Twelve. Ibid., 11–12.
76. Ibid., 12–13.
77. Ibid., 13.
78. Ruthven, "Apostleship," 218.

PART THREE—What We Should Make of It

who Christ is. Again, this is an archetypal event which is repeated by the apostles and prophets, and in turn by the Christian faithful.[79] Fourth, he is deeply concerned that according to many cessationists the "foundation" referred to in Ephesians 2:20 is "the established doctrine of the NT text." He counters this by arguing that nowhere in all of Scripture is it perceived as being the foundation. Instead, what is seen as being the core is the "ongoing series of revelatory encounters with Christ, which open our hearts to the Scriptures."[80] To support this he refers to Paul's comments in 1 Corinthians 2:14 and Galatians 3:3 as well as the nature of the last days which, according to the prophets, would be characterized by the prophetic Spirit who would "move the locus of perceiving God's mind and will into the heart (the spiritual centre of perception), away from the external coercion of the Law."[81]

As to 1 Corinthians 15:8 being proof that Paul saw himself as the last apostle, Ruthven argues that an unwarranted connection is being made as Paul is merely stating that he was the last of a particular group who saw the resurrected Jesus, and perhaps by implication he was the least of them; Paul is not arguing that he was the last apostle, rather he was making it clear "that his preaching was valid despite his lowly status among the witnesses."[82] What is notable from Ruthven's exegesis is that he allows Ephesians 4:11–13 and 1 Corinthians 12:28ff. to be the "boss" verses,[83] which in turn control his exegesis of Ephesians 2:20 and 1 Corinthians 15:8 respectively. Furthermore, viewed through these controlling lenses, Paul's apostolic ministry is no longer viewed as a once for all type but one that can be replicated.

There are scholars from across the denominational spectrum who similarly contend that the plain sense of Ephesians 4:11–13 is that the gift of apostle will continue to be given until the church reaches full maturity. The New Testament scholar Max Turner has written an article discussing the ecclesiology of the British Radical House Church Movement (HCM), in which he looks at their exegesis of Ephesians 4:11ff. He notes that the optimistic eschatology heralded by the HCM is firmly rooted in Ephesians; that the author does not foresee the maturing of the church

79. Ruthven, "'Foundational,'" 6–8.
80. Ruthven, "Apostleship," 219.
81. Ibid.
82. Ibid., 216.
83. I am grateful to Dr Sarah Sumner for this term which she uses to great effect in her discussion on differing perspectives on men and women in the church. See Sumner, *Men and Women*.

occurring post-Parousia, but rather as a result of each part doing its job in the now; Turner also draws attention to the word, *melchri*, usually translated "until" as being an indicator of when the gifts mentioned in verse 11 would cease to be given.[84] The Roman Catholic scholar, J. Burkhard, argues likewise,[85] as does the Baptist, Dr Michael Eaton[86] and the Anglican Evangelical, Kevin Giles.[87]

In regards to his exegesis of Ephesians 2:20, he does seem to have come up with a unique theory. It is supported in part by Marcus Barth,[88] who argues that a dynamic and eschatological relation between Christ as the keystone and the church is being described, and that the apostles and prophets mentioned are actively at work at the time of the epistle's writing. Nevertheless, Barth does not suppose the author sees other apostles and prophets being given after these ones, nor that the church will cease to be the church if they are not.[89] So although there is a convergence, Ruthven is arguing for a substantially new perspective.

The Pentecostal New Testament scholar Gordon Fee is cagey about offering a definitive interpretation of Paul's thinking on the subject, as he thinks Paul is rather fluid in his use of the term. Nevertheless, he argues that an integral part of Paul's understanding of an apostle's function was the founding of churches through evangelism—and in this regard 1 Corinthians 12:28 and Ephesians 2:20 are referring to the ministry of founding *local* churches.[90] With these interpretations in mind it is hard to see him not agreeing to the idea that this ministry is still functioning today. Nevertheless, Fee does not suggest what the implications are of his inter-

---

84. Turner, "Ecclesiology," 83–108. However, I have been using an unedited version that the author kindly e-mailed to me.

85. Burkhard makes a distinction between the apostles mentioned in 2:20/3:5 and those mentioned in 4:11. He refers to the apostles mentioned earlier as the "originary" apostles "whose preaching of the gospel accounts for the faith community's very existence"; however, those mentioned in 4:11 must be much later due to the dating of the epistle and due to wording used which refers to a present ministry. Burkhard, *Apostolicity*, 16–17.

86. Eaton, *Enjoying*, 74–75.

87. Admittedly, Kevin Giles is a little more hesitant; he writes in support of the idea that Paul saw apostles as being continually given to the church and looks to 1 Corinthians 12:28 and Ephesians 4:11 to support this view: "In 1 Cor. 12:28 and Eph. 4:11 apostles are said to be ministries given to the Church. The first passage certainly, and probably the second also, do not allow for any circumscription in the number of apostles." Giles, "Apostles Before," 251.

88. Ruthven, "Apostleship," 218, n. 3.

89. Barth, *Ephesians 1–3*, 316.

90. Fee, *Empowering*, 190–92, 688.

PART THREE—What We Should Make of It

pretations in regards to modern church practice. In correspondence with him I enquired further on this and asked the following questions: "1. Does Paul envisage other apostles being given by the risen Christ after his own call to that ministry—or did he see himself as last of all? 2. Does Ephesians 4:11–13 justify a belief held by many Charismatics today that Christ will continue to give apostles until he returns? 3. If apostles were still present in the church what would be the marks of discerning their validity or not?"

To which he answered, "These questions are all unanswerable on the basis of the biblical text itself; and I would not presume to answer on Paul's behalf. But since Paul tends to limit 'apostle' to those who have seen the Risen Christ, I doubt it!"[91] Therefore, I imagine that he would see Ruthven's interpretation of 1 Corinthians 15 as unlikely, and would be unwilling to claim as much as Ruthven does from Ephesians 4:11–13 and 1 Corinthians 12:28ff.

The strength of Ruthven's interpretation is that it does not require a differing understanding of apostle in 2:20/3:5 from that in 4:11, and does not unnaturally relegate the apostolic ministry mentioned in 4:11 to a past era when it appears to be a present reality to the Ephesians' author.[92] Nevertheless, it is possible to use the same word differently in two different contexts within the same document.[93] His contention that we should understand the "foundation" of apostles and prophets in a dynamic repeatable manner is plausible, although does not gain much scholarly support. In my opinion his arguments from Ephesians 4:11–13 are stronger than Grudem's in that *melchri* (until) determines how long the various gifts will be given and therefore are determinative to how we should understand the aorist tense that Grudem relies on for his position. Grudem's exegesis would lead to the idea that Christ gave all five ministry gifts once and for all at his ascension, a view that Grudem himself would not posit. Likewise, Ruthven's deduction on the basis of 1 Corinthians 12–14 also seems well placed, and an unbiased reader would naturally assume the same. Nevertheless, Ruthven's other arguments are less persuasive. For example, if

91. Gordon Fee, e-mail message to author, October 22, 2008.

92. Grudem's point that the aorist tense is used in 4:11 ("he gave") need not imply that these gifts are not still given, as he himself affirms that at least four of them still are; furthermore, the verses do imply that these gifts will continue to be given to equip God's people for service *until* the church reaches maturity. Markus Barth also thought that the epistle must have been relatively early because these verses imply that apostles and prophets were still at large in the Church. See Barth, *Ephesians 1–3*, 316.

93. For example, in Paul's letter to the Galatians he uses the word "law" sometimes to refer to the covenant consisting of the 613 statutes given to Israel at Mount Sinai (Gal 3:17), at other times to refer to the five books of Moses (Gal 4:21).

Biblical Counter-arguments and Legitimations

we see Ephesians 3:5–6 as enlightening us in what way the apostles and prophets were the foundation of the church, we could deduce that part of their foundational ministry was their reception of this essential revelation concerning the church's essence, that being that it was constituted by both Jew and Gentile as equals in one Body. It would therefore, seem superfluous for God to give this revelation to another group of "apostles and prophets" at another time, when it has already been given; all that needs to be done is to ensure that it is "traditioned" to the Saints who comprehend it by the Spirit.

As noted in the biblical counter-arguments section, it is not just Ephesians 2:20 that provides weight for the cessationist position—it is also the implication of Paul's statements in 1 Corinthians 15:8–9 and 1 Corinthians 9:1. Jon Ruthven tackles the cessation interpretation by arguing that in 1 Corinthians 15:8–9 Paul is not "attempting . . . to establish himself as the *last* in the circle of apostles, but only saying that he was the last . . . of a certain group who saw the resurrected Lord Jesus."[94] As to 1 Corinthians 9:1, he does not deny that apostles must have an encounter with the risen Jesus, in fact he believes that these encounters—if we compare them to Paul's visionary encounter—are not only in principle possible,[95] but have been claimed by individuals throughout the church's history.[96] This is a plausible interpretation, and not the only one countering the cessationist view. For example, Dr Michael Eaton has made the case that Paul's questioning in 1 Corinthians 9:1 is making "two points, not one"; so that he is in effect saying, "Am I not an apostle? And furthermore have I not also seen Jesus . . . ?," rather than, "Am I not an apostle by virtue of the fact that I have seen Jesus?"[97] Witness Lee takes a similar line arguing that Paul is not stating a "requirement or qualification for being the Lord's apostle," but it does "constitute some glory and dignity to" him as a "seer"; nevertheless, because Scripture calls Barnabas an apostle who did not have this experience then Paul cannot be viewing it as an apostle's qualification.[98] Kevin Giles similarly severs the link between seeing the risen Lord and being an apostle: "It is nowhere argued that Barnabas, Junia and Andronicus, Silvanus, Timothy or Apollos had seen the Lord. Furthermore, 1 Cor. 12:28 and Eph. 4:11 do not list qualifications for those whom the Spirit

94. Ruthven, "Apostleship," 215.
95. Ibid., 213. Contra Michael Eaton and Witness Lee.
96. Ibid., 215–16.
97. Eaton, *Enjoying*, 75.
98. Lee, *Recovery*, 713, n. 1.4. If Ruthven is correct on this, then there is no reason to assume that Barnabas did not have a visionary experience as well.

Part Three—What We Should Make of It

will raise up as apostles—the implication is that the Spirit can empower any Christian for this work."[99]

Yet both writers are making an explicit assumption about Barnabas' lack of an experience; it is an argument from silence and as such is not weighty enough to dismiss Ruthven's proposition. Eaton's idea is on one level quite compelling, yet the context of 1 Corinthians 9:1 would seem to support the linking with Paul's apostleship as he is undoubtedly trying to affirm his apostolic authority. This difficulty is surmounted if one takes a more "liberal" perspective—for example, Schnackenberg assumes a multiplicity of views in the NT, none of them as necessarily authoritative; therefore, he sees the appearance of the risen Lord as being a qualifying factor only in certain circles, notably the Jerusalem one and not a requirement for Paul.[100]

Ruthven insists that Paul does not view an association with the incarnate Lord as vital for apostleship, as the apostle undercuts "the significance of mere physical association with Jesus as determinative for apostleship by the principle that 'we no longer know [experience/interact with] [Jesus] according to the flesh, but according to the Spirit' (2 Cor. 5.16)."[101] As a result, Ruthven sees the disciples' decision to see Judas' position filled by someone who had witnessed the resurrection and had been with Jesus since John's baptism, as misguided. He argues this on the basis that the Holy Spirit clearly calls both Paul and Barnabas apostles after Matthias' election, even though they did not fulfill these criteria. This is an intriguing perspective, which does not actually affect the debate of whether more apostles are possible or not, as many proponents of apostles today suppose a difference between the twelve apostles of the Lamb who must have been witnesses of the resurrection and been with Christ during his earthly ministry, and those who were called apostles after Christ's ascension; for example, this is the position of Virgo (see chap. 3), Nee, Eaton, and I have heard Roger Forster use it as well. The popular Baptist Bible teacher David Pawson assumes this distinction as well by differentiating between five types of apostle in the New Testament: "1. Jesus the Chief apostle. . . . 2. The 12 apostles, witnesses of the resurrection. . . . 3. Paul, apostle number 13 . . . , writing inspired Scripture. 4. A pioneer church planter who builds new churches with new converts—the apostle Paul would be among this kind too, as would Barnabas and others, who were always sent out in a

---

99. Giles, "Apostles Before," 248.
100. See Schnackenberg, "Apostles Before," 293–95.
101. Ruthven, "Apostleship," 213.

team. 5. Any Christian sent from A to B to do anything is an "apostle", e.g., Epaphroditus."[102]

Ruthven's argument that Paul does not see himself as the "last" of the apostles to be called is very contentious. Most scholars think that is one of the points that Paul is making. It is not straightforward though; Fee notes the ambiguity of the phrase, "last of all", and outlines possibilities that have been suggested: "last of all in the sense of least significant"; or "last of all the apostles"—he doesn't think either—"More likely it is the final link in the chain that began with Peter and means 'finally.'"[103] However, if it could be proved that Paul viewed Timothy as a bona fide apostle too then Ruthven's interpretation is more plausible as it is indisputable that Timothy came to embrace Christianity much later than Paul; coupling 1 Thessalonians 2:6 with 1 Thessalonians 1:1 gives this impression and has convinced Gordon Fee that Paul did see Timothy in this light[104]—similarly Prince, Wagner (see chap. 3), and Hamon view him as an apostle.[105] But it is inconclusive and scholars such as Lightfoot[106] and Grudem[107] have made a strong enough case to put severe doubt over it. The fact that Ruthven himself does not argue for Timothy's apostolic ministry would suggest he recognizes this,[108] nevertheless he does recognize Apollos as an apostle who was a later convert than Paul. Lightfoot dismisses the evidence for Apollos being an apostle on the basis that a contemporary, Clement of Rome, does not call him one, and that his own interpretation of 1 Corinthians 15:8 means that it would not be possible for another apostle to be given to the church after Paul.[109] As it stands, Ruthven's reasoning is possible but the case made is far from watertight.

Ruthven's lack of interaction with Revelation 21:14 is notable, he mentions it in passing and sees the reference as representing "the complete people of God in Christ."[110] The book of Revelation with all its

102. Pawson, *Unlocking*, 877. He argues that it is only the fourth and fifth types that are still functioning today.
103. Fee, *Corinthians*, 732, n. 98.
104. Ibid., 729.
105. Hamon, *Apostles*, 5.
106. Lightfoot, *Galatians*, 96.
107. Grudem, *Systematic*, 909.
108. Ruthven identifies the following as "apostles" in the New Testament: Barnabas, James, "brothers of the Lord," Andronicus and Junia, Silas, "unnamed apostles of churches," Judas and Silas, and Apollos. Ruthven, "Apostleship," 215. Virgo does not include Timothy in his list either.
109. Lightfoot, *Galatians*, 96, n. 2.
110. Ruthven, "Apostleship," 215.

PART THREE—What We Should Make of It

symbolism is very hard to decipher, and Ruthven is not wrong in seeking a more symbolic interpretation; he comes to a similar view as Lightfoot who thinks it might represent "the general body of Christian pastors."[111] Nevertheless, it does seem unlikely considering the rich tradition within the New Testament concerning the Twelve that there is not some direct link being made with the Twelve apostles made mention of in the Gospels, Acts, and 1 Corinthians. Ruthven is keen to downplay the significance of the Twelve, but in so doing I think he goes too far; furthermore, one does not have to adopt a cessationist approach by embracing this as a reference to the Twelve. This is plainly seen in the exegesis of Giles who argues that there are two main types of apostle in the New Testament: non-repeatable foundational ones, and an ongoing charismatic apostolate; these "two lines" of apostleship are clearly present in the New Testament and are evident in Revelation itself: "In Rev. 21:14 the Twelve apostles are seen to be foundational in the establishment of the New Jerusalem but in Rev. 18:20 and 2:2 the term apostle is used much more widely."[112]

What Ruthven has done is produce a scripturally informed, well-reasoned case for an ongoing charismatic apostolate,[113] fully incorporating the difficult passages that are the planks in the formidable cessationist argument. What is satisfying about his position is that it answers the question that must be put to the cessationists, which is why the New Testament writers do not use the knock-down argument against the false apostles which cessationists use today—namely: they cannot be apostles as Paul was the last one; they were not witnesses of the resurrected Lord; we know who these apostles were: The Twelve, Paul, and possibly a couple of others who we can name. Yet this is never the approach the New Testament writers take; Paul seems to point to their character and teaching as being indicative of whether they were true apostles or not.[114] Although this is a significant fact, it remains an argument from silence. Furthermore, there is the possibility that Paul chose not to focus on these qualifications because

111. Lightfoot, *Galatians*, 95. I do, however, think this is an unlikely interpretation—due to the rich tradition within the New Testament concerning the Twelve. I think it likely that Lightfoot is trying to undermine the common view prevalent in his day that there were only twelve apostles (see his comments on ibid., 94), and therefore this suggested interpretation highlights that you cannot build your theory of New Testament apostleship on this one highly "symbolic" verse.

112. Giles, "Apostles Before," 249.

113. What he has not done, is present the ramifications of his interpretation onto the modern church scene, or provided an illustration of how a modern-day apostolic ministry might appear.

114. See his discussion in 2 Corinthians 11–12.

these false apostles might claim they had seen the risen Christ and had been commissioned by him—a claim that could not be disproved. Possibly Paul did not dispute the false apostles' encounter with the risen Christ and their commissioning but knew that currently they were operating as false apostles because their actions denied Christ; therefore, it was vital to point to those characteristics that could be objectively verified—such as their actions and their character. Alternatively, we take the path of Barrett and Schnackenberg and recognize a myriad of views on apostleship in the early church which explains why some quarters hold certain qualifications as being indispensable whereas others see other features that way. Or we take Giles and Burkhard's approach and see two distinct types of apostleship, which explains the tension between the once for all nature of certain Apostolic ministries, but also does justice to those verses that imply there is an ongoing charismatic apostolate.

Conclusion

On balance Ruthven's exegesis of Ephesians 4:11–13 and the implications of 1 Corinthians 12:28 would appear to be correct and make his assertion that the New Testament foresees an ongoing charismatic apostolate as the more likely interpretation. Therefore he provides a strong case for the exegesis that underpins Apostle Type 1, Apostle Type 2, and Apostle Type 3. However, Grudem and Stott are correct in giving the Twelve, Paul, and other first-generation apostles a unique role which can never be repeated due to their "originary" function. There is a middle ground between these two positions that needs to be reached which Burkhard and Giles occupy. It is a view that not only does justice to Ephesians 4:11–13 by affirming a continuing charismatic apostolate but at the same time recognizes, along with the church fathers, the Reformers, and the majority of Christian churches today, the non-repeatable work of the originary apostles. By coming to this conclusion I am suggesting that the basis that the popular authors have for advocating an ongoing charismatic apostolate is a biblically legitimate position. I think how they present their understanding of that ministry is more open to debate, and some of their conceptions are ecumenically damaging and theologically questionable. Therefore, in the next chapter we will consider the place the current concepts of the charismatic apostolate should have within the wider Body of Christ.

7

Theological/Ecclesiological Critique of Popular Evangelical Conceptions of the Charismatic Apostolate

Introduction

THE CASE HAS BEEN set out in chapters 1 and 2 that the charismatic apostolate has become a feature of modern Charismatic/Evangelical church life. Aside from the odd Scriptural critique of certain popular forms of the charismatic apostolate, there has not been a wider theological and ecumenical appraisal of them. Yet for many in older denominations who are flirting with the idea, considerable wisdom is needed in translating popular assertions about the charismatic apostolate into workable, ecumenical forms. Such a process needs to take account of the shared assumptions undergirding the idea, as well as to be aware of the potential positive and negative effects the charismatic apostolate could bring to the wider church. Our popular authors have not written books explaining how you incorporate apostles into mainstream churches—that was not their aim; however, they have aimed to describe what a genuine apostle's ministry should look like and how it functions and are writing for a wide Christian audience, not for a particular denomination; it is therefore up to the reader to consider how and whether the vision can be translated into reality within their ecclesial context. This chapter aims to help in that by discussing the merits of key shared theological assumptions undergirding the popular forms and highlighting the general pitfalls of this "fashionable" concept

Theological/Ecclesiological Critique of Popular Evangelical Conceptions

from a scholarly and ecumenical vantage point; then, I will critically consider whether there is an edificatory place in the catholic church for the three types of apostle being advocated.

Part 1: Appraising Charismatic Apostolates Generally

From my overview of five popular conceptions of the charismatic apostolate we saw distinct differences being promoted; however, I also noted that there were some shared conclusions:

1. The church needs apostles.
2. God is still giving apostles post the apostolic era.
3. No specified number of apostles.
4. This is scripturally legitimated.
5. Ephesians 4:11–13 is the key text and source of the underlying theology that drives this emphasis.
6. There is enough in Scripture to paint a picture of how an apostle functions.
7. They exercise spiritual authority based upon an empowering by the Spirit rather than delegated authority via church hierarchy.
8. All modern apostles are "under" Scripture and not authors of it.
9. Paul is a model apostle par excellence and his gift is evidenced through his spiritual fatherhood of initiating and nurturing churches.

Putting aside for the moment what form of apostle is being advocated, I will argue that each one of these points is a reasonable inference from Scripture and is not unfounded within Christian tradition; problems come when particular forms of charismatic apostolate are promoted that rely on dubious exegesis and inadequate interactions with history/tradition which in turn leads to ecumenical complications.

Underpinning our authors' thinking are Evangelical convictions concerning the primacy of Scripture in determining doctrine, and that the New Testament is indispensable in helping the church recognize its calling and modus operandi. There is belief that the New Testament provides us with enough concrete information about this ministry; and that the ministry so described should be expected and desired for the health of the church and for its mission within the world. This belief in the primacy of

PART THREE—What We Should Make of It

Scripture is not contentious; and their practice of mining the New Testament to help us be the church more effectively is not a unique Protestant drive, the same impulses are present within the church catholic and are esteemed. For example, Hans Küng writes, "The New Testament message, as the original testimony, is the highest court to which appeal must be made in all the changes of history."[1] They have tapped into a thoroughly catholic belief that we can find in the genesis of the church, as seen in the New Testament, principles and patterns that are clearly meant to guide the Christian community as it seeks to live out its life under the Lordship of Christ. Küng speaks for many when he states that the New Testament church "is the essential norm against which the Church of every age has to measure itself. The New Testament Church, which, beginning with its origins in Jesus Christ, is already the Church in the fullness of its nature, is therefore the original design; we cannot copy it today, but we can and must translate it into modern terms. The Church of the New Testament alone can show us what that original design was."[2]

Therefore, these principles, values and practices are fundamental to the health of the community and it is to our detriment if they are sidelined. Obviously, we still have the problem of working through which principles and practices and values are relevant today.

They all reject a "broad" (my term) cessationism—this is the idea that all the miraculous gifts and ministries died out with the first generation apostles and when the Scripture was completed. Some of them, like Hagin, affirm a "narrow" cessationism where they affirm all the charismatic ministries of Ephesians 4:11–13 as still available today but argue that there were some ministries present in the early church—the foundational apostles and prophets—which once fulfilling their purpose were never to be repeated again. Broad cessationism is a view most in vogue within the Conservative Evangelical wing of the church that asserts that all miraculous gifts died out with the first apostles. B. B. Warfield espoused this view, and it is still heralded by influential Evangelical pastor/theologians such as John MacArthur and J. I. Packer. Nevertheless, in the worldwide church the wholesale rejection of miraculous spiritual gifts is repudiated—both the Catholics and Orthodox have always believed that God continues to work miracles amongst the faithful, and have a host of saints that they revere accredited with signs and wonders.

---

1. Küng, *Church*, 24.
2. Ibid.

Theological/Ecclesiological Critique of Popular Evangelical Conceptions

Our authors' explicit Charismatic ecclesiology is in full accord with developments that have occurred amongst leading ecclesiologists who have reclaimed the fundamentally charismatic nature of the church as seen in Scripture. Roman Catholic scholars such as Küng, Anglicans such as Michael Ramsey, and Free Church scholars such as Miroslav Volf have all argued for the essential organic charismatic/pneumatic nature of church.[3] The importance of the charisms of the Spirit and their incorporation into the life of the church has become an accepted dogma amongst ecclesiologists of all church backgrounds. Within the Evangelical Protestant world there are a number of scholars showing the faulty exegesis on which Warfield and others have based their thinking. Two important works in this regard are Max Turner's *Spiritual Gifts Then and Now* and John Ruthven's *On the Cessation of the Charismata*. The cessationist argument has more plausibility on the basis of lack of experience of miraculous gifts than Scriptural testimony; it is eisegesis that leads to a broad cessationist reading of Scripture and not exegesis. Likewise, it is a selective reading of church history that does the same. However, the churches that have held to this theology still encourage ministries that many in the Charismatic world would call apostolic. It is amongst these churches that some of the most mission-minded and pioneering leaders are fashioned, and they have a rich tradition of sending people out as missionaries to start and nurture churches. (Two notable bases of mission and missional leaders in the Anglican Church are St Helen's Bishopsgate and Emmanuel Church, Wimbledon; both are thoroughly Reformed and non-Pentecostal theologically.) Arguably, therefore, they instinctively recognize this gift, but will choose an alternative name for it because of their prior convictions concerning cessationism.

It is not just Conservative Evangelicals who reject the charismatic apostolate on exegetical grounds. The Barthian Charismatic, former leader of Fountain Trust, Tom Smail, takes Ephesians 4:11–13 as referring to a select group of apostles who fit Luke's description in the beginning of Acts, and therefore cannot be applied to an ongoing charismatic apostolate. Being a witness of the resurrection is a fundamental aspect of being an apostle and that is not to be repeated, the episcope continues an element of the apostolic function, but it is a mistake to call them apostles; like most Conservative Evangelicals he is all for church planting, but to call such people apostles is a mistake; he hoped that this trend concerning the charismatic apostolate would be a passing fad.[4]

3. Küng, *Church*; Ramsey, *Gospel*; Volf, *Likeness*.
4. Tom Smail, interview with author, 8 April, 2009.

PART THREE—What We Should Make of It

What is important to Evangelicals is the belief that the Scriptures are complete and are to be submitted to with no further authoritative revelation for God's people needed. In this respect all of our popular authors agree regardless of the level of authority they ascribe to the apostle. Therefore, their view that all modern apostles are "under" Scripture and not authors of it (point 8) is uncontentious within Evangelical circles and should come as a welcome relief for that constituency. Obviously the idea that apostles are still given is an intractable problem for those whose hermeneutic rules it out. However, if we put the question of terminology aside, and describe the type of ministry being advocated by our popular authors, highlighting the main functions that are being brought to the fore (church planting; overseeing; evangelizing) then we have a form of ministry that even cessationists would be hard pressed to reject. With this in mind if we take their first point that the church needs apostolic leaders, there is not a branch of the Christian church that does not recognize the need to have Spirit-empowered, Spirit-sent-pioneering, church-initiating, spiritual-parenting figures. All of our authors would recognize these facets of a genuine apostle, and these functions are appreciated by all sectors of the church; furthermore, as shown in chapter 5 there is a particular desire at this time for more of these types of figures in places where the church is in decline and not reaching people. Therefore, Paul as a model apostolic ministry—aside from his authoritative words recorded in Scripture—is not and should not be a problem for Christians of all backgrounds. Even those who have not advocated an ongoing charismatic apostolate have seen the worth and importance of emulating Paul and seeing functions of his ministry replicated within the church. New Testament scholar Colin Kruse reaches a similar conclusion: "Unlike the Twelve, for instance, his call, commissioning and empowering for ministry all fall within the post-Pentecost era of the Spirit and of the world-wide mission. There is, therefore, every reason to believe that the sort of involvement on the part of our Lord evident in the ministry of Paul can and ought to be found in our ministries today."[5]

Nevertheless, our authors are not content to advocate ongoing apostolic functions; they want an ongoing charismatic apostolate on the basis of the New Testament, particularly Ephesians 4:11–13. From my earlier discussion in chapter 5, I show that the case for supposing that this passage does advocate an ongoing charismatic apostolate, along with the other three/four gifts until the church reaches unity and full maturity, is

5. Frost and Hirsch, *Shaping*, 187.

very strong, and is preferable to cessationist interpretations that deny it. Although it has not been the majority view through the church's history, it has increasingly been recognized across a wide sector of the church as a viable and reasonable inference of the text. Similarly, there is nothing from this passage or anywhere else to put a cap on how many of these apostles can be present; all of those movements that have capped the number of apostles have relied on very dubious typology which falls apart under scrutiny.

Their conviction that there is enough in the New Testament to give us a description of an apostle's ministry is well founded in that there is a fair amount written about this ministry, however, there still needs to be a healthy degree of skepticism for as Fee has argued there simply is not enough information from the New Testament to understand in detail what some of the early ministries were and how they functioned.

Even though some of their exegesis is suspect, and there is a lack of interaction with modern scholarship they still have some genuine insight in highlighting practices and principles utilized beneficially within the early church that might be effectively used today. Furthermore, some of their assumptions are in full accord with New Testament scholars; for example, their proof texting to argue that there were numerous itinerant apostolic ministries apart from the apostles (the Twelve and Paul) in the New Testament, is widely affirmed within scholarly circles—Eduard Schweizer in particular did an excellent job of highlighting the variety of church ministries present in this era including the itinerant charismatic apostolate;[6] however, Schweizer and other scholars have not done the task of trying to re-imagine such ministries for today which our popular authors have done.

Our authors' conviction that this ministry is to be Spirit-empowered if it is to be genuine runs in full accord with standard catholic theology, where all churches hold that God calls people into acts of service and empowers them by the Spirit. How the church both local and universal affirms or recognizes this gift is another matter. Their assumption that spiritual authority is derived from God and not connected with an ecclesiastical position is more controversial from an ecumenical perspective. Although as shown in chapter 4 the idea that this is a way in which God has and does work has been affirmed by renowned and respected figures within the church catholic, for example, St Symeon. On the other side, Orthodox, Catholic, and some Anglican thinkers would want to affirm

---

6. Schweizer, *Church*.

the ontological dimension to Holy Orders that confers spiritual authority. This type of thinking is foreign to Evangelical Protestantism where all of our popular authors locate themselves. With their Protestant background our authors have a natural tendency to bypass the historical development of the church and to encourage primitivism in reference to the New Testament, which, as Os Guinness argues, leads to a naive simplistic faith and the "Evangelical bias against history."[7] As a result there appears a casual dismissal of the historical development that occurred within the first few centuries of the church's existence where the use of the term "apostles" in describing contemporary leaders died out, and the focus shifted to their successors the "bishops." This is an undeniable fact, and one has to explain it. There are a number of alternative explanations: 1. This was a historical aberration where the church was drifting from the apostolic pattern laid down in epistles such as Ephesians and therefore should be abandoned; 2. this development was an apostolic tradition with roots in apostolic practice, the "seed" form being able to be discerned in the New Testament which took mature shape in the centuries that followed and it therefore remains God's pattern for his church; 3. it was a post-New Testament development and not in conflict with it and was useful for the sake of the church's mission in that particular era, therefore, it is not an authoritative pattern for other ages but can be utilized if needed.

If we assume that it is 1 or 3 then it is arguably not binding for any church on the basis of New Testament teaching to embrace this development today. Yet, however one approaches this subject, to not interact with it shows a profound disregard for a tradition that has strong catholic credentials. Episcopal succession and Episcopal office may well be the best way to organize the church as Lutheran ecclesiologist Carl Braaten argues,[8] and even be a natural outworking of the Gospel as Ramsey contends;[9] if we are attempting to work ecumenically we need to have something to say on this front. Likewise, there needs to be a robust explanation of how one is signifying unity with other members of the Body of Christ. This was a central concern of Paul's, and has remained so within apostolic-succession churches, and also amongst Protestant luminaries, as Braaten has pointed out: "There may have been some wild reformers who intended to start a bible church without catholic substance, but Luther, Calvin, and Wesley were not among them."[10]

7. Guinness, *Bodies*, 43.
8. Braaten, *Mother Church*, chap. 2.
9. Ramsey, *Gospel*, chap. 6.
10. Braaten, *Mother Church*, 144.

Theological/Ecclesiological Critique of Popular Evangelical Conceptions

On the other side, those who are committed to the historic succession as being the only way in which the apostolic charism is passed on need to be reminded of both the ecumenical developments that have placed "apostolicity" and "apostolic ministry" on a much wider plane,[11] as well as the "shape" of apostolic ministry in the New Testament. There also has to be a recognition that the "pipe-line" perspective stands on very shaky ground exegetically, theologically and historically.[12] In this regard the work of Roman Catholic John Burkhard is very important. His book *Apostolicity Then and Now* affirms historic succession as being an important part of what constituted apostolicity amongst early Christian theologians; however, it was by no means the only thing. Like Zizioulas and Francis Sullivan he has studied the relevant literature but in spite of his Catholic commitment he does not hold to historical succession as a direct apostolic tradition. Burkhard highlights the serious shortcomings of Sullivan's detailed defense of historic succession and conclusively shows that for all the claims made for historic succession it is nigh on impossible to find a solid basis for it prior to Irenaeus.[13] Alongside this, Burkhard makes a compelling case for the following: There is evidence both in Scripture and early Christian writings for a secondary charismatic apostolate differentiated from the "originary" apostles;[14] the early churches variously understood themselves as apostolic on the basis of origin, doctrine, life and apostolic succession;[15] the understanding of the apostolicity of the church has differed widely throughout history in accordance with the governing worldviews, that is, classical, modern and postmodern.[16] In discussing the recent fruit of ecumenical dialogues on this subject Burkhard states: "The ecumenical statements of the last forty years make it abundantly clear that on the question of apostolicity, primacy is to be given to the apostolicity of the whole church. The claim seems to be well supported by what we observed in the church of the early centuries. Only later was apostolic office separated out from the encompassing apostolicity of the community and understood as fundamental."[17]

---

11. See section on these developments in chap. 5.
12. Küng, *Infallible?*, 77.
13. Burkhard, *Apostolicity*, chap. 3.
14. Ibid., chap. 1.
15. Ibid., chap. 2.
16. Ibid., chaps. 3–6.
17. Ibid., 236.

Burkhard also challenges the Roman Catholic Church, and inadvertently other communities, to recognize the validity of other church's ministries on the basis of their own "ecclesial" and "Charismatic" validation, and only finally to consider the "ritual validation."[18]

Burkhard has made a significant ecumenical contribution to the ongoing discussions concerning the church's apostolic nature. He has highlighted the fruit of ecumenical reports that are calling for a fuller view of the apostolicity of the church, and thereby recognizing other ministries as apostolic. Yet he shows that this is not an aberration but in full accord with the early church where "there is more than just one orthodox understanding of episcopacy in the church and therefore of apostolic succession in the ministry."[19] The one major weakness in an otherwise outstanding book is Burkhard's lack of interaction with Pentecostalism's understanding of "apostolicity." Veli-Matti Kärkkäinen has done much to unpack Pentecostalism's understanding of "apostolicity," and show that it has a significant contribution to the wider ecumenical discussion concerning this subject.[20] This is a major omission particularly as Burkhard opens wide the debate on apostolicity in light of his commitment to postmodernity and ecumenism. Although Burkhard does not engage with the independent Charismatic churches (he does with the Free Churches, in particular the work of Miroslav Volf) he indirectly gives support to their contention that an ongoing charismatic apostolate is true to both Scripture and early church tradition.

The danger present in all our popular charismatic apostolate advocates is that of promoting blueprint ecclesiology which is problematic both biblically and historically. As Küng has rightfully stated, "To reflect on the New Testament . . . does not mean that we should try unhistorically to return to the Church's origins or try to imitate the New Testament community. . . . The New Testament Church is not a model which we can follow slavishly without any regard to the lapse of time and our constantly changing situation."[21]

In comparison with the other authors Breen appears very culturally aware. He's not tied up with a Restorationist agenda and less prone to blueprint ecclesiology with its inherent problems of a seeming dismissal

---

18. Burkhard is consciously drawing on Killian McDonnell's work which advocated these "three ways of validating ministry." Ibid., 226; see also 226–37.

19. Ibid., 217. In this he builds on the research and conclusions of Zizioulas.

20. Kärkkäinen, "Apostolicity"; Kärkkäinen, "Ecumenism."

21. Küng, *Church*, 24.

Theological/Ecclesiological Critique of Popular Evangelical Conceptions

of church history and development, idealistic views of the New Testament church, and a disregard of the diversity within the early church.

All of them rely upon a couple of verses from Ephesians to form the bedrock of their convictions concerning ministry in the worldwide church. Should these sentences be so universally applied? Supporters of this idea argue that Paul is describing principles for the church universal not merely for one New Testament local congregation. Breen, in particular, argues this as justification for his idea that all Christians are characterized by one of these "base ministries." Even though, the author of Ephesians does address a local situation in the epistle (for example, see Eph 6:21), there are theological themes that rightfully have a wider application and 4:11–13 appears to be appealing to a universal act of Christ toward the church post-ascension. In this regard Frost and Hirsch make a valid case by arguing that it is illegitimate to follow the logic of the author in asserting the necessity of one Lord, one Faith, one Baptism, and then question the legitimacy of his statements later concerning the four/fivefold ministry gifts:

> The Pauline logic that asserts the church is gathered around one Lord/faith/baptism is the same logic that says God has specifically and deliberately (and with purpose) placed this pattern of ministry/gifting in the church. We therefore claim that this text is grammatically, theologically, and thematically indivisible. . . . It seems that the doctrine of the church's unity and faith is therefore inextricably linked with a comprehensive understanding of the function of APEPT (Apostle Prophet Evangelist Pastor Teacher) in the life of the church. The church and its fundamental ministry are one. In fact the mission is here directly related to its ministry structure.[22]

Yet our popular authors have not just called the wider church to embrace the charism of apostle, they have also described the shape of that ministry and its place within the church; whether their type of apostle is good for the church at large and whether it is ecumenical is a different matter.

What I intend therefore to consider is whether the three types of charismatic apostolate identified in chapter 3 (Apostle Type 1, "hierarchical apostle"; Apostle Type 2, "non-foundational apostle"; Apostle Type 3, "non-select apostle")[23] should be endorsed within the wider church, in a

---

22. Frost and Hirsch, *Shaping*, 168.
23. See glossary for more detail.

PART THREE—What We Should Make of It

time when ecumenism is important. This is not to suggest that the least offensive view is embraced—as truth must be allowed to challenge and shape ecclesiastical tradition rather than be subservient to it—but the way truth is expressed is as moral an issue as the substance of it. While I have no doubt that there are advocates of Apostle Type 1, Type 2, and Type 3 whose motives are not pure, in my considerations I am going to assume that what they are putting forward in terms of their theology is honestly motivated and judge it on that rather than the assumption that they are all crooked and purposely misinterpreting Scriptures for their own end. As will become evident, there is more space given to critique Apostle Type 1 than the other two, for the reason that it is more contentious exegetically, ecclesiologically, and ecumenically.

PART 2: APPRAISING SPECIFIC TYPES OF CHARISMATIC APOSTOLATES

Apostle Type 1

There is substantial overlap between the popular types of charismatic apostolate and it is hard to classify them as a result;[24] however, the main feature distinguishing 1 from 2 and 3 is the unusual amount of spiritual authority that is attributed to the apostle. Advocates of all three types are agreed that the function of apostle is what identifies someone as a bona fide apostle; however, proponents of Apostle Type 1s stress the hierarchical nature of this ministry, whereas promoters of Apostle Type 2 and Type 3 do not. There are a host of Charismatic celebrities who advocate Apostle Type 1s: Peter Wagner, Terry Virgo, Derek Prince, Colin Urquhart, Barney Coombes, alongside most advocates of the New Apostolic Reformation. Joining this company would be the scholar Jon Ruthven. The following groups both past and present have encouraged Apostle Type 1: The Catholic Apostolic Church, the New Apostolic Church, the Apostolic Church; Latter Rain denominations; R1 churches;

---

24. There are some which simply cannot be boxed in the categories I have described—for example, Frank Viola shares elements of Apostle Type 1 exegesis in regard to seeing apostles as foundational to churches but is thoroughly opposed to the hierarchical reading and structure that Apostle Type 1 advocates propose. His description of apostleship is more in line with Apostle Type 2 views, however, unlike their typical exegesis in that he does not differentiate between the apostles of Ephesians 2:20 and those of Ephesians 4:11.

Theological/Ecclesiological Critique of Popular Evangelical Conceptions

some of the Apostolic Networks in Britain, and most recently those associated with the New Apostolic Reformation both in the West and in Africa and Asia.

Although it is essential to recognize that each one of these people and groups have different views on the exact nature of a bona fide apostle, some arguing for greater authority than others, even within this banding. Similarly, there are certain trends evident in Apostle Type 1 circles such as calling oneself or being referred to openly as an apostle that are more prevalent and important to certain advocates than to others. Therefore, I will concentrate on the core features as well as prevalent trends amongst this group. What unites them is that their apostles are viewed as indispensable, their spiritual authority takes precedent over all other ministries in the church and they provide "foundational" input without which the church local and universal will never become all that God desires. The Scriptures undergirding this type of apostle are Ephesians 2:20, 1 Corinthians 12:28 and Ephesians 4:11–13; and it is a hierarchical reading of these Scriptures that is used.

Even though there are serious theological and ecumenical questions with this type of apostle, it is a form of leadership that is having a noticeable impact on the church worldwide. It is important to note in evaluating Apostle Type 1s that there are frequently related theological dogmas that tie into their conception of the apostle. For example, Restorationism is often an overriding theological motif, with its positive and dominionist eschatology. These underlying convictions are not always explicitly put forward in their writings on apostles, but it is the framework within which they are operating. This does affect their thinking on apostles, and therefore is naturally concerning for all those groups opposed to Restorationism and Dominionism. In my opinion there are serious issues with these theological narratives, and where it does impinge upon their understanding of apostles I will address some of their problems.

Scripture and Apostle Type 1

Those who advocate this form of apostle believe that the Scriptural case for it is watertight. Yet it is on that ground that so many have rejected it. Nevertheless, I see no problems with their use of Ephesians 4:11–13 to stipulate that apostles are still given to the church as that is the most natural reading of the text, and the onus is on those who dispute this reading. However, when that same text is used to justify a form of church

PART THREE—What We Should Make of It

government then it stands on flimsier ground. K. T. Resane has studied and critiqued the New Apostolic Reformation's church polity, and argues that at its core there is a misunderstanding of Ephesians 4:11–13. She argues that these ministries are not concerned with church government; rather they are "intended for maturity, not for the government of the church."[25] Based solely upon Ephesians 4:11–13 that is a correct assessment; however, she omits discussion of 1 Corinthians 12:28 and Ephesians 2:20, which are the texts that Wagner and others see as tying the ministry to church government. A stronger argument would be appeal to Acts and the Pastoral letters and show how church polity developed in the course of the early church; the evidence of that and of later church tradition give the impression that the more mature church did not ascribe governmental positions to apostles and prophets.

Wagner and other Apostle Type 1 advocates rely heavily on Ephesians 2:20 and equate the apostles mentioned in that verse with those in Ephesians 4:11. This equation would appear prima facie to be correct and numerous scholars take this position, for example Dunn, Grudem, Stott, and Ruthven. Furthermore, Wagner and others argue that it is not the universal church that is in view, but local churches. Again there is a strong case for this, and Gordon Fee believes that is the correct interpretation. However, even if one does see it as descriptive of a local church's founding within the apostolic era it does not mean it is prescriptive for all proper church founding. The reality is that apostles and prophets did not always found individual churches within the New Testament era, and there is no indication within the narratives that they had to. As Rick Joyner has pointed out, the fellowship at Antioch was not begun by apostles,[26] nor was it seen as vital that an apostle go there to stabilize it. The fact that this church is often seen as the model church par excellence within Charismatic circles[27] makes this fact extremely significant; furthermore, it is out of this fellowship that Paul and Barnabas are "apostled" out by the Holy Spirit. Wagner's proposal leads to the dubious conclusion that very few churches throughout church history have ever been rightfully "founded."

It is therefore very understandable that Hagin and others have made a sharp delineation between the apostles mentioned in these verses and those promised in Ephesians 4:11–13; furthermore, it explains why Hagin

---

25. Resane, "Ecclesiology," v.

26. Joyner, *Apostolic Ministry*, 82.

27. The following are titles of books centering on the Antioch church: Paterson, *Antioch Factor*; Hemphill, *Antioch Effect*.

et al will argue that the universal church is in view here and in 1 Corinthians 12:28. Wagner and others' hierarchical use of Ephesians 2:20 and 1 Corinthians 12:28 magnifies Apostle Type 1s position and authority in a way that can be used to usurp the authority of other churchmen, and make individuals and churches overly reliant upon what these figures declare are the God inspired authoritative messages determining the direction and future of that person/community. There is a logic to their interpretation, but these verses do not have to be read that way. For example, Hagin argues (unconvincingly) that this is a description of the historical development of the universal church. Frank Viola's interpretation is more plausible; he argues that it reflects "a logical priority rather than a hierarchical one. . . . [T]he order reflects greater gifting with respect to church building";[28] this is because the apostle is the one who plants the new community. As an organic description of the formation of a local community Paul's ordering makes sense as even though it is not the only way a church is formed, it is the norm as presented in the New Testament—therefore, to see it as solidifying an authoritarian order is dubious.

There are also concerns with particular trends claiming to have Scriptural backing, associated with differing Apostle Type 1 authors. For example, Wagner broadens the concept of apostle so widely that many of his apostles appear unlike those in the New Testament. To start thinking of apostles of this and that unrelated to the local church community seems to be misguided, and unhelpful. This is not to undermine the rightness of encouraging a Christian vision of the workplace and of affirming God-given gifts in that sphere; or upon valid denominational ministries but it is to put a limit on what constitutes an apostle. From a cynical perspective, all this talk of "horizontal apostles" and "workplace apostles" is a means to give recognition to gifted individuals who are thereby instantly accorded status within certain Charismatic circles. On one level it is no different from the various ecclesiastical titles given to people in the older churches—especially if the older title/offices are likewise viewed as having spiritual authority. In a similar vein Virgo raises valid concerns with Wagner's work. He writes,

> Peter Wagner often observes large successful churches and describes their leaders as apostolic. In *Churchquake!* he highlights many distinctive features that he has noticed in churches that relate to apostolic ministry. But in his further book *The New Apostolic Churches*, there seems to be little attempt to rediscover

28. Viola, *Reimagining*, 285.

> the biblical principles of apostolic ministry, but rather to take note of highly successful modern churches that have strong and gifted leaders with some influence beyond their own congregation. . . . So his approach does not really help to shed light on those who want to build from a truly biblical perspective.[29]

Virgo is correct in his observations, although to be fair to Wagner, he does attempt to give a fuller description from the Bible of what apostolic ministry is in *Apostles Today*,[30] although even within that book there are assertions that do not have much backing from Scripture.

Another area that stands on flimsy New Testament ground is Wagner's concern that the title apostle should be used in reference to bona fide charismatic apostolates. Yet the attempt to justify it from Paul's example is misguided as Paul's claim to apostleship was integrally tied up with the authoritative revelation concerning the gospel that was revealed to him. He knew that for a congregation, to move away from the revelation that he brought would be detrimental to their spiritual wellbeing. Orthodox Christianity is united in its belief that the faith has once for all been delivered to the saints, and therefore no one is needed to unveil anything new from God to save humanity—that has been done through the revealed gospel. So using Paul's need to justify his apostolic calling cannot be transposed to today's "apostles." However, there is a Scriptural basis for referring to someone's function/ministry as an apostle; Viola argues that Paul never used it in any other way, even in regards to himself.[31]

Prince and Virgo are more rooted within the New Testament; both assume that apostles lay the foundation of churches—clear allusions to Ephesians 2:20 mixed with 1 Corinthians 3:10. They interact with the New Testament in much more depth and, although recognizing the unique authority and role that the Twelve and Paul had, like Wagner, they posit great authority into contemporary apostles' hands. In essence the command for a community to do something can rest on the fact that a "contemporary apostle" has commanded them to do this or that—the justification being found in Scripture based on the example of Paul and his use of apostolic authority. To suggest that an apostle today might have the same apostolic authority of Paul is highly questionable, and moves away from a well-established tradition and safeguard seen in the early church with figures like Clement who state, "I don't command you as an apostle." Prince and Virgo

---

29. Virgo, *Future*, 117.
30. Wagner, *Apostles Today*, 30–34.
31. Viola, *Reimaging*, 291.

Theological/Ecclesiological Critique of Popular Evangelical Conceptions

fail to interact properly with the Scriptures that pose problems for their thesis—in particular Ephesians 2:20 and 3:5—but they do provide a more solid biblically based conception of an apostolic ministry than Wagner.

Although they all do affirm the uniqueness of the Twelve and to some degree Paul, they do not do so sufficiently. It is this blurring of the boundaries that most concerns me from an exegetical and applicatory vantage point. The well-established tradition from Scripture that links the very incorporation into the church via connection with the original apostles' message must be given sufficient weight and emphasized, otherwise despotic apostles can manipulate through their pronouncements. Abraham Kuyper explains the utter uniqueness of the original authoritative apostles very well: "Life was manifested in such a way that it could be seen and handled. They who saw and handled it were the apostles; and they were also to declare this life unto the elect. By this declaration the required fellowship between the elect and the apostolate is established. And in consequence of this, there is fellowship also for the elect with the Father and the Son."[32]

Even though there are plausible elements to the hierarchical reading and some grounds to make a case for it, there is a lack of appreciation of the developments within the early church and not enough emphasis on the uniqueness of Paul. Therefore, it is naive to translate that into action now without taking into account nearly two millennia of church history/tradition and the worldwide ecclesiastical situation of today; interaction with those realities will help determine whether Apostle Type 1 can have a positive contribution to the church catholic and her mission.

Tradition, History, Church Development and Apostle Type 1

Apostle Type 1s hold that the pattern of church government headed by Apostles is divinely inspired and prescribed. There is nothing new in believing that one's particular church order is divinely mandated—that idea is present in most churches old and new. Furthermore, the idea that the fullness of the church can only be experienced when the church government is in divine order is not unique to Apostle Type 1s. The irony is that Apostle Type 1 advocates are arguing for a similar ministry to offices that they reject, that of a Roman Catholic or Orthodox bishop: a successor of

---

32. Kuyper, *Holy Spirit*, 141. Thanks to Tim Bradshaw for drawing my attention to this; see Bradshaw, *Olive*, 154.

the apostles, a leader of God's people, appointing and anointing elders/priests and deacons, teaching the truths of the faith, correcting doctrinal error, given titles that underline their authority. Like an Orthodox/Roman Catholic bishop, being an apostle is more than a function; it becomes an ontological phenomenon with great authority. This often results in a similar structure, with a similar chain of command. In many ways some of the Apostolic Network leaders have a role similar to the Pope, as they oversee their international sees.

It is important that this idea of a divinely decreed nature of church government is questioned, both on exegetical, historical and experiential grounds. New Testament scholar Dunn has falsified the supposition that there was a prescriptive pattern of church order instituted by the apostles which was to be followed by all churches;[33] the church's early traditions and practices similarly put this into question. Furthermore, if we were to adjudicate whether "outpourings of the Spirit" have been synonymous with correct church order, we would most likely conclude that they were not. This is an idea that has strong currency within the church's history but is found wanting. This is not to suggest that we do not work hard at learning from the principles revealed in the New Testament, and the lessons learnt from church history and current experience, but it does warn that the panacea of right church order is elusive.

Most advocates of this form of apostle do not believe it vital that there is historical precedent post New Testament for their belief. However, from a catholic, ecumenical perspective it is important, and we cannot get away from the fact that an ongoing office of apostle was not set up and the focus of apostolic gifts was uncontroversially transferred to the bishop. Similarly, we need to recognize that there has been this type of apostle before, and they have not brought the maturity or unity promised; in fact they have often done the opposite. The fact that most advocates of Apostle Type 1 are caught up within a Restorationist paradigm brings its own baggage. Restorationists esteem those movements that brought back doctrines that their present movement cherishes, but will effortlessly dismiss other movements that brought some other feature back—you do not hear many in Evangelical circles talking about the restoration that occurred during the Oxford Movement. In this regard William Abraham points out that Wagner has overlaid history with a highly problematical theological narrative, and concludes that "Wagner is so caught up in a whirl of romantic exuberance, and so immersed in his odd dispensationalist trappings, that

---

33. Dunn, *Unity*.

he is blind to the work of God in the more fixed and continuous forms of the Church's life."[34] Abraham rightly disputes Wagner's theological narrative and is correct in his assessment that Wagner and others in the movement are too dismissive of the signs of grace evident in other sectors of the church;[35] however, it would be foolish to conclude on that basis that much of what Wagner is applauding in these new apostolic leaders and their networks is of no benefit to the wider church, as these leaders may indeed herald signs of the kingdom. Of course there is a mixture of fallen humanity as well as divine enabling; there is no pure stream in any movement and Luther's famous dictum *simul iustus et peccator* can be applied to the New Apostolic Reformation.

People have been concerned about the New Apostolic Reformation's propensity for serious spiritual abuse because of the Pope-like status that the apostles are accorded, and there have been those who have seen similarities with the Shepherding movement that caused so much damage. I do think the similarities are overplayed as generally they do not seem to be encouraging the same intrusiveness that that movement did; however, the unquestioning obedience to the apostle that sometimes is put forward has the same "odor." This is a real problem, built into their very high view of the apostle, and demanded by their hermeneutic. Nevertheless, the same concern could be said for the high view of bishops that the older churches have. As has long been recognized by the older churches, the supposed divine authority inherent in that office must be demonstrated by the humility and service practiced and taught by Jesus. Therefore, there is no reason why Apostle Type 1s cannot follow suit. The underlying danger is to so exaggerate the "office" that all sense of proportion is lost making the apostles the central plank in the church edifice leading to an inevitable depreciation of the rest of the Body. This is a huge pitfall in regards to Apostle Type 1, but it can apply equally to bishops in the historic succession.

As Apostle Type 1s tend to be starting their churches afresh they do not have the accumulated baggage and constrictions laid upon them by ecclesiastical regulations and history. Yet, at the same time they have to accrue certain safeguards that the older churches have taken time to put in place; this is particularly the case in regards to power and accountability. I asked a prominent UK apostle who he was accountable to, and he said he could pick up the phone and talk to another apostle if need be, but the answer was sufficiently vague to make me question how accountable

---

34. Abraham, *Renewal*, 126.
35. Ibid.

PART THREE—What We Should Make of It

these apostles are. To Wagner's credit he recognizes this, and has tried hard to form and nurture accountable relationships amongst the emerging apostles; with such authority vested in individuals a very clear accountability structure must be in place. Positively, Prince advocates a team-working conception of apostles and elders that provides accountability and highlights the indispensable role of the pastor and his office that other Apostle Type 1 advocates appear to bypass. For example, according to Ian Stackhouse, Wagner sets up a "derisory, lackluster image of the traditional pastor's role, against which the new apostolic pastor appears as a healthy and welcome alternative"; in effect, Wagner argues that "church leaders need to be far more visionary, throwing aside the sedentary and all too pedestrian nature of the pastoral office."[36] Stackhouse contends for the indispensable nature of the pastor and accuses Church Growth enthusiasts of doing a disservice to the church by undermining this tried and tested spiritual form of leadership.[37]

All sorts of issues surround the recognition of Apostle Type 1s. Although most advocates think that the fruit of each person's ministry is the determining factor, that is not how it always appears in practice; there is frequent recourse to prophetic words, or even personal visions and visitations. This is not to deny that these things might happen, but the potential for abuse is vast. The fact that a couple of high profile leaders[38] who have been associated with the New Apostolic Reformation have been exposed for serious moral failings highlights how easy it is for charisma to undermine genuine discernment.

One problem that has beset churches, which many have finally woken up to and have been addressing, has been the stifling of the laity. For many, that was the chief benefit of the Charismatic Movement, as there was an emphasis on mobilizing all the people of God to serve utilizing their God-given gifts. This is still a central element in many Charismatic churches; however, there is a danger in this regard with Apostle Type 1s. Ironically the haughty authority perceived to be theirs can end up undermining the very purpose for these apostles. These groups argue on the basis of Ephesians 4:11–13 that apostles and all the other ministries are given for the maturing of the Body of Christ so that the saints can be equipped for ministry. However, as Wimber discovered, a new elite of apostles and prophets undermines the priesthood and prophethood of all believers.[39]

36. Stackhouse, *Gospel-Driven*, 221.
37. Ibid., chap. 7.
38. Todd Bentley and Ted Haggard.
39. Jackson, *Quest*, 230.

There becomes an overdependence upon these super apostles for direction and revelation. This is not to suggest that people cannot become mature apostles and prophets who can and should be sought for their input, but it does raise questions about the way these people are presented. The fact that Paul often encouraged his fledgling congregations to judge things for themselves would seem to suggest that Paul did not want to become *the* lifeline for the community—rather he was calling them to grow up and take responsibility.

There is also sometimes a naivety that things will be different this time as if God is doing something so utterly fresh and new with this restoration that the same usual ossification that occurs after a new movement is sparked will not happen. The challenge for these "apostolic" groups is to keep that momentum going into the next generation, for the reality is that today's fresh movement becomes tomorrow's ossified denomination. Percy's perceptive points in regards to the Restorationist movements in Britain which were headed by apostles could equally apply to the next generation with the New Apostles, "These once-new radical expressions of Christianity find themselves, in their second phase of development, led by an emerging system (not a person), bequeathed them by the original founding Charismatic leader—who *de facto*, could find no equal to replace them."[40]

Wagner is well aware that these networks may become denominations, and is trying to formulate ways of preventing this. He is very wary of the routinization of charisma and believes that it is not inevitable and he proposes three prescriptions for "preserving vitality": "keep a ceiling on the number of churches in each network"; "constantly cultivate new charisma"; "multiply apostolic networks."[41] His rationale for these points seem reasonable[42] and may well enable apostolic networks to avoid some of the pitfalls that he and others perceive as hindering the older church's mission; nevertheless, it is hard not to predict that, despite Wagner's endeavors, all of these networks will inevitably either disband, join with others, or become recognized denominations. K. T. Resane argues that this is the case in churches where catechesis is not taken seriously which is a fault she has identified in New Apostolic Reformation churches.[43]

---

40. Percy, *Clergy*, 6.
41. Wagner, *Churchquake*, 140.
42. Ibid., 140ff.
43. Resane, "Ecclesiology," 120ff.

Part Three—What We Should Make of It

In spite of all these pitfalls and inherent problems with Apostle Type 1s, it is worth recalling that the church universal has esteemed people that have evidenced unusual spiritual authority and gifting, and as a result have made their mark on church history. Many of these past figures have been ordained as well as unordained. In light of this it would be foolish to doubt that God cannot and does not grant individuals unusual spiritual authority to pioneer works that actively extend the church's mission and build up communities. However, if these figures and this theology of the charismatic apostolate promote ecumenism or work against it will highlight whether it is a positive contribution to the church catholic or not, for ecumenism is important, not only theologically but also missionally.

Ecumenism and Apostle Type 1

Any group that believes that they are the cutting edge of what God is doing, is bound to have unecumenical traits—for they instinctively see themselves as associated with God's present purposes, whereas those not caught up in their new "paradigm" are yesterday's people. Apostle Type 1s are presented as having God given spiritual authority, in opposition to a "fleshly" authority mediated by stagnant institutions. Although not actively opposing denominations, Wagner and others are supporting a rival Charismatic network of "pneumatic" individuals who are having a noticeable impact within their "sphere of influence." Wagner's insistence on using the title "apostle" is unhelpful ecumenically as it raises all sorts of issues which are an unnecessary stumbling block. For example, in Britain where the church scene is not yet dominated by an independent Charismatic stream it is very important that new traditions interact healthily with the old. In parts of Africa it has become a more "solid" tradition and does not seem to be so contentious; although from those I know who have worked in Africa, ecumenism is not a strength of the African Church. It does not necessarily bring the benefits that Wagner foresees and is not akin to calling someone "pastor," "teacher" or even "bishop," as it is a notion that has a variety of meanings within the New Testament, and therefore can cause unnecessary confusion. The fact that they are evolving their own terminology and structures again makes them suspect to the charge of being unecumenical and divisive. Nevertheless, most Christian churches before them have done similar things, so, it would be uncharitable to shoot them down on that basis. However, whether Apostle Type 1s are at core unecumenical will depend on the lenses being worn by the adjudicator.

Theological/Ecclesiological Critique of Popular Evangelical Conceptions

If we wear the more Catholic/Orthodox lenses any new independent structure is by its very nature unecumenical. For to them church should be visibly united in structure, as well as organically related in Spirit. If we wear this lens then Apostle Type 1s run into all sorts of problems. For inherent within this form of apostleship is a justification for a new form of church with a claimed authentication given by God. Obviously, this type can only come from a Protestant perspective which holds that historical affiliation with the older churches is unimportant in determining whether one is part of the true church. Wagner and others are very happy for the existence of older denominations but believe that they need to structurally change to incorporate the new wine that God is giving to the church. As it stands Orthodox/Roman Catholic and most Protestant Churches are not in a position to do this.

Therefore, this form of apostleship appears unecumenical and judgmental of other forms of church. There is substance to this, but the weight of that accusation needs to be balanced by wider ecclesiological and confessional issues. Of course, any uprooting from the historical churches leaves a void in the signification of historical continuity. Yet, how important is this signification? Peter Hocken thinks it is important and argues that just as God was (and is) committed to his historic people Israel, so he is committed to "whatever witness there is of the Holy Spirit in each Christian family and tradition."[44] As a result if we assume he has abandoned these groups then we undermine the witness of God's faithfulness to that community. This is an attractive idea, as long as we do not assume it to mean that God is committed to historical expressions of the faith irrespective of their biblical veracity. One can justifiably advocate that he is faithful to his people within the historic churches, but not necessarily to the forms however "good" they appear.

The standard response from most Protestant Evangelicals is that what constitutes the church is not being connected to a particular form of church, but whether you are in Christ and therefore in a living communion with the Holy Trinity. If it is the latter, the denominational affiliation that you have is of secondary importance, and God is committed to those who are his people; as I have heard Colin Urquhart state, it is they who he seeks to revive, not the historic institutions. The continuity that is important is that of faith, not of historical lineage. This is not to mean disparaging the historical forms as pointless, nor to mean necessarily separating from them but it is to raise the pertinent question of how central they are

---

44. Hocken, *Glory*, 115.

PART THREE—What We Should Make of It

theologically to what constitutes God's people in Christ, and whether God really is committed to them. However, I have yet to encounter an advocate of this form of apostle who sees any issue with the proliferation of new independent networks. From the outside looking in, Wagner and others do not appear ecumenical in the traditional sense at all. This is a concern for "it is vital that ecumenism be kept alive"[45] out of obedience to Christ and for the sake of mission. Wagner does not think it an issue if pastors break away to link into existing apostolic networks or form their own—to his mind it is more important to embrace the new move of God, than to continue within a dead tradition seeking to bring life there.[46] Both Virgo and Prince appear to have a similar conviction, and it is one increasingly shared by former denominational loyalists—an example of this can be seen in Lutheran Renewal's Paul Anderson's statement where he highlights that the former word within the Charismatic Movement was "to bloom where you are planted," but that this word is no longer universally appropriate given the situation within the denominations.[47] Yet even though there is a realization that there have been and will be splits from older churches in this new movement, there is the belief that "genuine" Christian unity can still be nourished although in a different form.

The implication therefore, which is increasingly the case in the USA, is there will be even more church franchises flooding the Christian "market." One's ecclesiology will determine whether this is an issue or not. For most "older" churches this is a travesty and a further indictment of the Protestant church in general in its tendency to splinter and fragment and pursue individualistic visions. However, this is not the only ecclesiological appraisal possible; another set of lenses can be worn. Roger Forster, founder of Ichthus, and an influential figure in the New Church networks in Britain, has downplayed this issue, arguing that relationship between Christian churches is what matters not a visible organizational unity. Forster uses the framework of the nation of Israel to lend weight to this idea. The people of Israel were one people under Yahweh, however, they were different tribes with differing characteristics and roles but collectively making up the nation of Israel. Could the various churches not be akin to the differing tribes of Israel? This is an attractive idea, although for Forster the concern for unity seems to be limited to Evangelicals; he writes:

45. Abraham, *Renewal*, 129.

46. Wagner does think it possible for denominations to reshape themselves to become new wineskins to hold the new wine, but he does not hold out much hope for this.

47. Anderson, "Stay."

> One of my lifelong heart-concerns is for Evangelical unity, so that Jesus' evangelistic prayer may be answered: "I in them, and you in me, that they may become perfectly one, so that the world may know that you have sent me, and have loved them, even as you have loved me" (John 17:23). That prayer of Jesus was answered, not by our trifling and petty efforts at cooperation in the 20th century (the thought is almost blasphemous), but on the cross, within a few hours of its utterance, when by his death, Jesus broke down all dividing walls and made reconciliation through his blood, so that people could be one with God and with each other. Evangelical unity is therefore a gift to be received, cherished and enjoyed . . .[48]

Elsewhere he has commented, "There will always be denominations. There will always be Paul, Apollos and Cephas."[49]

If Forster is correct, visible unity, which is central to the eschatological and missionary vision of Jesus, can be still seen in this arrangement. This is worth contemplating as the hoped for structural unity so central to Roman Catholicism and other historic churches is not a model that currently works. Not only do Foster et al. have a problem with it biblically and ecclesiologically but they are likely aware of the natural impasse that these older churches have reached in their pursuit of structural unity. In practice, fraternal unity seems to work better amongst the older churches, as well as the newer churches. However, it is strange that Forster would quote Paul concerning "Apollos, Peter and Paul" in a justificatory manner for his view, as Paul was fundamentally opposed to this factionalism that was occurring in Corinth. Nevertheless, it is apparent that within the New Testament era there were marked differences in belief as well as practice between the different congregations.[50] They were united in their common allegiance to Jesus the Lord, but as to their patterns of worship they were not uniform. What was vital though was the sharing and communion that existed between the different Christian communities. Paul is at pains to keep the Gentile and Jewish communities in good supportive relationships—hence, his desire for the Gentile communities to support the Jewish ones in Jerusalem. These new apostolically-led churches may well promote and foster an experiential unity based on shared experience and some united core beliefs but beyond this it is hard to envisage any

---

48. Forster, "Evangelical?"
49. Marfleet, "New Churches," 78.
50. See Dunn, *Unity*, for an excellent description of the main uniting factors as well as the marked differences.

substantial unity between old and new churches, and it is hard to square that with Jesus' vision of a visibly united people that cause the world to believe.

Although there are unecumenical dimensions to this type of apostle, it is important to affirm that there are Apostle Type 1s and apostolic networks actively seeking to work with other groups of Christians;[51] notable in this regard are Ulf Ekman and Bill Johnson. Similarly, Peter Wagner himself works with whomever, and does not advocate that they cut off their denominational links unless there is a conflict of allegiances. Obviously, there tend to be better relationships and stronger ties with those who share similar values and core beliefs. In this regard they are no different from other Christian churches whether Evangelical/Charismatic or not. Where further ecumenical problems will arise is when denominational churches and leaders are forging personal/discipleship links with apostles and apostolic networks but are caught between two loyalties. I recall hearing an Apostle Type 1 asked about this by a denominational pastor and the apostle responded by advocating going with the apostle over and above denominational loyalty. This attitude would cause chaos within the historic churches where ordinands are required to give their allegiance on oath to their bishop.

From all appearances many of these Apostle Type 1 churches and networks are focused on mission and extending the influence of the kingdom of God—as they understand it. It is in this context that they have real advantages, there is an inherent "freedom" of not being restricted by denominational regulations, buildings and traditions; and in reading Prince, Wagner and Virgo, one is struck by the simplicity of the models that they promote. Therefore, it is unsurprising that many "apostolic networks," such as Newfrontiers International, have been able to grow so rapidly and keep the missionary impulse at the forefront of their work.

Although the freedom and the simplicity that Apostles Type 1s typify is attractive and challenging, the basis on which it is founded is questionable exegetically and brings problems ecumenically. If there was a way to harness the passion, zeal and freedom evidenced by many of these Apostle

---

51. Kay highlights the diversity of approaches of his studied apostolic networks in relation to membership, some being very exclusive (e.g., Bryn Jones), others less so: "New Frontiers has congregations that retain a Baptist connection and Kingdom Faith incorporates Baptist, Roman Catholic and Anglican congregations." Kay, *Networks*, 255. Similarly, less authoritarian networks such as Ichthus and Pioneer are openly embracing of and enthusiastic about ecumenical gatherings such as Spring Harvest—see ibid., 256–57.

Type 1s and their networks into more ecumenically friendly forms then the wider church might benefit immeasurably—but its current theological basis makes it hard for that to happen. Whether Apostle Types 2 or 3 can help in this regard is what we now turn to.

Apostle Type 2

Unlike Apostle Type 1, Apostle Type 2 draws a sharp distinction between foundational and non-foundational apostles; or in Wimber's case "big A" Apostles and "little a" apostles. These "little a" apostles do not have the right or ability to make authoritative decisions in light of their "apostolic gifting" on behalf of the church universal, nor are current apostles the "foundation of the church" alongside prophets. As a result the hierarchical nature of apostleship is downplayed, and the pioneering functional aspect is brought more to the fore. It is a form of apostleship that has been popularized by the first mainstream Pentecostal churches (Elim and Assemblies of God), and has continued to be the default position of such groups. It has also been popularized in gift courses such as SHAPE and Network, and is the type of apostolic ministry advocated by influential new churches such as Vineyard. Of our popular teachers, Hagin is the one who supports this view; other significant advocates have been Gee, Lindsay and Synan. Outside the Pentecostal movement the following scholarly authors propose a similar charismatic apostolate: Burkhard, Warner and Giles.

Like Type 1 advocates, they use Ephesians 4:11–13 as the proof of an ongoing apostolate and an indicator of its purpose. Again there is no concern with this. They tend not to have a hierarchical reading of 1 Corinthians 12:28. Most Apostle Type 2 advocates make a clear differentiation between the apostles mentioned in Ephesians 2:20 and those in 4:11. It is not such an easy reading of the text, but it has good credentials in that a number of scholars from a variety of church backgrounds are identifying a difference between the two groups: Burkhard (Catholic); Giles (Anglican); Warner (Baptist). Apostle Type 2 advocates tend to assume that the four or five ministry gifts are given to only certain members of the body of Christ. This idea fits with the Acts narrative and appears the most straightforward reading of the Ephesians text, and hence is the majority perspective in Charismatic circles. For example, in Acts, only certain individuals are singled out as being Prophets or Evangelists or Apostles and the same is true in Paul's writings. In comparison with Apostle Type 1, Apostle Type 2 seem less focused on spiritual authority and more on functions:

PART THREE—What We Should Make of It

proclaiming the gospel and forming new communities around "the faith once delivered." In this regard they are remarkably uncontroversial from a catholic perspective—in fact, even those like Stott and Grudem, who are opposed to an ongoing charismatic apostolate based on their interpretation of Scripture, are active supporters of all of these things, as are all Conservative Evangelicals.

None of the advocates try to make a case from church history for their viewpoint, although Burkhard sees the Didache as upholding his interpretation of Ephesians 4:11–13; nevertheless, Hagin and others think there are examples of such ministries functioning throughout the church's history. This is not a foolhardy view as church history is filled with daring, church-planting pioneers bringing the Gospel to new areas and initiating new communities of Christians. Therefore, although the categorization and linking with Ephesians 4:11 may be new, the reality and function of lower case apostles has been an integral part of the catholic church over nearly two millennia. Where there have been missionary impulses throughout the church's history there have been such leaders emerging. Whether it is wise to start identifying *current* missionary, church-planting figures as apostles is another matter—particularly in the light of ecumenism.

The very idea of a non-authoritarian pioneer ministry has nothing intrinsically to make it unecumenical or divisive. Obviously, it very much depends on the individual "apostle" and his/her way of doing things whether it would lead to further schisms or not. However, the function in and of itself should not. It is surely telling that a Roman Catholic scholar (Burkhard), a Baptist (Warner), and an Anglican (Giles) all come to a similar position as Hagin, and none of them view it as impossible for their respective communions to make space for this charism. Warner notes that many are indeed doing so and my own research suggests the same thing. Like Hagin they all do justice to Ephesians 4:11–13 by affirming a continuing charismatic apostolate but at the same time recognizing, along with the Church Fathers, the Reformers and majority of Christian churches today, the non-repeatable work of the "originary" apostles, and making an absolute distinction between their authority and the far lesser authority of a current charismatic apostolate.

The fact that they specifically equate this pioneering church planting ministry with that of the apostle as mentioned in Ephesians 4:11-13 inevitably brings problems for groups who are very precious about apostolic succession or cessationism. However, this is an area that the church universal may need to move cautiously forward on in light of Scriptural teaching as well as the increasing openness amongst groups to reclaim both the language and practice of apostolic ministries. Martin Garner thinks it is important to reclaim the biblical language and challenges the situation of happily using the word "missionary" (from *missio*—Latin for "sent one"), which is the same as "apostle" (from *apostolos*—Greek for "sent one").[52] There would be benefits if we were to reappropriate this terminology without bestowing titles as it would be easier for people to recognize themselves and their ministry within the New Testament—which in turn could help churches recognize, train and release people into apostolic ministries.

Yet it does bring a negative knee-jerk reaction from older churches and Evangelical groups to so label people. As mentioned before, it is one of the reasons for the development of the term "pioneer minister." This new title has the advantage of avoiding any kind of confusion about what is being referred to. From my various interviews it appeared that most advocates of Type 2 are unconcerned about the terminology. One of the hallmarks of Hagin's apostle is the unimportance of titles, and that the fruit should be the indicator of whether someone has this charism or not. The high office that he accords the pastor would also work well within traditional structures whether Anglican, Catholic, Orthodox, or Baptist, as it does not undermine the order which has served those communities well, and is a natural safeguard from so-called apostles who turn up and attempt to direct churches without a proper working knowledge of them. There is wisdom to this indifference to titling or referring to people as apostles as there are negative connotations connected to both past groups and present authoritarian ones that make the terminology unhelpful. On the other side, the word "apostle" has much more to it than the word "pioneer" and, as already noted, it has a rooting within Scripture that the newly-used term does not. As long as there is appropriate teaching highlighting the distinction between originary/foundational and non-originary/non-foundational apostles, this need not be a problem, and it may also help pastors and teachers exegete and apply the Scriptures more easily. In time, right use can correct misuse and abuse.

The less authoritarian Type 2 Apostle lends itself to being transposed into a variety of ecclesial settings. Obviously, one has to take into account all of the ecclesiastical baggage that each author has—for example, there cannot be a straight transferring of Hagin's language and churchmanship, as his use of the word "office of apostle" and his non-episcopal tradition

---

52. Garner, *Apostles Today*, chap. 3.

would clearly not be able to be embraced by episcopal churches. The same could be said for the Free Church traditions of Stuart Murray-Williams (Anabaptist) or Rob Warner (Baptist). Nevertheless, with the fear of an elite people who might see themselves as having the God-given authority over the rest of the Body removed, the church initiating functions and charisms associated with this gift can be readily embraced by Episcopal or non-episcopal churches.

Therefore, a charismatic apostle can in principle be a bishop, priest, deacon, superintendent, and so on. The gift will shape how you are in those positions, and unless the structures are so rigid there is no reason why they cannot flourish in those roles. Even Conservative Evangelicals do not have to be as concerned as there is a very clear differentiation between the authoritative apostles who were the deliverers of the faith given once for all, who were granted a unique place in salvation history that is never to be repeated, and these mission-driven individuals. However, they would struggle with the terminology and the belief held by many Type 2 advocates that signs and wonders would be an aspect of this gift.

Apostle Type 3

In some ways there is very little to discuss in light of the similarities with Type 2. In fact, aside from their exegesis of Ephesians 4:11–13, advocates of Type 3 share virtually everything in common, and therefore will encounter the same problems in being transposed into old or new churches. The one significant difference is their (Breen, Frost, Hirsch, Hopkins) contention that all members of the Body of Christ are charismatically gifted as apostle, prophet, pastor, teacher, or evangelist. This idea is very uncommon within the Pentecostal Charismatic Movement. Breen removes the usual distinction between the "clerical" five-fold ministers and the laity in his interpretation of Ephesians 4:11–13; it is an interpretation that I have not found in any Ephesians commentary and is harder to justify from the witness of the rest of the New Testament where only certain individuals are recorded as apostles, prophets, and evangelists.

Yet there is a plausible logic to his interpretation, and if its purported success is anything to go by it should not be dismissed too quickly. Breen argues his case exegetically by suggesting that if we omit verses 9 and 10, there would be the natural assumption that "to each one of us grace has been given" is a reference to all Christians, and that those grace gifts described in verse 11 are a description of the grace that has been given.[53] Verse 9 does appear as a universal statement encompassing all Christians. Nevertheless, the interpretation encounters problems as there is no indication elsewhere in Scripture that all Christians are one of these gifts. Breen does not try to show how it harmonizes with the rest of Scripture; the only way I can see it doing so is if we suppose that only those who have become so mature in their "base ministry" are referred to as apostles or prophets (or one of the other five ministries) in the New Testament. They have become defined through their function, and as a result the New Testament authors name them as apostles or prophets; needless, to say this is an inference and an argument from silence and is not the most natural reading of Scripture and therefore is weak.

Breen identifies plausible apostolic ministerial patterns within Scripture. Like Wagner, Breen does not tie down recognition of an apostle's gift to initiating church communities, but, in the main, sees it as one of the core features of an apostolic ministry. As with Apostle Type 2 advocates, they see no need to draw attention to titles, or suppose that the encouragement of this ministry will inevitably conflict with traditional church orders. What is clear from Breen's writing, as well as Frost and Hirsch's, is that we are not dealing with "big A" apostles; the focus is more on function, rather than ontology or position. As a result there is no inherent threat to existing church offices instead a potential ecumenical contribution enabling more pioneering leaders through providing helpful principles from Scripture to facilitate the initiating and growing of healthy communities.

A Proposal

In my estimation there is a valid place for a lower case charismatic apostolate (Apostle Type 2 and 3), and I think that this not only has strong exegetical weight behind it, but it has actually been part and parcel of how the church itself has operated—that is, with charismatically gifted pioneering/church-planting leaders. Therefore it is good and right that the church in the USA and Britain in its multi-faceted forms embraces this charism and makes room for it. For this to be done ecumenically there needs to be a careful use of language and an appropriate sifting of popular models with a determination to present scripturally shaped forms of ministry.

Clearly, how this gift is presented will either make it more accessible or divisive—therefore, whilst the theology and scholarship and talk

53. Breen, *Notebook*, 150–51.

of apostles is becoming more recognizable and commonplace the use of language such as "pioneer" or "missional" rather than "apostle" will avoid unnecessary stumbling blocks for older churches and Evangelical ones; although for training purposes I think it is important to ground the ministry in Scriptural categories and therefore use the word "apostle" and "apostolic," but be very careful to differentiate between originary and non-foundational apostles, focusing on function rather than titles. The realization that these types of gifts might emerge amongst the people of God will help the church to more readily recognize and release people into this enabling ministry. Modified forms of Apostle Type 2 or 3 can work within the structures, still readily submitting to the orders above them, at the same time likely challenging their "superiors" and the church as a whole to pioneer new communities where the church is not visible; as long as "apostles" in those structures recognize their place under the authorities in place within their denomination there should be no threat to unity.

All our popular authors have some good ideas that are worthy of being considered and potentially embraced by mission-minded communities: Prince's two-legged vision of apostles and elders working in unison; Wagner's call for firm accountability structures amongst apostles; Virgo's emphasis on apostles being preachers of the grace of God; Hagin's differentiation of foundational and non-foundational apostles; Breen's various images of pioneering, planting, bridging and building. Obviously, there needs to be a critical embracing of the various popular apostle types, even beyond the necessary changes that need to be taken into account in relation to the denominational context they come into, but also as there are other aspects common to all of them that are questionable from a rounded biblical perspective. If there is one feature above all others that Paul was determined to impress upon the Corinthian church in proof of the genuineness of his apostolic ministry, it was the place of suffering. It is this non-triumphalistic attitude that is central to his understanding of a genuine apostolic ministry, and it seems comparatively undwelt on in modern popular conceptions. Again, this challenge must be put to all in ecclesiastical positions as well as to the unordained follower of Christ: "Where is the cross in your life and ministry?"

Although I think our authors are correct in highlighting certain patterns that elucidate what an apostolic ministry looks like, there is an overcertainty of what a biblically defined apostle is; this oversteps the mark and there needs to be a recognition that there is not one controlling motif. Martyn Percy puts it helpfully: "it is not as if the word "apostle" ever had a precise meaning, other than the one the church (eventually) gave it. The noun from which the word is derived was borrowed from nautical terminology, and can mean "ambassador," "delegate" or "messenger."[54]

This does not undermine their conceptions but it does point out the need for authors to let their readers know that there is more ambiguity connected to the New Testament portrayal than is often acknowledged. Percy has convincingly argued the necessity of recognizing the impact that culture has and should have on the shape of Christian ministry; he also highlights the problematic nature of taking either a "blueprint" approach based on Scripture or Tradition which does not do justice to the present-day context; instead he argues for an evolutionary model of ministry.[55] This approach avoids the danger of straightjacketing apostolic ministry into a "one size fits all" form. The fundamental insight that the charism of apostle is still being given is correct but there needs to be a corresponding recognition that the shape that that ministry takes will be affected by the leader and his context.

Meeting the Challenge

As seen in chapter 2 many churches in Britain are seeking to bring an apostolic dimension more prominently back into their modus operandi. Increasingly, the Western church is recognizing the need to enable forms of ministry that are actively going out and establishing new communities in the power of the Spirit. This missionary impulse, always present and often affirmed within the Universal church, but rarely in ways that directly equate with the charismatic apostolate, is now so widely appreciated that the provocative actions of new church movements with charismatic apostolates no longer appear so threatening, but rather as groups to learn from. The challenge of this new emphasis is not so felt amongst those pentecostal denominations and independent Charismatic fellowships that have always argued for a continuing charismatic apostolate, but it is for apostolic succession churches and local autonomous free churches. Are there plausible ways in which they can incorporate Apostle type 2/Apostle type 3 into their church structures? To a certain degree we already see it happening through the introduction of "pioneer ministers," however, there are still factors that stifle this type of ministry within these forms of

---

54. Percy, *Clergy*, p. 8.
55. Ibid., 1–6; 179ff.

Part Three—What We Should Make of It

church as well as facets in their tradition that can inspire them to embrace the charismatic apostolate.

It is much harder for established churches where dioceses and parishes are already a part of the landscape to adopt a more pioneering edge to their work, as buildings and maintenance can limit their mission.[56] However, in Britain and elsewhere there has been a recognition by the established church that a "mixed economy"[57] is a positive way forward, that we are in dire need of advocating apostolic leaders to initiate church where the traditional parish church is unable to impact the area. It is in light of this that pioneer ministers have been trained and are being ordained as both priests and deacons. There is no pioneer bishop as yet, although the Church of England has managed to incorporate Sandy Millar as Bishop in Mission through links with the Anglican Church in Uganda.

The theology associated with apostolic succession as propounded by leading Catholic, Orthodox and Anglican theologians recognizes that an "apostolic" charism is given in ordination and therefore should be utilized and given space to flourish. This is especially the case in regard to bishops and there are aspects in the Tradition that could help facilitate more charismatic apostolates within the bishopric. First, it is important to accept the fact that the historic churches have had and do have "missionary bishops." Worldwide, particularly in Anglicanism, there are some fine examples of missionary bishops who have been actively involved in planting churches. The Anglican Church of Nigeria is to be noted for its bold missionary initiatives, combining both a high ecclesiology centered on the bishop yet rooted within Evangelicalism. The recent emergence of the Anglican Church of North America (ACNA) with their commitment to church planting, and their decision to pursue that by making the former Vineyard church planter and national leader Todd Hunter a bishop with a vision of him helping plant 200 churches is another example of how the charismatic apostolate can operate within an apostolic succession framework.

Second, in regards to the Anglican Church, it is incumbent upon the bishop to be actively involved in mission. This challenge has been spelt out

---

56. Although it is important to recall that their historic buildings can also enhance their mission, too.

57. This is a phrase used by Rowan Williams to advocate the two forms of mission—one through the traditional parish church system; the other through Fresh Expressions not necessarily linked to normal parish ministry. There have been many questions raised about the ecclesiological nature of Fresh Expressions, but nothing substantial enough to shut the whole endeavor down. As a result bishops are being given much more space to develop missionary works within their own dioceses.

Theological/Ecclesiological Critique of Popular Evangelical Conceptions

in a practical way in *Mission-Shaped Church* where it is stated that bishops should be "sufficiently free from administrative overload to be able to invest time in a more apostolic role, developing mission strategy and taking the lead in the discernment of priority mission initiatives."[58] This aspect may not be emphasized in the ordination liturgy but it is there. The Baptist Paul Campion argues from his study of the liturgy for the Church of England's ordination of a bishop that it is primarily concerned with "overseeing" functions rather than missional ones; as a result he would make a sharp distinction between the charism associated with a bishop/presbyter and an apostle. He believes that the church made an error by absorbing apostolic ministry into an episcopal mode, arguing that as a result what is assumed to be apostolic in shape is not.[59] Campion is correct in that the weight given to "overseeing" functions is more prominent than the missionary dimension, but he goes too far in not recognizing the aspects of the liturgy that point to an "apostolic" charism. The missionary dimension is there; the bishop is charged "to seek out those who are lost and lead them home with rejoicing, declaring the absolution and forgiveness of sins to those who turn to Christ"; likewise, "they are to proclaim the gospel boldly."[60] So there is room within this charge to be actively missional, as well as encouraging it in others through their role as "overseer." Even within the ordination rites of the Roman Catholic and Orthodox communions there is an emphasis on their role of proclaiming the gospel,[61] which is central to any conception of the charismatic apostolate; however, Campion's critique could be as applicable to the Roman Catholic and Orthodox vision of the bishop enshrined in their liturgy, where the focus is clearly on the function of overseeing and serving the flock rather than going out into the world. Liturgical revision in the near future would be unlikely within those two communions; however, the fact that they both treasure and laud missionary bishops highlights that they are not averse to that type of charism being manifested in the episcopal office, and they recognize the centrality of the missionary imperative which, however clouded it is in their liturgy, is still there. Therefore a refocusing on the missionary and pioneering dimensions of the apostolic charism does not undermine the historic orders of bishop, priest and deacon; there

---

58. Cray et al., *Mission-Shaped Church*, 135.
59. Campion, "Apostolic Leadership," chap. 2.
60. See Church of England, "Ordinal—Bishops."
61. See Greek Orthodox Archdiocese, "Holy Sacrament," for Greek Orthodox liturgy for ordination to the priesthood.

is only an affirmation of aspects of the apostolic gift bestowed upon the church that may not have received enough attention.

However, if these communions are to encourage the charismatic apostolate within their clergy there is a need to think afresh concerning selection of appropriate candidates. In seeking more pioneer ministers, it would be wise to see whether there is evidence of this type of vocation already. Are they visionaries? Do they have a desire to proclaim the gospel and initiate church communities? Are they already showing apostolic traits within their ministry? These types of selection criteria are actively used in other parts of the world—Michael Green writes enthusiastically about the test used by certain Indonesian denominations of whether someone has started a Christian community and grown it to thirty in discerning whether someone is called to the ordained ministry.[62] Whilst the Church of England is established and its dioceses remain intact, it is hard to imagine that the bishop will ever have opportunity to be a church planter firsthand in his role as bishop. The situation is different abroad, particularly in Africa and South East Asia where bishops have been the personal initiators of Christian communities. However, there is plenty of scope for Church of England bishops to encourage their clergys' apostolic charisms; their very facilitating of this is "apostolic" in its vision and inclination. How bishops make the most of that in light of their "apostolic" calling will inevitably vary—there could be initiatives started or encouraged by the bishop that facilitate people to start communities exploring the Christian faith, that in time culminate in them being incorporated into the Sunday worship of the parish church.

Free Churches can encourage apostolic church planters without compromising their convictions concerning the autonomy of the local church, nor capitulating to the need to have an outside leader/bishop to whom they are accountable. With this current emphasis, it is an ideal time to go with the missionary imperative, to make use of the various resources that are helping communities recognize, affirm and practically utilize the differing charisms distributed amongst God's people. However, there needs to be a fresh appreciation and affirmation of a different form of minister/ministry alongside the Pastor/teacher, as the context demands.

---

62. Green, *Tigers*, 70.

Conclusion

Although certain popular conceptions of the charismatic apostolate are dubious on Scriptural grounds and are disastrous ecumenically; there are some which work, which are biblically legitimate, traditionally acceptable and are flexible enough to work within older church structures as well as new ones. Rather than work against the church's unity there is no reason why they cannot help foster it as well as extend the church's mission. The Scriptural case for a charismatic apostolate to continue is strong enough to warrant both petitionary prayer for such a ministry, and to create space or orders within church structures that allow such ministries to function. Added to this is direct and indirect support from the church's history where there has been a consistent recognition of apostolic type ministries who have pioneered the church's mission in unchartered areas, parenting new communities. If there is such a thing as *sensus fidelium*, then surely this type of ministry has always been recognized and the challenge is to give it its due recognition. Particularly, in light of our declining churches and the need to proclaim the gospel afresh in incarnational ways, this refocus on the apostolic and apostolic ministry should be welcomed; and its knock-on effects, such as the recent push to reaffirm the missionary nature of the bishop within Church of England circles, to be encouraged.[63] However, in light of Scripture, Tradition, and our present ecumenical context, the apostolic ministry itself should always be seen with a "small a" rather than a "big A." It would be more helpful to group the Twelve and Paul as being "big A" Apostles in light of their unique role in salvation history and being the initial bearers of the "faith delivered once for all to the saints"; nevertheless, we should encourage and expect to see "apostles" being raised up by Christ for the sake of his church and his ongoing mission in our world. The church has always instinctively recognized the place of pioneer/missionary ministers—and to view them as "apostles" with a "small a" is helpful in locating their gift and calling within Scripture.

If a further re-ordering of the church leads to more mission-shaped communities and encourages fresh initiatives and church planting, then it is a positive step and should be nurtured. However, if new charismatic

---

63. There is an increasing awareness that the bishop's role should not just be about looking over the flock, but actively encouraging mission. This can be seen in *Mission-Shaped Church*, the writings of Steven Croft and Christopher Cocksworth. I have heard a number of people praise the work of Richard Chartres, Anglican Bishop of London, for his active encouragement in promoting mission and pioneering expressions of church within London.

Part Three—What We Should Make of It

apostolate enthusiasts encourage elitism, spiritual superiority and disdain for other Christian groups then it is a sad state of affairs and reminiscent of too many past movements that have not given the Christian faith a good name. From an ecclesiological perspective therefore there is nothing inherently wrong with promoting "apostolic" ministries; conversely, there is a lot wrong with stifling this much needed gift in a time where mission is a central concern of the church in a post-Christendom society. Churches which are not embracing a charismatic apostolate should do so; there needs to be openness amongst these older churches to reimagine their own orders in light of this charism making full use of the historical fact that changing eras have necessitated different-shaped ministries. There is nothing innovative in adopting this principle—the bishopric itself has always done that, as A. G. Hebert puts it: "there are great differences between the pre-Nicene bishop and the missionary monk of the Dark Ages, and the medieval prelate, and the Hanoverian grandee, and the hard-worked pastor of today, and the missionary bishop among the Pacific islands, and a Japanese bishop in his own native land."[64]

However, whether the church in Britain will continue to move forward with the idea or abandon it is another question which we will look at in our concluding chapter.

---

64. Hebert, *Apostle and Bishop*, 15.

Part Four

Where It Might Go

Summary and Conclusion

Summary

THIS STUDY HAS BEEN making sense of contemporary charismatic apostolates, giving evidence of the current situation, and showing in chapters 1 and 2, that the charismatic apostolate is on the agenda in the USA and in Britain. It is well established in the independent Charismatic and Pentecostal sector, as well as being accepted in principle if not form in denominational Charismatic circles. Renewal organizations on both sides of the Atlantic are promoting the idea, as are prominent gift courses. It was noted that overall the historic Pentecostal Church is paying more attention to this ministry, and some are using the adjective and title in a manner that is out of step with where early Pentecostalism, the Apostolic Church aside, has historically been. Within Britain the burgeoning Black Pentecostal Church is similarly advocating this ministry sometimes overtly and other times more discreetly. It is part of the DNA of independent Charismatic New Churches, and has become commonplace amongst Charismatic groups in the older churches except for the Catholics and Orthodox; yet even within these circles there is an affirmation of the phenomena associated with the charismatic apostolate. The concept is even being disseminated in other Evangelical and non-Evangelical settings within Britain through Fresh Expressions and pioneer ministry. If we were to measure significance in regards to popularity, we must concede that the charismatic apostolate is indeed noteworthy as it is very firmly on the agenda internationally[1] and becoming part of common Christian vocabulary for a great number.

---

1. For example, leading African Pentecostal scholar, Allan Anderson, told me that the "phenomenon is widespread in Africa and there is not really much controversy about it." (Allan Anderson, e-mail message to au- thor, February, 2008). Chris Ross' MA dissertation highlights that running parallel to Wagner's New Apostolic Reformation is the "Third World" New Apostolic Reformation, which has its leading

PART FOUR—Where It Might Go

As demonstrated in chapter 3 there are now detailed descriptions of what a biblical apostolic ministry looks like which are being propagated by influential Bible teachers arguing that it can be replicated today. While they differ in details they are all convinced that Ephesians 4:11–13 demands this ministry today. To them and others involved in the Pentecostal Charismatic Movement, apostleship is a vital element on the agenda for the church. Charismatic apostolates come in different guises undergirded by different theologies embraced under different titles.[2] Chapter 4 illustrated how although the church both East and West has for a long time termed saintly, pioneer missionary leaders as "Apostles" posthumously; the belief in and recognition of charismatic apostles has historically been a fringe phenomenon based upon exegesis that was seen as suspect and unorthodox by the majority.

Chapter 5 highlighted a number of different factors that have led to an openness to this idea and its increasing acceptance in quarters that in the past would not have had much time for it; there are theological/missional and societal shifts that have made the concept timely—underlying this shift has been the extraordinary growth and influence of the Pentecostal Charismatic Movement. The shifts that have occurred as a result of the Pentecostal Charismatic Movement both academically and experientially have given a grounding and justification to a concept that for most of Christian history was only held by minority pietistic groups who were unafraid to swim against the tide of the mainstream church and her formidable traditions. Today, the charismatic apostolate has been widely disseminated through popular books, gift courses, radio, TV, tapes/CDs and the internet.[3] Furthermore, even though the majority of popular advocates are not scholars, as chapter 6 shows there is a strong biblical case to be made for an ongoing charismatic apostolate.

Chapter 7 explained how some popular forms of charismatic apostolate are questionable on exegetical grounds and are detrimental in terms of ecumenism, but other forms not only can be justified biblically, but

---

proponents in Africa, Asia and Trinidad. See Ross, "Apostolic Reformation," chap. 2. Wherever Pentecostalism has gone so has a commitment to the charismatic gifts and ministries. Furthermore, in light of Barrett and Johnson's figures associated with "denominationalism" and "Post-de- nominationalism", Neo-apostolic churches are the fastest growing megabloc; see Barrett and Johnson, Trends, 302. See ibid., 296–306 for a fuller discussion of the Neo-apostolic churches and how they figure in the Independent megabloc.

2. Ibid.

3. See my research in chap. 5.

Summary and Conclusion

can be incorporated within older forms of church without doing them violence. The concept is grounded enough scripturally, theologically and missionally[4] to enable certain types of charismatic apostolate to become accepted as orthodox even outside overtly Charismatic churches. It was argued that for such an idea to really take root amongst the church catholic there needs to be sensitive engagement with well-established traditions and church orders, nevertheless, there are forms of the charismatic apostolate that are conducive to working within the structures as well as without. There remains therefore the challenge to the historic churches to be willing to incorporate such ministry into their way of being; as well as to popular advocates of the charismatic apostolate to consider ways in which they package the charism so as to both encourage and build up the wider Body of Christ.

Mapping the Future of the Charismatic Apostolate

Undoubtedly, this current fascination with the charismatic apostolate is a new "fashion" within the church, and therefore carries with it a warning sign as "faddism" has often beset the church—particularly the Charismatic branch—with promises that are not borne out in reality.[5] Yet *this* fashion may bring an important dimension to church life and ministry, however, interpreting charismatic apostolates as *the* recipe for success is foolhardy. It seems likely that talk of charismatic apostolates and promotion of differing types will not be a passing fad, but will indeed become more established within the British church. So far our three types of apostle (Apostle Type 1, "hierarchical Apostle"; Apostle Type 2, "non-foundational apostle"; Apostle Type 3, "non-select apostle") have been receiving a varied reception in many quarters of the British church; whether it will embrace them more and more is what I will be considering in this concluding section in light of all of the evidence of the preceding chapters. This is not an exact science, as the future is unknown but I think there are indicators in the present that help give an idea of what might lie ahead.

Whether the church in Britain will be filled with "charismatic apostles" will depend in part upon what forms of churchmanship will be in the ascendancy, as well as which theological and ecclesiological trends are

4. See my research in chaps. 6–7.
5. Stackhouse, *Gospel-Driven*, chap. 1.

most prominent. Will independent Charismatic churches and apostolic networks continue to grow and multiply? Will the Pentecostal Charismatic Movement continue to inspire and shape the ecclesiology of Charismatics/Evangelicals in mainstream churches? Will Fresh Expressions and pioneer ministries become fully established within the British church thereby implicitly and explicitly promoting a charismatic apostolate? Will the wider church appreciate the biblical and theological justification for a charismatic apostolate?

According to Peter Brierley's research,[6] the only two groups that are expected to continue to grow are the Orthodox and the Pentecostals.[7] Even the new churches collectively are not predicted to.[8] He paints a grim picture of overall decline in church attendance across all forms of churchmanship;[9] nevertheless, the three forms of churchmanship that easily could embrace (if they have not already) a type of charismatic apostle (Broad Evangelical, Mainstream Evangelical and Charismatic) would still remain a formidable block within British Christianity.[10] Coupled with the continued growth of Pentecostalism and more experimentation across the denominations with Fresh Expressions and pioneer ministry[11] there is plenty of ground for the seeds of a charismatic apostolate to germinate. Which types of charismatic apostleship will grow and flourish I will consider now.

Apostle Type 1 in Britain

My guess is that independent Apostle Type 1s are unlikely to find enough support to make a noticeable difference on the structures of the

---

6. Dr Peter Brierley's latest collection of research recorded in *UK Christian Handbook Religious Trends 7* has been the subject of controversy—nevertheless, it is based upon well-researched statistics. Obviously, that does not mean that his predictions will be right; nevertheless, they are not wanting for data to be based on.

7. Brierley, *Trends 7*, 2.13, fig. 2.13.4.

8. Ibid. In an e-mail exchange, Peter Brierley told me that this had partly been to do with a number of church splits that have occurred in that sector. (Peter Brierley, e-mail message to author, August 21, 2009). Brierley also highlighted that the two new church groups that were noticeably bucking this trend and growing were Vineyard and Newfrontiers International.

9. Ibid., 12.2ff.

10. Brierley, *Trends 7*, 2.13, fig. 2.13.5.

11. The biggest issue for both these is funding; that in large measure may determine its longevity. Will the churches get behind it monetarily or not?

Evangelical/Charismatic side of the church in Britain. One only has to see the makeup of New Wine and Soul Survivor to recognize that there are many Charismatics who are at home within their denomination and have no desire to break away from them—certainly not because a Charismatic "outsider" is inviting them to. Therefore I think it unlikely that Peter Wagner's International Coalition of Apostles will ever take off in Britain[12] in the manner that it has in the USA. The Lakeland "revival" that ended in widespread disappointment due to the antics of the evangelist Todd Bentley has tarnished that particular stream as some of the leading "apostles" actively endorsed both Bentley and the "revival."[13] Furthermore, the fact that many of the older churches are specifically trying to make room for pioneer ministers, makes it less incumbent upon people so gifted to seek out alternative independent Charismatic churches which affirm their "calling." The widespread acceptance of the term "pioneer minister" gives good ground for thinking that the older denominations will be increasingly accepting and promoting the gift of apostle but not necessarily using that terminology. The emphasis will be on the function and not the office. Significantly, many of the Charismatic hubs in this country—St Thomas Crookes, St Andrews Chorleywood, Holy Trinity Brompton, New Wine, Soul Survivor, Spring Harvest—are integrally related to the older churches as well as resourcing newer ones, and do not advocate abandoning the historic churches or see themselves as providing authoritative oversight of churches. This is not to say that the big "apostle" will no longer find room in the British church—he/she undoubtedly will; there is no indication that New Wine and other influential networks will stop inviting "revival" leaders such as John Arnott and Bill Johnson to their conferences. Their teaching will continue to be influential too through the internet, radio, satellite TV as well as books. The day of the superstar is still very much amongst us and there is no sign that our obsession with spiritual "celebrities" is slowing down; yet the appeal of these characters is limited to Charismatic churches; whereas the *Mission-Shaped Church* and its offshoot, "pioneer ministers," have managed to win the confidence of Christians from diverse backgrounds and traditions.

---

12. From an interview I conducted I am aware of a well-known British Charismatic leader who was approached to be the leader of the European branch. He refused, and told Wagner that it would not work in Europe.

13. The list of those who came and supported Lakeland appears like a "who's who" in the independent Charismatic world: John Arnott, John Kilpatrick, Paul Cain, Bob Jones, Rick Joyner, Randy Clarke, Peter Wagner, Bill Johnson, Ché Ahn, and Stacey Campbell.

PART FOUR—Where It Might Go

In spite of Brierley's predictions of decline I think it likely that new independent "apostolic networks" will be initiated due to positive precedents set by others, the need for mission and the ease of receiving support via Charismatic hubs or conferences. Many of the existing ones will continue to exert influence—although, undoubtedly some of them will crumble as others have done before them. With all the networks that Kay studied it is relatively early days; even though some of the "apostolic networks" are now entering into their second generation it remains to be seen whether the "successful" networks will be able to survive the transition. Interestingly those groups that are doing this seem to be undergoing the usual change into a more ossified institutional structure. For example, it is hard not to see both Newfrontiers International and Kingdom Faith[14] as anything but new denominations—something that both groups have tried not to become. A further proliferation of independent Charismatic churches is likely as they are more flexible and can use financial resources more efficiently to further church growth rather than being funneled away into expensive maintenance. Nevertheless, smaller independent Charismatic churches may well find it necessary, in order to gain support and become more established, to link themselves into a wider network.[15] The phenomenal growth of the black Pentecostal Church shows no signs of abating, and therefore I think it very likely that within some of those networks we will encounter Apostle Type 1s.

Therefore, there will be areas in which Apostle Type 1s will thrive and continue to exert influence. This will be the case in independent apostolic networks, some black Pentecostal branches and attenders of overt Charismatic conferences which invite in the apostolic "super-stars." Nevertheless many of the apostolic networks will struggle to make the transition to the next generation and likely fragment and disband. Wagner's International Coalition of Apostles will not take off except within some fringe groups, and most of the denominational churches will stay rooted within their structures and not look to alternative "bishoprics" amongst the apostles.

---

14. Colin Urquhart insists that this has not happened with Kingdom Faith, as it has resisted attempts to solidify the structure binding the Kingdom Faith churches together. Each one is still very much autonomous, and Colin Urquhart does not hire or fire individual leaders. (Colin Urquhart, interview with author, May 13, 2009). Nevertheless, it is still an alternative church network, which to my mind therefore constitutes a denomination—even if it is not as tightly bound as others.

15. It was Professor Synan who got me thinking along these lines as it was his judgment that this was very much happening in the USA. Vinson Synan, telephone conversation with author, December 15, 2009.

Summary and Conclusion

Apostle Types 2 and 3 in Britain

The equation made by *Mission-Shaped Church* between a "church planter" and the gift of apostle mentioned in Ephesians 4:11–13 typifies a general trend that accepts a charismatic apostolate within traditional structures without doing violence to the inherited orders. This document has been widely read and has helped refashion the terrain for mission in a variety of contexts.[16] The Church of England has clearly endorsed this form of ministry and is seeking to resource and train church planters. They are not alone, the Methodists, the United Reformed Church and others have climbed on board by actively embracing "Fresh Expressions," and training up "pioneer" leaders. Older denominations are very aware that churches are closing in Britain, and that church planting and Fresh Expressions are vital if the church is going to infiltrate this country again with the gospel. With such support behind them these Apostle Type 2s will find it easier to flourish particularly as the nomenclature of apostle does not tend to be important in the circles that buy into this form of leader, nor is there a threat to received authorities within the church structures. For these reasons, unless the funds dry up to support these initiatives, I predict that this type of "apostle"[17] will become an even more accepted part of the church landscape.

I see no slowing down amongst Evangelical/Charismatic churches in their use of gift courses due to the commitment to mobilize the laity, which in turn will continue to popularize Apostle Type 2 and Apostle Type 3 apostles, making "apostle/apostolic" language more commonplace amongst churches. There will be inevitable differences on the basis of personality and theological conviction on the level of authority attributed to the apostle, and there will likely be overlap with Type 1 Apostles through adopting similar styles of ministry. Conservative Evangelical churches will remain wary of talk about "apostles," but will continue to advocate missionaries and church planters. Due to its breadth the Anglican Church will accommodate these types of ministries in various forms. The Orthodox

---

16. In 2008 the report had sold over 25,000 copies. Its influence being felt across the UK in a variety of denominations as well as in "northern Europe, North America, Australia and New Zealand." See Croft, "Persuading Gamaliel," 36.

17. I asked Dave Male—who has led a Fresh Expression as a pioneer minister and now trains pioneer ministers at Ridley Hall and Westcott House, Cambridge—whether he thought Fresh Expressions and the Church of England were in essence advocating a "charismatic apostolate" through promoting "pioneer ministers"—to which he replied, "basically, yes." Dave Male, e-mail message to author, May 18, 2009.

PART FOUR—Where It Might Go

and Catholic Churches in Britain will find it hard to incorporate a charismatic apostolate into their way of being. It is unlikely that the language of charismatic apostles will ever take off in Catholic Charismatic circles for the reasons that Charles Whitehead outlined;[18] the same can be said for the Orthodox. However, it also seems likely, given the Roman Catholic Church's past history in making room for new movements[19] that they will continue to give space to "apostolic" gifts yet call them by a different name. With the establishment of the Antiochian Church within the Orthodox Church which has had a number of Evangelical/Charismatic converts such as Michael Harper and Peter Gillquist, the push for mission has become more prevalent; obviously there is no talk of a charismatic apostolate, however, with a renewed missionary focus maybe we will see more pioneering Orthodox bishops in Britain, or bishops who actively support missionary initiatives on these shores.

It appears that most prominent independent Charismatic churches tend toward more hierarchical Apostle Type 1 figures; however, there are some that try and avoid this. Arguably, Roger Forster's Ichthus with its low-level doctrine of apostleship, where the emphasis is on function, would be an example. However, how long that movement and others associated with it will last is questionable due to the splits that have occurred within it.[20] Another form of church that will continue to advocate Apostle Type 2s is the so-called "organic house church" movement based upon the writings of Viola[21]/ Edwards and Nee. I think it unlikely that it will become very widespread, but it is a stream to be aware of that joins into the river of charismatic apostolate propagators.

---

18. See chap. 2.

19. Consider the way in which the Roman Catholic Church made room for the Franciscans, or more recently the L'Arche communities or Cor Lumen Christi amongst many others.

20. Significantly I have a friend who was very involved in Ichthus during the schism, and although grateful for his time within that movement decided to go for Anglican ordination rather than lead an Ichthus church due in part with the fact that he could not envisage a long-term future for it.

21. I have observed the rising interest in Viola and his works and have encountered a number of web discussions amongst people who have been disappointed with the institutional church linking to him and his writings. .

Summary and Conclusion

A Final Word

In summary, the charismatic apostolate is becoming a feature of the church scene in Britain; this will not be a short-lived fad, but rather something that will remain commonplace in the independent churches and become more so in the older mainstream ones. The desire for mission, for a new shape of leader, for more organic expressions of church life will make it inconceivable that the charismatic apostolate in its various guises will disappear from the scene. In Britain the metamorphism from a less missional church to a more apostolic one is happening and as a part of that the charismatic apostolate is integral. The way in which it makes this transition is fraught with difficulties as churches work through the ecclesiological, theological and ecumenical implications of incorporating types of charismatic apostolate into their way of being, but the need within the declining Western church is plain for all to see. This study has shown the biblical and theological grounds for a charismatic apostolate is robust enough to facilitate and encourage forms of it, but for it to be carried forward in a helpful manner the ecumenical dimension should be taken into account.

Although this study has done much to locate, describe, make sense of and appraise modern popular charismatic apostolates, it has only scratched the surface of an idea that needs to be looked at in even greater depth from a global perspective. The numerous forms of charismatic apostolate that are central to the indigenous African and Asian churches which are growing at a phenomenal rate are needed to balance out this Western picture and conceptions that I have depicted. Much more needs to be done on the subject of the charismatic apostolate, more in-depth research needed, strengthening (or weakening) the cords and threads that have formed this study, focusing in on topics that I have only looked at superficially and generally—specialized studies looking at the genesis and development of gift identification courses; the on-the-ground effects on congregations of incorporating different types of charismatic apostolates. Or historical studies looking at how the Church of England embraced the charismatic apostolate in the form of pioneer ministry, or how Baptist Mainstream developed their overt acceptance of the charismatic apostolate and how the ministry structure has been shifting within that denomination in relation to charismatic apostolates. This study has the opportunity to be a springboard for numerous research projects in relation to both theology and history.

Part Four—Where It Might Go

In spite of vast chasms of knowledge that need to be explored and unearthed this study has provided enough to make the case that contemporary charismatic apostolates in their diverse forms are here to stay. It is an often idealized form of ministry that has been increasingly embraced by all churches that have been impacted by the Pentecostal Charismatic Movement, as well as indirectly sparking other initiatives not directly involved with the Pentecostal Charismatic Movement. This new "ministry" stands tenuously on the shoulders of controversial movements; however, charismatic apostolate depictions have been increasingly honed in light of Scripture and history to make them acceptable to large segments of the church. Although there is a multiplicity of interpretations surrounding this ministry, an important charism has been brought to the fore, one that has a rooting within Scripture and one that is timely and needed in the West, particularly in Britain. The factors that have caused this gift to come to the surface and be focused on are several, but the widespread appeal and impact of the Pentecostal Charismatic Movement is central. Popular Charismatic depictions of this gift range from being insightful, ecumenical and Scriptural, to fantastical and contentious. Yet there is enough Biblical and theological support for the concept to have a lasting future within the church in Britain, both mainstream and non. The case has been made, the need is clear, the question remains will churches in Britain continue to commit to investing in this form of ministry or not. Will we fan into flame the gift of God, or quench the apostolic Spirit?

> While they were worshipping the Lord and fasting, the Holy Spirit said, "Set apart for me Barnabas and Saul for the work to which I have called them." Then after fasting and praying they laid their hands on them and sent them off. Acts 13:2–3 NRSV

> For there is no distinction between Jew and Greek; the same Lord is Lord of all and is generous to all who call on him. For, "Everyone who calls on the name of the Lord shall be saved." But how are they to call on one in whom they have not believed? And how are they to believe in one of whom they have never heard? And how are they to hear without someone to proclaim him? And how are they to proclaim him unless they are sent? As it is written, "How beautiful are the feet of those who bring good news!" Romans 10:12–15 NRSV

Glossary

Apostle type 1. "Hierarchical/supreme apostles" advocated by Wagner, Virgo, and Prince. Their primary Scripture for justifying an ongoing CA is Ephesians 4:11–13. These are more prominent in New Apostolic Reformation (NAR) churches and Apostolic Networks, and are part of the DNA of the Apostolic Church's view of apostles. Many of them look to the following Scriptures to assert the supremacy of the apostle in all church matters: 1 Corinthians 12:28 and Ephesians 2:20. Their authority can be exercised in relation to those that they have founded and even amongst those they have not (if so invited). Their authority is capable of being on a par with the apostolic authority seen in the Twelve and Paul in their dealings with the church—not in relation to their capacity to issue Scripture.

Apostle type 2. This is a "non-foundational apostle" who is under the authority of the local pastor. Advocates of this position are Hagin, Gee, Lindsay, Synan; it would be the default position of most Assemblies of God (exception being Assemblies of God Australia) and Elim churches. Their primary Scripture for justifying an ongoing CA is Ephesians 4:11–13. Current apostles are still part of the five-fold elite and therefore clearly separated from the non-five-fold "laity," but they are to be subservient to the Presbyter/elder/pastor of a church that they are ministering in.

Apostle type 3. This is the "non-select" form, in that, along with the other four ministry gifts they are not reserved for a select group; every member of the church is either an apostle, prophet, pastor, teacher or evangelist. Breen, Frost, Hirsch and Hopkins advocate this view. The primary Scripture for justifying an ongoing CA is Ephesians 4:11–13. The apostle is an equal partner with the other ministries; there are times when his/her leadership gifts should be heeded by others for the sake of mission but there is no assertion that the apostle is the "top dog" due to his gifting.

Charismatic apostolate. This is not necessarily used by popular writers who often refer to them simply as "apostles"; nevertheless, the assumption underlining all of the contemporary charismatic/evangelical accounts of modern apostles is that these are Spirit-empowered ministers of the ascended Christ whose vocation and ministry has its origin in God and who are wholly reliant upon the strengthening of the Holy Spirit to do what they are called to do. This charismatic "gift"/"ministry"/"office" of apostle that some are called to is not in popular charismatic conceptions to be equated with ordained ministry. This calling and ministry can coincide with an official church position—such as bishop, priest, deacon, elder, superintendent, and so on—but the tying of the "gift" to a church position is rejected. The evidence of what the person does is likely to indicate whether they are a charismatic apostle, not their title or position in a church.

Cessationism. The belief that certain spiritual gifts and ministries have ceased from being active in the church as they are no longer needed in light of the completion of the canon.

Dominionism. The belief that the church will rule over all things prior to the second coming of Christ.

Ecclesiology. The doctrine concerning the church.

"Five-fold ministry." This is a reference to the list of gifts given by the ascended Christ in Ephesians 4:11–13: "apostles, prophets, evangelists, pastors and teachers."

"Four-fold ministry." This is related to the same passage but thinks of "pastors and teachers" as being one ministry/gift/person.

New Apostolic Reformation (NAR). Term coined by Peter Wagner to describe a trend that he believes can be seen since the 1990s of new types of churches/networks that are headed up by apostles.

Renewalism. The belief that God wishes to renew congregations and individuals by spiritually enduing them with the Holy Spirit and His various gifts without necessarily destroying historic structures and denominations.

Restorationism. The belief that during church history the church has fallen away from God-given truths in the New Testament and that God has been, is and will continue to restore the church to the divine pattern until it reaches perfection.

Bibliography

Abraham, W. J. *The Logic of Renewal*. London: SPCK, 2003.
Adogame, A. "Germany." In *The New International Dictionary of Pentecostal and Charismatic Movements*, rev. ed., edited by S. M. Burgess, 109–11. Grand Rapids: Zondervan, 2002.
Aldersgate Renewal Ministries. "History of Aldersgate Renewal Ministries," accessed October 27, 2010, http://www.aldersgaterenewal.org/who-we-are/history.
Allen, R. *Missionary Methods. St Paul's or Ours?* Cambridge: Lutterworth, 2006.
———. *The Spontaneous Expansion of the Church and the Causes which Hinder It*. Cambridge: Lutterworth, 2006.
Alliance of Renewal Churches. "About Alliance of Renewal Churches," accessed October 27, 2010, http://www.allianceofrenewalchurches.org/About/dna.html.
———. "History of Alliance of Renewal churches," accessed October 27, 2010, http://www.allianceofrenewalchurches.org/About/About/history.html.
Anderson, A. *An Introduction to Pentecostalism: Global Charismatic Christianity*. Cambridge: Cambridge University Press, 2004.
Anderson, P. "To Stay or To Leave," accessed November 9, 2010, http://www.lutheranrenewal.org.
Anglican Church in North America. "The 1,000 Churches Proclamation," accessed November 12, 2010, http://anglican1000.org/media/Proclamation2.pdf.
———. "ACNA—What We Stand For," accessed November 22, 2010, http://acnaassembly.org/media/ACNA_-_What_we_stand_for_-_June_09_-_fact_sheet.pdf.
Anglican 1000. "Anglican 1000," accessed November 12, 2010, http://anglican1000.org.
———. "Anglican 1,000—Who We Are," accessed November 12, 2010, http://anglican1000.org/?/main/who_we_are.
Ankerberg, J., and J. Weldon. *Encyclopaedia of Cults and New Religions*. Eugene, OR: Harvest House, 1999.
Anonymous. "Basic Stott," accessed December 9, 2010, http://www.christianitytoday.com/ct/2003/septemberweb-only/9-1-51.0.html?start=6.
———. "Britain's Largest Black Churches." *The Voice*, 2005.
———. *Didache*. Translated by Roberts and Donaldson. Accessed October 27, 2010, http://earlychristianwritings.com/text/didache-roberts.html.
———. "Gene Edwards," accessed December 8, 2010, http://www.tyndale.com/authors/authorbio.asp?id=184.
———. "Joining Forces, Blazing Trails: An Interview with Peter Wagner." *Renewal* 290 (2000) 30–32.
———. *The Life of the Great Martyr Thecla of Iconium, Equal to the Apostles, as Recorded in the Acts of Paul*, n.d. Translated by Jeremiah Jones? http://gbgm-umc.org/umw/corinthians/thecla.stm.
———. "Ministries Today Update for March 2004," accessed October 27, 2010, http://www.cephas-library.com/assembly_of_god/assembly_of_god_orlando_statement.html.
The Apostolic Church UK. "The Constitution of the Apostolic Church UK." In *Pentecostal and Charismatic Studies: A Reader*, edited by W. K. Kay, and A. E. Dyer, 168–70. London: SCM, 2004.

Bibliography

Armstrong. *Armstrong Tracts 1831–54*. London, n.d.
Arsenal Books. "Books—Apostolic," accessed October 27, 2010, http://arsenalbooks.com/category/Apostolic.
Ashworth, J., and I. Farthing, *Churchgoing in the UK*. Teddington, UK: Tearfund, 2007.
Assemblies of God UK. "Meet the Leaders," accessed October 27, 2010, http://www.aog.org.uk/pages/16-meet-the-leaders/content.
———. "Statement of Faith," accessed October 27, 2010, http://www.aog.org.uk/pages/17-statement-of-faith/content.
Athanasius. *Life of St Anthony*, n.d. http://www.fordham.edu/halsall/basis/VITA-ANTONY.html.
Bales, J. D. *Apostles or Apostates: Have the Latter Day Saints Perverted the New Testament Teachings concerning Apostles of Christ?* Whitefish, MT: Kessinger, 2004.
Barrett, C. K. *The Signs of an Apostle*. Carlisle, UK: Paternoster, 1996.
Barrett, D., and T. Johnson. *World Christian Trends AD 30–AD 2200: Interpreting the Annual Christian Megacensus*. Pasadena, CA: William Carey Library, 2001.
Barrett, D., et al. *World Christian Encyclopedia*. New York: Oxford University Press, 2001.
Barth, M. *Ephesians. Translation and Commentary on Chapters 1–3*. New York: Doubleday, 1974.
———. *Ephesians. Translation and Commentary on Chapters 4–6*. New York: Doubleday, 1974.
Bartlett, A. *A Passionate Balance. The Anglican Tradition*. London: Darton, Longman & Todd, 2007.
Battle, J. A. "Charles Hodge, Inspiration, Textual Criticism, and the Princeton Doctrine of Scripture." *Western Reformed Seminary Journal* 4.2 (1997) 28–41.
Beckwith, R. *Elders in Every City: The Origin and Role of the Ordained Ministry*. Carlisle, UK: Paternoster, 2003.
Beeson, T. "Liberating Leaders for Mission." In *Setting the Church of England Free*, edited by M. Mills-Powell, 226–31. Alresford, UK: Hunt, 2003.
Berkhof, L. *Systematic Theology*. Edinburgh: Banner of Truth, 1958.
Best, E. *Ephesians: A Shorter Commentary*. Edinburgh: T. & T. Clark, 2003.
Bicknell, E. J. *A Theological Introduction to the Thirty-Nine Articles of the Church of England*. London: Longmans, Green and Co., 1936.
Blackhouse, R. *The Classics on Revival. An Anthology of Classic Writings on the Holy Spirit and Renewal*. London: Hodder & Stoughton, 1996.
Blake, C. E. "A Centennial Proclamation—An Apostolic Missive," accessed October 27, 2010, http://www.cogic.com/pdfs/apostolic-missive-I.pdf.
Blake, W. "Alexander Campbell, Apostle of Truth," accessed December 8, 2010, www.dabar.org/SemReview/Volume06/issue1/V6I1A2.htm.
Blomgren, D. K. *Prophetic Gatherings in the Church: The Laying on of Hands and Prophecy*. Portland, OR: Bible Temple, 1979.
Blumhofer, E. L., and C. R. Armstrong. "Assemblies of God." In *The New International Dictionary of Pentecostal and Charismatic Movements*, rev. ed., edited by S. M. Burgess, 333–40. Grand Rapids: Zondervan, 2002.
Booth, R. "Religion: Praise the Lord and Pass the Business Plan as God Embraces Mammon." *The Guardian*, August 29, 2008. http://www.guardian.co.uk/world/2008/aug/29/religion

Bibliography

Bosch, D. J. *Transforming Mission: Paradigm Shifts in Theology of Mission*. New York: Orbis, 2000.

Bouyer, L "Bishops in the Church: The Catholic Tradition." In *Bishops: But What Kind? Reflections on Episcopacy*, edited by P. Moore, 25–40. London: SPCK, 1982.

Braaten, C. E. *Mother Church: Ecclesiology and Ecumenism*. Minneapolis, MN: Fortress, 1998.

Bradshaw, T. *The Olive Branch. An Evangelical Anglican Doctrine of the Church*. Carlisle, UK: Paternoster, 1992.

Bray, G., editor. *1–2 Corinthians*. Ancient Christian Commentary on Scripture, New Testament 7. London: Dearborn, 1999.

———. *Romans*. Ancient Christian Commentary on Scripture, New Testament 6. London: Dearborn, 1998.

Breen, M. *The Apostle's Notebook*. Eastbourne, UK: Kingsway, 2002.

Breen, M., and W. Kallestad. *The Passionate Church*. Eastbourne, UK: Kingsway, 2005.

———. *A Passionate Life*. Eastbourne, UK: Kingsway, 2005.

———. *A Passionate Life Workbook*. Eastbourne, UK: Kingsway, 2005.

Bridge, D., and D. Phypers. *Spiritual Gifts and the Church*. London: InterVarsity, 1973.

Brierley, P. *UK Christian Handbook, Religious Trends 7—2007/2008: British Religion in the 21st Century; What the Statistics Indicate*. Swindon, UK: Christian Research, 2008.

Brotherhood of St. Symeon the New Theologian. "Brotherhood of St. Symeon the New Theologian," accessed October 27, 2010, http://www.stsymeon.org.

Brown, C. "Note on Apostleship in Luke-Acts." In *New International Dictionary of New Testament Theology*, edited by C. Brown, 1:135–36. Carlisle, UK: Paternoster, 1986.

Brown, J. "Divisions in Eastern Orthodoxy Today." *East-West Church & Ministry Report* 5.2 (1997). http://www.eastwestreport.org/articles/ew05201.htm.

Brown, R. "Latter-day Saints/Don't Understand," accessed May 6, 2011, http://en.allexperts.com/q/Latter-day-Saints-958/Dont-understand.htm.

Bruce, F. F. *1 and 2 Corinthians*. London: Marshall, Morgan and Scott, 1984.

———. *The Epistles to the Colossians, to Philemon, and to the Ephesians*. Grand Rapids: Eerdmans, 1984.

Bryman, A. *Social Research Methods*. Oxford: Oxford University Press, 2004.

Buchanan, C. *Is the Church of England Biblical?* London: Darton, Longman & Todd, 1998.

Bugbee, B. *What You Do Best in the Body of Christ: Discover Your Spiritual Gifts, Personal Style, and God-given Passion*. Grand Rapids: Zondervan, 1995.

Bugbee, B., D. Cousins, et al. *Network Participant's Guide*. Rev. ed. Grand Rapids: Zondervan, 2005.

Bundy, D. D. "Irving, Edward." In *The New International Dictionary of Pentecostal and Charismatic Movements*, rev. ed., edited by S. M. Burgess, 803–4. Grand Rapids: Zondervan, 2002.

———. "United Methodist Charismatics." In *The New International Dictionary of Pentecostal and Charismatic Movements*, rev. ed., edited by S. M. Burgess, 1158–60. Grand Rapids: Zondervan, 2002.

Burgess, S. M. *The Holy Spirit: Eastern Christian Traditions*. Peabody, MA: Hendrickson, 2000.

Bibliography

———. "Holy Spirit, Doctrine of: The Medieval Churches." In *The New International Dictionary of Pentecostal and Charismatic Movements*, rev. ed., edited by S. M. Burgess, 747. Grand Rapids: Zondervan, 2002.

———. "Stephanou, Eusebius A." In *The New International Dictionary of Pentecostal and Charismatic Movements*, rev. ed., edited by S. M. Burgess, 1106-7. Grand Rapids: Zondervan, 2002.

Burkhard, J. J. *Apostolicity Then and Now. An Ecumenical Church in a Postmodern World*. Collegeville, MN: Liturgical, 2004.

Butte College. "Deductive, Inductive and Abductive Reasoning," accessed December 1, 2011, http://www.butte.edu/departments/cas/tipsheets/thinking/reasoning.html.

Buttner, C. "The Latter Rain Movement." In *Encyclopedia of American Religions*, edited by G. J. Melton, 84. Detroit: Gale Research, 1996.

Calvin. J. *Commentary on Corinthians*, Vol. 2. http://www.ccel.org/ccel/calvin/calcom40.i.i.html.

———. *Commentary on Galatians and Ephesians*. http://www.ccel.org/ccel/calvin/calcom41.iv.v.iii.html.

Cameron, E. *Waldenses. Rejections of Holy Church in Medieval Europe*. Oxford: Blackwell, 2000.

Campbell, A. *The Christian System*, 1956. http://www.piney.com/AcCSMinistry.html.

Campion, P. H. F. "Apostolic Leadership in Contemporary Baptist Ministry." MTh diss., Spurgeon's College, London, 2008.

Capper, B. J. "Order and Ministry in the Social Pattern of the New Testament Church." In *Order and Ministry*, edited by C. Hall, and R. Hannaford, 61-103. Leominster, UK: Gracewing, 1996.

Cartledge, D. *The Apostolic Revolution: The Restoration of Apostles and Prophets in the Assemblies of God in Australia*. Chester Hill, Australia: Paraclete Institute, 2000.

The Catholic Apostolic Church. *The Catechism of the Catholic Apostolic Church*, n.d. http://www.apostolic.de/eng/files/doc/b-027.pdf.

Christenson, L. *A Message to the Charismatic Movement*. Minneapolis, MN: Dimension, 1972.

Christenson, L., and P. Anderson. "Lutheran Charismatics." In *The New International Dictionary of Pentecostal and Charismatic Movements*, rev. ed., edited by S. M. Burgess, 847–51. Grand Rapids: Zondervan, 2002.

Christian Church (Disciples of Christ) in the United States and Canada. "The Design of the Christian Church (Disciples of Christ)," accessed December 8, 2010, http://www.disciples.org/AboutTheDisciples/TheDesignoftheChristianChurch/tabid/228/Default.aspx.

Christian, J. T. *A History of the Baptists*. Sunday School Board of the Southern Baptist Convention, 1922. http://www.pbministries.org/History/John%20T.%20Christian/vol1/history_19.htm.

Church of England. "Ordinal—Bishops," accessed July 21, 2011, http://www.churchofengland.org/prayer-worship/worship/texts/ordinal/bishops.aspx.

The Church of Jesus Christ of Latter Day Saints. *Doctrine and Covenants*, n.d. http://lds.org/scriptures/dc-testament?lang=eng.

Clark, A. C. "Apostleship: Evidence from the New Testament and Early Christian Literature." *Vox Evangelica* 19 (1989) 49–82.

Clendenin, D. "The Journey with Jesus: Book Notes," accessed July 20, 2012, http://www.journeywithjesus.net/BookNotes/Alister_McGrath_Christianitys_Dangerous_Idea.shtml.

Bibliography

Clifton, S. J. "An Analysis of the Developing Ecclesiology of the Assemblies of God in Australia." PhD diss., Australian Catholic University, 2005.
Cloud, D. "Charismatic Southern Baptists," accessed July 27, 2012, http://www.wayoflife.org/index_files/category-charismatic-movement.html.
Coates, G. "Growing in the Spirit." *Library of Lives* 13 (2008) 6–9.
Cocksworth, C. *Holding Together: Gospel, Church and Spirit—The Essentials of Christian Identity*. London: Canterbury, 2008.
Cohn, N. *The Pursuit of the Millennium. Revolutionary Millenarians and Mystical Anarchists of the Middle Ages*, 1970. http://watch.pair.com/anabaptist.html.
Conn, C. W. "Church of God (Cleveland, TN)." In *The New International Dictionary of Pentecostal and Charismatic Movements*, rev. ed., edited by S. M. Burgess, 530–34. Grand Rapids: Zondervan, 2002.
Cooke, B. *Ministry to Word and Sacraments: History and Theology*. Philadelphia, PA: Fortress, 1980.
Cottrell, S. *From the Abundance of the Heart: Catholic Evangelism for all Christians* London: Darton, Longman & Todd, 2006.
Cray, G., et al. *Mission-Shaped Church: Church Planting and Fresh Expressions of Church in a Changing Context*. London: Church House, 2004.
Croft, S. *Ministry in Three Dimensions. Ordination and Leadership in the Local Church*. London: Darton, Longman & Todd, 2008.
———. "Persuading Gamaliel: Helping the Anglo-Catholic Tradition Engage with Fresh Expressions of Church." In *Fresh Expressions in the Sacramental Tradition*, edited by S. Croft, and I. Mobsby, 36–51. Norwich: Canterbury, 2009.
Damazio, F. *Seasons of Revival: Understanding the Appointed Times of Spiritual Refreshing*. Portland, OR: BT, 1996.
Department in the Laity. "Christ's Ministry through His Whole Church and Its Ministers." In *Theological Foundations for Ministry*, edited by R. S. Anderson, 430–57. Edinburgh: T. & T. Clark, 1979.
Derek Prince Ministries. "Derek Prince Ministries," accessed October 27, 2010, http://www.derekprince.com.
Derek Prince Ministries UK. "About Derek Prince," accessed July 27, 2012, http://www.dpmuk.org/Groups/10379/DPM/Derek_Prince/Derek_Prince.aspx.
———. "Derek Prince Ministries UK," accessed July 27, http://dpmuk.org.
DeWaay, B. "The Roots and Fruits of the New Apostolic Reformation," accessed November 17, 2011, http://www.ukapologetics.net/10/1NAR.htm.
Diocese of Ely. "All Good Gifts around Us: Ministry Strategy for the Diocese of Ely." Ely, UK: Church of England, 2002.
Dobb, K. *The Blackwell Guide to Theology and Popular Culture*. Oxford: Blackwell, 2005.
Dorries, D. W. "Catholic Apostolic Church." In *The New International Dictionary of Pentecostal and Charismatic Movements*, rev. ed., edited by S. M. Burgess, 459–60. Grand Rapids: Zondervan, 2002.
Douglas, A., et al. "Concluding Statements." In *Are Miraculous Gifts for Today? Four Views*, edited by W. Grudem, 309–40. Leicester, UK: InterVarsity, 1996.
Dowse, J. "Monksthorpe Baptist Church," accessed December 8, 2010, http://homepage.ntlworld.com/bh.keyworth/History.htm.
Dunn, J. D. G. "Ephesians." In *The Oxford Bible Commentary*, edited by J. Barton, and J. Muddiman, 1165–79. Oxford: Oxford University Press, 2000.
———. *The Theology of the Apostle Paul*. Edinburgh: T. & T. Clark, 1998.

Bibliography

———. *Unity and Diversity in the New Testament. An Inquiry into the Character of Earliest Christianity.* 2nd ed. London: SCM, 1991.

DuPree, S. S. "Church of God in Christ." In *The New International Dictionary of Pentecostal and Charismatic Movements*, rev. ed., edited by S. M. Burgess, 535–37. Grand Rapids: Zondervan, 2002.

Dye, C. "What is Apostolic Leadership?" Accessed October 27, 2010, http://www.revivaltimes.org/index.php?aid=379.

Eaton, M. *Enjoying God's Worldwide Church: The Biblical Doctrine of the "Universal Church."* N.p.: OM, 1998.

Eberle, H. R. *The Complete Wineskin: Restructuring the Church for the Outpouring of the Holy Spirit.* Tunbridge Wells, UK: International Media for Ministry, 1998.

Edwards, D. L. *Christianity: The First Two Thousand Years.* London: Cassell, 1997.

Edwards, M. J., editor. *Galatians, Ephesians, Philippians.* Ancient Christian Commentary on Scripture, New Testament 8. London: Dearborn, 1999.

Ehrhardt, A. *The Apostolic Succession.* London: Lutterworth, 1953.

Ekklesia. "News Brief," accessed December 15, 2010, http://www.ekklesia.co.uk/node/10860.

Ekman, U. *The Apostolic Ministry.* Uppsala: Word of Life, 2002.

Elim UK. "What We Believe," accessed October 27, 2010, http://www.elim.org.uk/Groups/112249/What_we_believe.aspx.

England, E., et al. "The House Church Question." *Renewal* 120 (1985–86) 4–10.

Eusebius. *The History of the Church from Christ to Constantine.* Translated by G. A. Williamson. Harmondsworth, UK: Penguin, 1965.

Evangelical Alliance UK. "Evangelical Alliance Church Search," accessed November 3, 2011, http://www.eauk.org/churchsearch/index.cfm.

Fee, G. *The First Epistle to the Corinthians.* Grand Rapids: Eerdmans, 1987.

———. *God's Empowering Presence: The Holy Spirit in the Letters of Paul.* Peabody, MA: Hendrickson, 1994.

Flegg, C. G. *"Gathered under Apostles": A Study of the Catholic Apostolic Church.* Oxford: Clarendon, 1992.

Forster, R. "What is an Evangelical?" Accessed November 17, 2011, http://www.ichthus.org.uk/Articles/105523/Home/Free_Resources/Articles/What_is_an.aspx.

Fresh Expressions. "Big Night for Fresh Expressions," accessed September 24, 2010, http://www.freshexpressions.org.uk/news/media-big-night-fresh-expressions.

Fresh Streams. "How Fresh Streams was launched," accessed August 9, 2013, http://www.freshstreams.net/about-us/fresh-streams-is-launched/.

Frost, M., and A. Hirsch. *The Shaping of Things to Come: Innovation and Mission for the 21st-Century Church.* Peabody, MA: Hendrickson, 2004.

Gaffin Jr, R. B. "A Cessationist View." In *Are Miraculous Gifts for Today? Four Views*, edited by W. Grudem, 25–64. Leicester, UK: InterVarsity, 1996.

Garner, M. *A Call for Apostles Today.* Cambridge: Grove, 2007.

Gee, D. *Wind and Flame.* Croydon, UK: Assemblies of God, 1967.

Gelder, C. V. *The Essence of the Church: A Community Created by the Spirit.* Grand Rapids: Baker, 2000.

General Presbytery of the Assemblies of God. "Apostles and Prophets," accessed July 27, 2012, http://ag.org/top/beliefs/position_papers/pp_downloads/pp_4195_apostles_prophets.pdf.

Bibliography

Gibbs, E. *Church Next: Quantum Changes in How We Do Ministry*. Downers Grove, IL: InterVarsity, 2000.

———. *Leadership Next: Changing Leaders in a Changing Culture*. Leicester, UK: InterVarsity, 2005.

Gibbs, E., and R. K. Bolger. *Emerging Churches: Creating Christian Community in Postmodern Cultures*. Grand Rapids: Baker Academic, 2005.

Giles, K. "Apostles Before and After Paul." *Churchman* 99 (1985) 241–56.

Goppelt, L. *Apostolic and Post-Apostolic Times*. London: Black, 1970.

Grass, T. *Modern Church History*. London: SCM, 2008.

Graves, C. S. "Anointing or Apostasy: The Latter Rain Legacy," accessed December 8, 2010, http://www.birthpangs.org/articles/background/Chas-Graves-Anointing-Apostasy.pdf.

Greek Orthodox Archdiocese of America. "The Holy Sacrament of Ordination to the Priesthood," accessed March 25, 2011, http://www.goarch.org/en/chapel/liturgical_texts/ordination-priesthood-en.asp.

Green, M. *Asian Tigers for Christ: The Dynamic Growth of the Church in South East Asia*. London: SPCK, 2001.

———. *Called to Serve: Ministry and Ministers in the Church*. London: Hodder & Stoughton, 1964.

———. *The Corinthian Agenda*. Eastbourne, UK: Victor, 2004.

———. *I Believe in the Holy Spirit*. Eastbourne, UK: Kingsway, 2004.

Greenslade, P. *Leadership: Reflections on Biblical Leadership Today*. Farnham, UK: CWR, 2002.

Grudem, W. "Conclusion: Wayne A. Grudem." In *Are Miraculous Gifts for Today? Four Views*, edited by W. Grudem, 341–50. Leicester, UK: InterVarsity, 1996.

———. *Systematic Theology: An Introduction to Biblical Doctrine*. Leicester, UK: InterVarsity, 1994.

Gruen, E. "Documentation of Aberrant Practices and Teachings of Kansas City Fellowship (Grace Ministries)," accessed October 27, 2010, http://www.birthpangs.org/articles/kcp/Abberent%20Practises.pdf.

Guinness, O. *Fit Bodies, Fat Minds: Why Evangelicals Don't Think and What to Do about It*. London: Hodder & Stoughton, 1995.

Hagin, K. E. *He Gave Gifts unto Men: A Biblical Perspective of Apostles, Prophets, and Pastors*. Tulsa, OK: Faith Library, 1994.

———. *I Believe in Visions*. Tulsa, OK: Faith Library, 1996.

———. *The Ministry Gifts: Fifteen Lessons on the Ministry Gifts*. Tulsa, OK: Faith Library, 2006.

———. *Understanding the Anointing*. Tulsa, OK: Faith Library, 1995.

Hall, J. L. "United Pentecostal Church, International." In *The New International Dictionary of Pentecostal and Charismatic Movements*, rev. ed., edited by S. M. Burgess, 1160–5. Grand Rapids: Zondervan, 2002.

Halliburton, J. "The Laity in the Ministry of the Church." In *Order and Ministry*, edited by C. Hall, and R. Hannaford, 105–24. Leominster, UK: Gracewing, 1996.

Hamon, B. *Apostles, Prophets and the Coming Moves of God: God's End-Time Plans for His Church and Planet Earth*. Shippensburg, PA: Destiny Image, 1997.

Hamon, D. B. *The Eternal Church*. Shippensburg, PA: Destiny Image, 2003.

Hannaford, R. "Foundations for an Ecclesiology of Ministry." In *Order and Ministry*, edited by C. Hall, and R. Hannaford, 21–60. Leominster, UK: Gracewing, 1996.

Hanson, A. *Church, Sacraments and Ministry*. Oxford: Mowbrays, 1975.

Bibliography

Harlan, R. "John Alexander Dowie and the Christian Catholic Apostolic Church in Zion." PhD diss., University of Chicago, 1906.

Harper, M. "Apostles Today—Yes and No." *Renewal* 118 (1985) 26–27.

———. *Let My People Grow: Ministry and Leadership in the Church*. London: Hodder & Stoughton, 1988.

———. *That We May Be One*. London: Hodder & Stoughton, 1983.

Harrell Jr., D. E. "Healers and Televangelists after World War II." In *The Century of the Holy Spirit: 100 Years of Pentecostal and Charismatic Renewal*, edited by V. Synan, 325–47. Nashville, TN: Thomas Nelson, 2001.

Harrell Jr., D. E. *Oral Roberts: An American Life*. Bloomington, IN: Indiana University Press, 1985.

Harriman, N. H. "Inside Story of Sanfordism and Shiloh." *Lewiston Saturday Journal*, September 26, 1903. http://www.fwselijah.com/harriman.htm.

Harrington, D. J. *The Church according to the New Testament: What the Wisdom and Witness of Early Christianity Teach Us Today*. Wisconsin: Sheed and Ward, 2001.

Hays, R. B. *First Corinthians*. Louisville, KY: John Knox, 1997.

Hebert, A. G. *Apostle and Bishop*. London: Faber and Faber, 1963.

Heine, R. E. *The Commentaries of Origen and Jerome on St. Paul's Epistle to the Ephesians*. Oxford: Oxford University Press, 2002.

Hemphill, K. *The Antioch Effect: 8 Characteristics of Highly Effective Churches*. Nashville: Broadman and Holman, 1994.

Hermas. *The Shepherd of Hermas*, n.d. http://www.earlychristianwritings.com/text/shepherd.html.

Hewett, J. A. "Apostle, Office of." In *The New International Dictionary of Pentecostal and Charismatic Movements*, rev. ed., edited by S. M. Burgess, 318–21. Grand Rapids: Zondervan, 2002.

———. "Baptist Pentecostals and Charismatics." In *The New International Dictionary of Pentecostal and Charismatic Movements*, rev. ed., edited by S. M. Burgess, 365–66. Grand Rapids: Zondervan, 2002.

Higton, T., and G. Kirby. "The Challenge of the House Churches." *Latimer Studies* 27 (1988) 46.

Hill, C. "Here Today, Where Tomorrow?" In *Blessing the Church? A Review of the History and Direction of the Charismatic Movement*, edited by C. Hill, 184–229. Guildford, UK: Eagle, 1995.

Hocken, P. D. "The Challenge of Non-Denominational Charismatic Christianity: Experiences of the Spirit." In *Conference on Pentecostal and Charismatic Research in Europe at Utrecht University 1989*, edited by J. A. B. Jongeneel, 221–38. Frankfurt am Main: Lang, 1991.

———. *The Challenges of the Pentecostal, Charismatic and Messianic Jewish Movements: The Tensions of the Spirit*. Farnham, UK: Ashgate, 2009.

———. "Charismatic Movement." In *The New International Dictionary of Pentecostal and Charismatic Movements*, rev. ed., edited by S. M. Burgess, 477–519. Grand Rapids: Zondervan, 2002.

———. *God's Masterplan: Penetrating the Mystery of Christ*. Stoke-on-Trent, UK: Alive, 2003.

———. *The Glory and the Shame: Reflections on the 20th-Century Outpouring of the Holy Spirit*. Guildford, UK: Eagle, 1994.

———. "House Church Movement." In *The New International Dictionary of Pentecostal and Charismatic Movements*, rev. ed., edited by S. M. Burgess, 773-4. Grand Rapids: Zondervan, 2002.

———. *One Lord One Spirit One Body*. Exeter, UK: Paternoster, 1987.

———. "Smail, Thomas A." In *The New International Dictionary of Pentecostal and Charismatic Movements*, rev. ed., edited by S. M. Burgess, 1074. Grand Rapids: Zondervan, 2002.

———. *The Strategy of the Spirit? Worldwide Renewal and Revival in the Established Church and Modern Movements*. Guildford, UK: Eagle, 1996.

———. *Streams of Renewal. The Origins and Early Development of the Charismatic Movement in Great Britain*. Carlisle, UK: Paternoster, 1997.

———. "Whitehead, Charles." In *The New International Dictionary of Pentecostal and Charismatic Movements*, rev. ed., edited by S. M. Burgess, 1194. Grand Rapids: Zondervan, 2002.

———. "Virgo, Terry." In *The New International Dictionary of Pentecostal and Charis-matic Movements*, rev. ed., edited by S. M. Burgess, 1178. Grand Rapids: Zondervan, 2002.

Hollenweger, W. J. *The Pentecostals*. London: SCM, 1972.

Holy Spirit Renewal Ministries. "Introducing Holy Spirit Renewal Ministries," accessed October 27, 2010, http://hsrm.org/roots.html.

Holy Spirit Teaching Mission. *New Wine*, June, 1969. http://www.csmpublishing.org/pdf/newwine/06-1969.pdf.

———. *New Wine*, February, 1970. http://www.csmpublishing.org/pdf/newwine/02-1970.pdf.

Hopkins, M., and B. Hopkins. "Institutional and Local Change through Church Plants." In *Setting the Church of England Free*, edited by M. Mills-Powell, 139-52. Alresford, UK: Hunt, 2003.

Horne, B. "The Republic, the Hierarchy, and the Trinity: A Theology of Order." In *Order and Ministry*, edited by C. Hall, and R. Hannaford, 1-20. Leominster, UK: Gracewing, 1996.

Horsley, R. G. "Obituary—Rob Frost," accessed October 27, 2010, http://www.churchtimes.co.uk/content.asp?id=47709.

House of Praise. "House of Praise—About Us," accessed October 27, 2010, http://www.houseofpraise.co.uk/02-about.html.

Humphrey, T. "Can these Bones Live?" In *Setting the Church of England Free*, edited by M. Mills-Powell, 29-35. Alresford, UK: Hunt, 2003.

Ibbotson, S. "Apostolic Leadership and Congregational Principles—Reflections for Discussion," accessed October 27, 2010, http://www.mainstream-uk.com/apostolic_articles.html.

Ignite Revival. "Ignite Revival History," accessed October 27, 2010, http://www.igniterevival.net/history.

———. "Ignite Revival Testimonies," accessed October 27, 2010, http://www.igniterevival.net/testimonies.

International Coalition of Apostles. "History of ICA," accessed October 27, 2010, http://www.coalitionofapostles.com/about-ica/history-of-ica.

International House of Prayer. "International House of Prayer," accessed October 27, 2010, http://www.ihop.org.

Bibliography

International Pentecostal Holiness Church. "Apostolic Biblical Statement and Practical Guidelines," accessed July 27, 2012, http://www.iphc.org/sites/default/files/ApostolicPositionPaper.pdf.
Irving, E. *The Collected Writings of Edward Irving*, Vol. 2, edited by G. Carlyle. London: Strahan, 1864.
———. *The Collected Writings of Edward Irving*, Vol. 3, edited by G. Carlyle. London: Strahan, 1865.
———. "On the Unity of Christ and His Members." In *Irving Sermons*, n.p. London: Harding, n.d., ca. 1832.
Jackson, B. *The Quest for the Radical Middle: A History of the Vineyard*. Cape Town: Vineyard International, 2006.
Jerome. "Epistle 146: About Deacons." Translated by Wm. Henry Fremantle, n.d. http://www.voskrese.info/spl/jerome146.html.
Jesus House Church. "Jesus House—About Us," accessed October 27, 2010, http://www.jesushouse.org.uk/about-us.
Johnson, B. *When Heaven Invades Earth: A Practical Guide to a Life of Miracles*. Shippensburg, PA: Treasure House, 2003.
Johnson, T. M., et al., editors. *World Christian Encyclopedia: A Comparative Survey of Churches and Religions in the Modern World*. 2 vols. New York: Oxford University Press, 2002.
John Stott Ministries. "Statement of Faith," accessed December 9, 2010, http://www.johnstottministries.org/about-us/statement-of-faith.
Jones, S. "Giving Shape to Intentional Discipleship." *Talk: The Mainstream Magazine* 6 (2006) 10–11. http://biblicalstudies.org.uk/pdf/talk/06-3.pdf.
Joyner, R. *The Apostolic Ministry*. Fort Mill, SC: MorningStar, 2006.
Kärkkäinen, V.-M. *An Introduction to Ecclesiology: Ecumenical, Historical and Global Perspectives*. Downers Grove, IL: InterVarsity Academic, 2002.
———. "Receptive Ecumenism and the Dynamics of Development within Pentecostalism." Paper presented at Ushaw College: Durham, January 2009.
———. "Unity, Diversity, and Apostolicity: Any Hopes for Rapprochement between Older and Younger Churches?" Unpublished paper, Louvain, 2007.
Kay, W. K. *Apostolic Networks in Britain: New Ways of Being Church*. Milton Keynes: Paternoster, 2007.
———. "Britain." In *The New International Dictionary of Pentecostal and Charismatic Movements*, rev. ed., edited by S. M. Burgess, 42–46. Grand Rapids: Zondervan, 2002.
———. "Dynamics of Church Life—Introduction." In *Pentecostal and Charismatic Studies: A Reader*, edited by W. K. Kay, and A. E. Dyer, 166–67. London: SCM, 2004.
———. *Pentecostals in Britain*. Carlisle, UK: Paternoster, 2000.
Kay, W. K., and A. E. Dyer. *Pentecostal and Charismatic Studies: A Reader*. London: SCM, 2004.
Kenneth Hagin Ministries. "Founder's Memorial," accessed October 27, 2010, http://www.rhema.org/index.php?option=com_content&view=article&id=8:founders-memorial&catid=100:leadership&Itemid=137.
KICC. "KICC Branches," accessed October 27, 2010, http://www.kicc.org.uk/Branches/tabid/61/Default.aspx.

Bibliography

KICC. "KICC Near You," accessed October 27, 2010, http://kicc.org.uk/Portals/0/Aug%2008%20KICC_NEAR%20reprint%2010000.pdf.
Kinnaman, G. D. *And Signs Shall Follow*. Tonbridge, UK: Sovereign World, 1992.
Kinnear, A. *Against the Tide: The Story of Watchman Nee*. Eastbourne, UK: Victory, 1974.
Kruse, C. G. "Apostle, Apostleship." In *Dictionary of the Later New Testament and Its Developments*, edited by R. P. Martin and P. H. Davids, 76–82. Downers Grove, IL: InterVarsity, 1997.
———. *New Testament Foundations for Ministry*. Basingstoke, UK: Marshall Morgan & Scott, 1985.
Küng, H. *The Church*. Tunbridge Wells, UK: Search, 1981.
———. *Infallible? An Inquiry*. London: Fontana, 1972.
Kuyper, A. *The Work of the Holy Spirit*, 1946. http://www.ccel.org/ccel/kuyper/holy_spirit.
Lane, T. *The Lion Concise Book of Christian Thought*. Oxford: Lion, 2002.
Langham Partnership. "John Stott Biography," accessed December 9, 2010, http://www.langhampartnership.org/john-stott/biography.
———. "Langham Partnership History," accessed December 9, 2010, http://www.langhampartnership.org/about-us/history.
Leadership Network. "European Church Planting Network," accessed July 31, 2012, http://leadnet.org/page/ecpn.
Lederle, H. I. *Treasures Old and New: Interpretations of "Spirit-Baptism" in the Charismatic Renewal Movement*. Peabody, MA: Hendrickson, 1988.
Lehanne, B. *Early Celtic Christianity*. London: Continuum, 1994.
Lee, W. *The New Testament Recovery Version*. Anaheim, CA: Living Stream Ministry, 1991.
Liardon, R. *God's Generals: Why They Succeeded and Why Some Failed*. Tulsa, OK: Albury, 1996.
Lie, G. "The Ecclesiology of Gene Edwards," accessed July 20, 2012, http://brethrenhistory.org/qwicsitePro/php/docsview.php?docid=423.
Lightfoot, J. B. *Saint Paul's Epistle to the Galatians*. London: Macmillan, 1896.
Lincoln, A. T. *Ephesians*. Dallas, TX: Word, 1990.
Lindsay, G. *Apostles, Prophets and Administrators*. Dallas, TX: Christ for the Nations, 1996.
———. *John Alexander Dowie: A Life Story of Trials, Tragedies and Triumphs*. Dallas, TX: Christ for the Nations, 1980.
Lings, G. "Nearing the Edge." In *Setting the Church of England Free*, edited by M. Mills-Powell, 16–28. Alresford, UK: Hunt, 2003.
Long, B. *In the Spirit's Power*. Plymouth, UK: Dunamis Project, 2009.
———. *Listening Evangelism*. Plymouth, UK: Dunamis Project, 2009.
Lowe, V. G. "Researchers Receive Millions to Study Pentecostal-Charismatic Movement," accessed October 27, 2010, http://www.charismamag.com/index.php/news/26663-researchers-receive-millions-to-study-pentecostal-Charismatic-movement.
Luther, M. *Commentaries on 1 Corinthians 7, 1 Corinthians 15, and Lectures on 1 Timothy*. In *Luther's Works*, American Edition. Vol. 28 of 55 vols. Edited by J. Pelikan and H. T. Lehman. Philadelphia, PA: Fortress/St Louis, MO: Concordia, 1973.

Bibliography

Lutheran Renewal. "Lutheran Renewal," accessed October 27, 2010, http://www.lutheranrenewal.org.
Lynch, G. *Understanding Theology and Popular Culture*. Oxford, Blackwell, 2005.
MacCulloch, D. *Christian History: An introduction to the Western Tradition*. Werrington, UK: Epworth, 2006.
MacDonald, G. *The Evangelical Universalist*. Eugene, OR: Cascade, 2006.
Mansfield, S. *Derek Prince: A Biography*. Milton Keynes, UK: Authentic Media, 2005.
Marfleet, D. "New Churches: The Restoration of Mission?" MA diss., All Nations Christian College, Ware, UK, 1999.
Martin, D. *Pentecostalism: The World Their Parish*. Oxford: Blackwell, 2002.
Matthew, D., editor. *Apostles Today*. Bradford, UK: Harvestime, 1988.
Mazur, E. M., and K. McCarthy. "Introduction." In *God in the Details: American Religion in Popular Culture*, edited by E. M. Mazur, and K. McCarthy, 1–16. London: Routledge, 2001.
McAlpine, R. *Post-Charismatic?* Eastbourne, UK: Kingsway, 2008.
McCallum, D. "Watchman Nee and the House Church Movement in China," accessed 8/12/2010 at http://www.xenos.org/essays/neeframe.htm.
McGee, G. B., and B. A. Pavia. "Wagner, Charles Peter." In *The New International Dictionary of Pentecostal and Charismatic Movements*, rev. ed., edited by S. M. Burgess, 1181. Grand Rapids: Zondervan, 2002.
McGrath, A. *Heresy*. London: SPCK, 2009.
McKay, J. *Movements of the Spirit: A History of the Prophetic Church*. Horsham, UK: Way of the Spirit, 2010.
———. "When the Veil is Taken Away: The Impact of Prophetic Experience on Biblical Interpretation." *Journal of Pentecostal Theology* 5 (1994) 17–40.
Menzies, W. W. "The Reformed Roots of Pentecostalism," accessed December 9, 2010, http://www.glopent.net/pentecostudies/2007/fall-2/menzies-2007a/view.
Miller, L. "49: E. A. Adeboye," accessed October 27, 2010, http://www.newsweek.com/id/176333/page/1
Mills-Powell, M. "Leadership for a New Generation." In *Setting the Church of England Free*, edited by M. Mills-Powell, 218–25. Alresford, UK: Hunt, 2003.
Ministries Today Symposium. "Orlando Statement," accessed October 27, 2010, http://web.archive.org/web/20050218110953/http://www.ministriestoday.com/OrlandoStatement.html.
Moberly, R. C *Ministerial Priesthood*. London: SPCK, 1969.
Moffatt, J. *The First Epistle of Paul to the Corinthians*. London: Hodder & Stoughton, 1938.
Moore. P., editor. *Bishops: But What Kind? Reflections on Episcopacy*. London: SPCK, 1982.
Moore, S. D. *The Shepherding Movement: Controversy and Charismatic Ecclesiology*. London: T. & T. Clark, 2003.
Muller, D. "Apostle." In *New International Dictionary of New Testament Theology*, edited by C. Brown, 1:128–35, 137. Carlisle, UK: Paternoster, 1986.
Mullings, L. J. "The Future of Theological Education—Theological Training Programmes for Migrant Churches/among Ethnic Minorities," accessed November 17, 2011, http://www.oikoumene.org/fileadmin/files/wcc-main/documents/p5/ete/Lynette%20Mullings%20-%20Theological%20training%20programmes%20for%20migrant%20churches.pdf.

Bibliography

Murray, F. S. "Was Frank Sandford an Egotist?" Accessed December 15, 2010, http://www.fwselijah.com/frank.htm.

Murray, I. *The Puritan Hope: Revival and the Interpretation of Prophecy*. Edinburgh: Banner of Truth, 1975.

Murray-Williams, S. "Anabaptism as a Charismatic Movement: Diverse Phenomena in Early Decades," accessed December 15, 2010, http://www.anabaptistnetwork.com/node/173.

———. *Church After Christendom*. Milton Keynes, UK: Paternoster, 2004.

Nee, W. *The Normal Christian Church Life*. Anaheim, CA: Living Stream Ministry, 1994.

Nelson, S. *Fair, Clear and Terrible: The Story of Shiloh, Maine*. New York: British American, 1989.

New Apostolic Church, United Kingdom & Ireland. "New Apostolic Church United Kingdom & Ireland," accessed September 19, 2011, http://www.nacukie.org.

Newbigin, J. E. L. *The Reunion of the Church: A Defence of the South India Scheme*. London: SCM, 1960.

New Wine. "Our Leadership," accessed December 9, 2010, http://www.new-wine.org/about_us/Our%20Leadership.htm.

Nichols, A. *Holy Order. Apostolic Priesthood from the New Testament to the Second Vatican Council*. Dublin: Veritas, 1990.

Oloyede, P. J. "The Emerging Black Church," accessed 27/10/2010, http://www.christiantoday.com/article/pastor.jonathan.oloyede.the.emerging.black.church/5037.htm.

Oss, D. A. "A Pentecostal/Charismatic View." In *Are Miraculous Gifts for Today? Four Views*, edited by W. Grudem, 239–83. Leicester, UK: InterVarsity, 1996.

Packer, J. I. "John Owen on Spiritual Gifts," accessed December 15, 2010, http://www.johnowen.org/media/packer_quest_for_godliness_ch_13.pdf.

———. *Keep in Step with the Spirit*. Leicester, UK: InterVarsity, 2002.

Paterson, R. *The Antioch Factor: The Hidden Message in the Book of Acts*. Lancaster, UK: Sovereign World International, 2000.

Patterson, R. M. R. "Designing the Last Days: Edward Irving, The Albury Circle, and the Theology of the Morning Watch." PhD diss., King's College London, 2001.

Pawson, D. *Unlocking the Bible Omnibus: A Unique Overview of the Whole Bible*. London: Harper Collins, 2003.

Payne, D. "Learning to Step Out in the Anointing," accessed October 29, 2010, http://ccr.org.uk/archive/gn1001/g01.htm.

Pentecostal Church of God. "What We Believe," accessed October 27, 2010, http://www.pcg.org/cgi-bin/gx.cgi/AppLogic+FTContentServer?pagename=FaithHighway/10000/7000/880PE/main_believe.

Percy, M. *Clergy: Origin of Species*. London: Continuum, 2006.

———. "Old Tricks for New Dogs? A Critique of Fresh Expressions." In *Evaluating Fresh Expressions: Explorations in Emerging Church. Responses to the Changing Face of Ecclesiology in the Church of England*, edited by L. Nelstrop and M. Percy, 27–39. Norwich, UK: Canterbury Press, 2008.

———. *Power and the Church: Ecclesiology in an Age of Transition*. London: Cassell, 1998.

Peters, J. *Colin Urquhart: A Biography*. London: Hodder & Stoughton, 1994.

Phoenix Seminary, Arizona. "Wayne A. Grudem, Ph.D.," accessed July 30, 2012, http://www.ps.edu/about-us/faculty-staff-board/resident-faculty/wayne-a-grudem.

Bibliography

Plumer, E. *Augustine's Commentary on Galatians: Introduction, Text, Translation, and Notes.* Oxford: Oxford University Press, 2003.
Plummer, A. "Apostle." In *Dictionary of the Apostolic Church: Aaron–Lystra*, edited by J. Hastings, 1:82–84. Edinburgh: T. & T. Clark, 1915.
Prince, D. *Rediscovering God's Church.* Baldock, UK: Derek Prince Ministries UK, 2006.
———. *Sound Judgement: What Judging Is, When We Should Do it and How.* Kingsfield, UK: Derek Prince Ministries UK, 2002.
Pytches, D. *Leadership for New Life.* London: Hodder & Stoughton, 1998.
Ramsey, M. *The Gospel and the Catholic Church*: London, SPCK, 1990.
Redeemed Christian Church of God. "Redeemed Christian Church of God," accessed October 27, 2010, www.rccg.org.
Rees, E. *S.H.A.P.E.: Finding and Fulfilling Your Unique Purpose for Life.* Grand Rapids: Zondervan, 2006.
Regent University. "Jon Ruthven, School of Divinity, Regent University," accessed September 30, 2011, http://www.regent.edu/acad/schdiv/faculty_staff/ruthven.shtml.
Resane, K. T. "The Ecclesiology of the Emerging Apostolic Churches—Fivefold Ministry." PhD diss., University of Pretoria, 2008.
Riss, R. M. "Hagin, Kenneth E." In *The New International Dictionary of Pentecostal and Charismatic Movements*, rev. ed., edited by S. M. Burgess, 687. Grand Rapids: Zondervan, 2002.
———. "Latter Rain Movement." In *The New International Dictionary of Pentecostal and Charismatic Movements*, rev. ed., edited by S. M. Burgess, 830–33. Grand Rapids: Zondervan, 2002.
River Fellowship International. "Bishop John Francis," accessed August 18, 2012, www.theriverdurham.com/rfi/francis.html.
Robeck Jr, C. M. "International Church of the Foursquare Gospel." In *The New International Dictionary of Pentecostal and Charismatic Movements*, rev. ed., edited by S. M. Burgess, 793–94. Grand Rapids: Zondervan, 2002.
Ross, C. "The New Apostolic Reformation: An Analysis and Critique." MA diss., Cape Town, 2005.
Rowell, A. "Ben Witherington on Frank Viola's *Pagan Christianity* and *Reimagining Church*," accessed December 8, 2010, http://www.andyrowell.net/andy_rowell/2009/04/ben-witherington-on-frank-violas-pagan-christianity-and-reimagining-church.html.
Rowell, J. "New Apostolic Reformation," accessed October 27, 2010, http://www.intheworkplace.com/apps/articles/default.asp?articleid=68277&columnid=1935.
Ruach Ministries. "Bishop John Francis (Ruach Ministries)," accessed August 18, 2012, http://www.boldbelieversforchrist.com/photo/bishop-john-francis-ruach.
Ruthven, J. "Does the Spiritual Gift of Apostleship Also Continue?" In *On the Cessation of the Charismata: Protestant Polemic on Postbiblical Miracles*, 213–20. Sheffield, UK: Sheffield Academic Press, 1993.
———. "The 'Foundational Gifts' of Ephesians 2:20," accessed December 1, 2011, http://hopefaithprayer.com/books/The%20Foundational%20Gifts%20of%20Ephesians%202-20.pdf.
———. *On the Cessation of the Charismata: Protestant Polemic on Postbiblical Miracles.* Sheffield, UK: Sheffield Academic Press, 1993.
St Barnabas Church, Kensington. *Bodywork Seminar Notes.* London: St Barnabas Church, n.d.

Bibliography

Saucy, R. L. "An Open but Cautious View." In *Are Miraculous Gifts for Today? Four Views*, edited by W. Grudem, 97–148. Leicester, UK: InterVarsity, 1996.

Schaff, P. *The Ante-Nicene Fathers 1: The Apostolic Fathers with Justin Martyr and Irenaeus*. Grand Rapids: Christian Classics Ethereal Library, 2002.

Schmaus, M. *Dogma 4: The Church. Its Origin and Structure*. London: Sheed and Ward, 1979.

Schmithals, W. *Office of Apostle in the Early Church*. New York: Abingdon, 1969.

———. *The Office of Apostle in the Early Church*. London: SPCK, 1971.

Schnackenberg, R. "Apostles before and during Paul's Time." In *Apostolic History and the Gospel: Biblical and Historical Essays Presented to F. F. Bruce*, edited by W. W. Gasque and R. P. Martin, 287–303. Exeter, UK: Paternoster, 1970.

———. *The Epistle to the Ephesians*. Edinburgh: T. & T, Clark, 1991.

Schweizer, E. *Church Order in the New Testament*. London: SCM, 1969.

Scotland, N. *Charismatics and the New Millennium*. Guildford, UK: Eagle, 2000.

Simmons, M. *The Complete Works of Menno Simmons*. n.c. http://www.mennosimons.net/fto64-mission.html.

St. Thomas' Church, "Our Core Values," accessed July 30, 2012, http://www.stthomaschurch.org.uk/our_core_values.

Stackhouse, I. *The Gospel-Driven Church: Retrieving Classical Ministries for Contemporary Revivalism*. Milton Keynes, UK: Paternoster, 2004.

———. "Revivalism, Faddism and the Gospel." In *On Revival: A Critical Examination*, edited by A. Walker, and K. Aune, 239–51. Carlisle, UK: Paternoster, 2003.

Stafford, T. "Evangelism Plus," accessed September 19, 2011, http://www.ctlibrary.com/ct/2006/october/32.94.html.

Stark, R. *For the Glory of God*. Oxford: Princeton University Press, 2003.

Stibbe, M. *One Touch from the King Changes Everything*. Milton Keynes, UK: Authentic Media, 2007.

Stone, D. *Episcopacy and Valid Orders in the Primitive Church: A Statement of Evidence*. London: Longmans, Green and Co., 1926.

Storms, C. S. "A Third Wave View." In *Are Miraculous Gifts for Today? Four Views*, edited by W. Grudem, 175–223. Leicester, UK: InterVarsity, 1996.

Stott, J. *Evangelical Truth*. Leicester, UK: InterVarsity, 1999.

———. *The Message of Acts*. Leicester, UK: InterVarsity, 2005.

———. *The Message of Ephesians*. Leicester, UK: InterVarsity, 2005.

Sullivan, F. A. *From Apostles to Bishops: The Development of the Episcopacy in the Early Church*. New York: Newman, 2001.

Sumner, S. *Men and Women in the Church*. Downers Grove, IL: InterVarsity, 2003.

Sweet, B. H. "The Didache (The Teaching) with comments by Ben H. Sweet," accessed August 25, 2011, http://bswett.com/1998-01Didache.html.

Swinton, J., and H. Mowat. *Practical Theology and Qualitative Research*. London: SCM, 2007.

Sykes, S., and J. Booty, editors. *The Study of Anglicanism*. London: SPCK, 1993.

Synan, H. V. "International Pentecostal Holiness Church." In *The New International Dictionary of Pentecostal and Charismatic Movements*, rev. ed., edited by S. M. Burgess, 798–801. Grand Rapids: Zondervan, 2002.

Synan, V. *The Century of the Holy Spirit: 100 Years of Pentecostal and Charismatic Renewal*. Nashville, TN: Thomas Nelson, 2001.

Bibliography

———. "The Holiness Pentecostal Churches." In *The Century of the Holy Spirit: 100 Years of Pentecostal and Charismatic Renewal*, 97–122. Nashville, TN: Thomas Nelson, 2001.

———. *In The Latter Days: The Outpouring of the Holy Spirit in the Twentieth Century*. Fairfax, VA: Xulon, 2001.

———. "Presbyterian and Reformed Charismatics." In *The New International Dictionary of Pentecostal and Charismatic Movements*, rev. ed., edited by S. M. Burgess, 995–97. Grand Rapids: Zondervan, 2002.

Tertullian. *The Prescription against Heretics*, n.d. http://www.newadvent.org/fathers/0311.htm.

3DM. "About 3DM," accessed July 30, 2012, http://weare3dm.com/about.

Tillin, T. "Plagiarism, Kenyon and the Word-of-Faith Movement," accessed July 30, 2012, http://thewordonthewordoffaithinfoblog.com/2010/10/14/hagin_copied_kenyon.

Turner, H. J. M. *St. Symeon the New Theologian and Spiritual Fatherhood*. New York: Brill, 1985.

Turner, M. "Ecclesiology in the Major 'Apostolic' Restorationist Churches in the United Kingdom." *Vox Evangelica* 19 (1989) 83–108.

Urquhart, C. *Faith for the Future*. London: Hodder & Stoughton, 1982.

———. *True Church*. Horsham, UK: Kingdom Faith, 2002.

———. *When the Spirit Comes*. London: Hodder & Stoughton, 1994.

Vatican II. *Dogmatic Constitution on the Church—Lumen Gentium*. Vatican City, 1964.

Viola, F. "Interview with Todd Hunter," accessed November 12, 2010, http://frankviola.wordpress.com/2010/02/05/interview-with-todd-hunter.

———. *Reimagining Church: Pursuing the Dream of Organic Christianity*. Eastbourne, UK: Kingsway, 2008.

———. "Rethinking the Five-Fold Ministry," accessed December 8, 2010, http://www.ptmin.org/fivefold.htm.

Virgo, T. "An Apostle by the Grace of God." In *Apostles Today*, edited by D. Matthew, 73–82. Bradford, UK: Harvestime, 1988.

———. "The Apostle is No Optional Extra." In *Apostles Today*, edited by D. Matthew, 37–44. Bradford, UK: Harvestime, 1988.

———. "Local Churches under Apostolic Authority." *Newfrontiers Magazine* 2 (2003) 5–10.

———. *Does the Future Have a Church?* Eastbourne, UK: Kingsway, 2003.

———. *No Well-Worn Paths: Restoring the Church to Christ's Original Intention—One Man's Journey*. Eastbourne, UK: Kingsway, 2007.

———. *Restoration in the Church*. Eastbourne, UK: Kingsway, 1985.

Volf, M. *After Our Likeness: The Church as the Image of the Trinity*. Grand Rapids: Eerdmans, 1998.

Von Eiken, E., and H. Lidner. "Apostle." In *New International Dictionary of New Testament Theology*, edited by C. Brown, 1:126–28. Carlisle, UK: Paternoster, 1986.

Wagner, C. P. *Apostles and Prophets: The Foundation of the Church*. Ventura, CA: Regal, 2000.

———. *Apostles of the City: How to Mobilize Territorial Apostles for City Transformation*. Colorado Springs, CO: Wagner, 2001.

———. *Apostles Today: Biblical Government for Biblical Power*. Ventura, CA: Regal, 2006.

———. *Changing Church: How God is Leading His Church into the Future.* Ventura, CA: Regal, 2004.

———. *Churchquake! How the New Apostolic Reformation is Shaking Up the Church as We Know It.* Ventura, CA: Regal, 1999.

———. "The Church's One Foundation, Part II." *American Society for Church Growth* 11 (2000).

———. "Lecture AP825, Session 4," n.d. Accessed October 27, 2010, http://www.wagnerleadership.org.

———. *Look Out! The Pentecostals are Coming.* Carol Stream, IL: Creation House, 1973.

———. "New Apostolic Churches," accessed July 27, 2012, http://www.thenetwork.org.nz/thenetwork/Article.html.

———. "New Apostolic Reformation," accessed October 27, 2010, http://www.globalharvest.org/apostref.html.

———. "The New Apostolic Reformation." In *The New Apostolic Churches: Rediscovering the New Testament Model of Leadership and Why It Is God's Desire for the Church Today,* edited by C. P. Wagner, 13–25. Ventura, CA: Regal, 1998.

———. *Spheres of Authority: Apostles in Today's Church.* Colorado Springs, CO: Wagner, 2002.

———. "Understanding How Apostles Minister in Different Spheres," accessed July 27, 2012, http://www.apostolicparadigms.com/C__Peter_Wagner/Spheres/spheres.html.

Wagner Leadership. "Wagner Leadership," accessed October 27, 2010, http://www.wagnerleadership.org.

Walker, A. "Pentecostalism and Charismatic Christianity." In *The Blackwell Encyclopedia of Modern Christian Thought,* edited by A. McGrath, 428–33. Oxford: Blackwell, 1993.

———. *Restoring the Kingdom: The Radical Christianity of the House Church Movement.* Guildford, UK: Eagle, 1998.

———. "Pentecostalism and Charismatic Christianity." In *The Blackwell Encyclopedia of Modern Christian Thought,* edited by A. McGrath, 428–34. Oxford: Blackwell, 2005.

Wallis, A. "Apostles Today? Why Not?" In *Pentecostal and Charismatic Studies: A Reader,* edited by W. K. Kay, and A. E. Dyer, 171–4. London: SCM, 2004.

———. *Rain from Heaven. Revival in Scripture and History.* Sevenoaks, UK: Hodder & Stoughton, 1979.

———. "When Faith Would Fail." *New Wine* 3 (1971) 12–13. http://www.csmpublishing.org/pdf/newwine/10-1971.pdf.

Ward, P. *Selling Worship: How What We Sing has Changed the Church.* Milton Keynes, UK: Paternoster, 2005.

Ware, T. *The Orthodox Church.* London: Penguin, 1993.

Warner, R. *Alive in the Spirit: A Biblical and Practical Guide.* London: Hodder & Stoughton, 1997.

———. *Reinventing English Evangelicalism 1966–2001: A Theological and Sociological Study.* Milton Keynes, UK: Paternoster, 2007.

Warner, W. E. "Pentecostal Church of God." In *The New International Dictionary of Pentecostal and Charismatic Movements,* rev. ed., edited by S. M. Burgess, 965–66. Grand Rapids: Zondervan, 2002.

Bibliography

Warren, R. *Building Missionary Congregations: Towards a Post-modern Way of Being Church*. London: Church House, 1995.
Watson, D. *I Believe in the Church*. London: Hodder & Stoughton, 1999.
Weaver, C. D. *In Search of the New Testament Church: The Baptist Story*. Macon, GA: Mercer University Press, 2008.
Weber, M. *Theory of Social and Economic Organization*. New York: Free, 1964.
Webster, J. *Holy Scripture: A Dogmatic Sketch*. Cambridge: Cambridge University Press, 2003.
———. *Word and Church: Essays in Church Dogmatics*. Edinburgh, T. & T. Clark, 2001.
Weddell, S. "The Challenge of Independent Christianity, Part 11," accessed July 20, 2012, http://www.siena.org/May-2007/the-challenge-of-independent-christianity-part-11-the-end.
Westminster Assembly. *Westminster Confession: Presbyterian Church Government*, 1646. http://reformedonline.com/view/reformedonline/formfpresbygov.htm#ofthe officers.
Williams, D. H. *Evangelicals and Tradition: The Formative Influences of the Early Church*. Grand Rapids: Baker, 2005.
Williams, G. H. *The Radical Reformation*. Ann Arbor, MI: Truman State University Press, 2000.
Williams, J. R. *Renewal Theology: The Church, the Kingdom, and Last Things*. Republished in *Renewal Theology: Systematic Theology from a Charismatic Perspective*. Grand Rapids: Zondervan, 1996.
———. *Renewal Theology: God, the World, and Redemption*. Republished in *Renewal Theology: Systematic Theology from a Charismatic Perspective*. Grand Rapids: Zondervan, 1996.
———. *Renewal Theology: Salvation, the Holy Spirit, and Christian Living*. Republished in *Renewal Theology: Systematic Theology from a Charismatic Perspective*. Grand Rapids: Zondervan, 1996.
Williams, R. "One, Holy, Catholic and Apostolic Church," accessed December 9, 2010, http://www.archbishopofcanterbury.org/965.
Wimber, J. "The Five-Fold Ministry." In *Vineyard Reflections*, 1–12. Anaheim, CA: Association of Vineyard Churches, 1997.
Woodhouse, F. V. *The Substance of the Ministry of the Office of Apostle in the Gentile Church*. London: Bosworth, 1882.
Woodward, J., and S. Pattison, editors. *The Blackwell Reader in Pastoral and Practical Theology*. Oxford: Blackwell, 2000.
World Council of Churches. *Baptism, Eucharist and Ministry*. Geneva: World Council of Churches, 1982.
Wright, A. *Christianity and Critical Realism: Ambiguity, Truth and Theological Literacy*. London: Routledge, forthcoming.
Wright, N. *The Radical Kingdom: Restoration in Theory and Practice*. Eastbourne, UK: Kingsway, 1986.
Wright, N. T. *The New Testament and the People of God*. London: SPCK, 1992.
———. *Scripture and the Authority of God*. London: SPCK, 2005.
Wright, T. *Paul for Everyone: The Prison Letters; Ephesians, Philippians, Colossians and Philemon*. London: SPCK, 2004.
Zizioulas, J. *Being as Communion*. London: Darton, Longman & Todd, 1985.

Index of Names

Abraham, William, 188, 189, 194, 223
Adedibu, Babatunde, 54
Adeleke, Andrew, 53
Adogame, A., 223
Ahn, Ché, 18, 215
Allen, Roland, 140, 223
Ambrosiaster, 100, 102
Anderson, Allan, ix, 8, 49, 125, 132, 211, 223
Anderson, Paul, 15, 16, 194, 223
Anderson, R. S., 227
Ankerberg, John, 117, 122, 223
Armstrong, C. R., 224
Armstrong, N., 7, 112, 113, 115, 123, 224
Arnott, Carol, 46 47
Arnott, John, 18, 19, 46, 47, 215
Ashimolowo, Matthew, 51, 52
Ashworth, J., 140, 224
Athanasius, 92, 97, 103, 224
Augustine of Hippo, 100, 101, 236

Baker, Heidi, 161
Baker, Rolland, 161
Bales, J. D., 4, 117, 224
Barna, George, 29
Barrett, C. K., 160, 171, 224
Barrett, David, 6, 22, 23, 25, 118, 132, 212, 224
Barth, Marcus, 165, 166, 224
Bartlett, A., 224
Basham, Don, 126
Battle, J. A., 148, 224
Baughen, Michael, 150

Baxter, Err., 64, 126, 127
Bickle, Mike, 18, 19, 26, 27, 71
Beckwith, R., 224
Beeson, T., 43, 224
Bell, Stuart, 37, 50
Bengel, Johann Albrecht, 113
Bennett, Dennis, 13
Bennett, Rita, 13
Berkhof, L., 224
Best, Ernest, 157-59, 224
Bevere, John, 30
Bicknell, E. J., 224
Billman, Frank, 18, 26
Blackhouse, R., 224
Blake, Charles, 8, 224
Blake, William, 109, 224
Blomgren, D. K., 137, 224
Blumhofer, E. L., 224
Bolger, R. K., 229
Bonnke, Reinhard, 30
Booth, Robert, 51, 52, 224
Booty, J., 237
Bosch, D. J., 4, 137, 225
Bosworth, F. F., 119
Bouyer, L., 108, 225
Bowring, Lyndon, 59
Braaten, C. E., 178, 225
Brackett, Wanda, 11
Bradshaw, Tim, 187, 225
Branham, William, 127
Bray, G., 100, 225
Breen, Mike, xvi, 6, 33, 34, 40, 58, 59, 72-77, 88, 180, 181, 200-202, 221, 225
Brewster, Percy, 38

Index of Names

Bridge, Donald, 40, 106, 225
Brierley, Peter, 49, 51, 214, 216, 225
Brooks, David, 150
Brow, Robert, 43
Brown, C., 10, 225, 234, 238
Brown, J., 21, 225
Brown, Raymond, 166
Brown, Romy, 117, 225
Bruce, F. F., 148, 157, 159, 225, 237
Bryman, A., 225
Buchanan, C., 225
Bugbee, B., 35, 41, 225
Bundy, David, 18, 58, 59, 225
Burgess, Stanley, 105, 106, 108, 223–32, 234, 236–39
Burkhard, John, 92, 93, 98, 102, 148, 165, 171, 179–80, 197–98, 226
Butler, Keith, 30
Buttner, C., 126, 226

Cain, Paul, 27, 215
Calver, Clive, 136
Calvin, John, 17, 20, 71, 106, 108, 113, 130, 178, 226
Cameron, E., 226
Campbell, Alexander, 109, 224, 226
Campbell, Stacey, 215
Campion, Paul, 205, 226
Capper, B. J., 226
Cardale, Emily, 112
Carlyle, G., 232
Cartledge, David, 9, 226
Chartres, Richard, 207
Christian, J. T., 111, 226
Christenson, Larry, 14, 15, 115, 226
Chrysostom, John, 100, 101
Clarke, Charles, 46
Clarke, Gary, 19, 110
Clarke, Randy, 18–20, 161, 215
Clement of Rome, 94, 95, 97, 169, 186
Clendenin, D., 22, 226
Clifford, Steve, 136

Clifton, S. J., 227
Cloud, David, 19, 227
Coates, Gerald, 36, 37, 50, 227
Cocksworth, Christopher, 43, 103, 207, 227
Cohn, Norman, 106, 107, 227
Coles, John, 40
Collins, Bruce, xvi, 56, 134
Colomba, 103
Conn, C. W., 227
Cooke, Bernard, 48, 227
Coombes, Barney, 69, 182
Cottrell, Stephen, 4, 227
Cousins, D., 225
Cray, G., 41, 58, 140, 205, 227
Croft, Steven, 41, 42, 207, 227

Daffe, Jerald, 10, 11
Damazio, F., 227
DeWaay, B., 127, 227
Dionysius of Corinth, 4
Dobb, K., 227
Dorries, D. W., 227
Douglas, A., 227
Dowie, John Alexander, 109, 118–21, 130, 131, 230, 233
Dowse, J., 110, 227
Drummond, Henry, 112
Duncan, Robert, 14
Dunmoye, Esther, 52
Dunn, James, 10, 92, 135, 148, 157, 158, 184, 188, 195, 227, 228
DuPont, Marc, 19
DuPree, S. S., 228
Dyer, A. E., 223, 232, 239
Dye, Colin, 6, 37, 38, 50, 59, 228

Eaton, Michael, xvi, 135, 165, 167, 168, 228
Eberle, H. R., 228
Edwards, D. L., 228
Edwards, Gene, 28, 29, 123, 130, 218, 223, 233
Edwards, Joel, 136

Index of Names

Edwards, M. J., 100, 101, 103, 228
Ehrhardt, A., 228
Ekman, Ulf, 6, 58, 59, 73, 196, 228
England, E., 40, 228
Eusebius of Caesarea, 92, 100, 228

Farthing, I., 140, 224
Fee, G., 10, 135, 165, 166, 169, 177, 184, 228
Flegg, C. G., 102, 112–15, 118, 228
Folds, Gary, 19
Ford, Clay, 18–20
Forster, Roger, 50, 136, 168, 194, 195, 218, 228
Francis, John, 52, 53, 236
Franciscans, 103, 218
Frost, Andy, 46
Frost, Rob, 46, 231
Frost, Michael, xi, 35, 36, 58, 88, 140, 176, 181, 200, 201, 221, 228
Fryer, Clifford, 40
Fullam, Terry, 13

Gaffin, R. B., Jr., 228
Garner, Martin, 36, 40, 122, 199, 228
Gee, Donald, 8, 82, 86, 87, 123, 124, 197, 221, 228
Gelder, C. V., 137, 140, 228
General Presbytery of the Assemblies of God, 10, 228
Geyer, Heinrich, 117, 118
Glass, John, 38
Gibbs, Eddie, 35, 140, 229
Gilles, Kevin, 48, 98, 103, 165, 167, 168, 170, 171, 197, 198, 229
Gooding, John, 42
Goppelt, L., 229
Gower, Nancy, 24
Grady, J. Lee, 31
Grantham, Thomas, 110, 111
Grass, T., 229
Graves, C. S., 125, 229

Green, Michael, 41, 93, 148, 206, 229
Greenslade, P., 229
Gregory of Nazianzus, 105
Grudem, Wayne, vii, 148–49, 151–58, 160, 161, 166, 169, 171, 184, 198, 227–29, 235, 237
Gruen, E., 71, 229
Guinness, Os, 178, 229
Gumbel, Nicky, 37
Gunstone, John, 40

Haggard, Ted, 24, 30, 190
Hagin, Kenneth, xvi, 5, 58, 81–87, 131, 153, 174, 184, 185, 197–99, 202, 221, 229, 236
Hagin, Kenneth, Jr., 82
Hahn, Ferdinand, 93
Hahn, Phillip Matthew, 113
Hall, C., 226, 229, 231
Hall, J. L., 229
Halliburton, J., 229
Hamon, Bill, xii, 24, 30, 38, 69–71, 125, 137, 169, 229
Hannaford, R., 226, 229, 231
Hanson, Alan, 229
Harlan, R., 109, 120, 121, 230
Harley, Brian, 17, 45
Harper, Michael, 40, 49, 122, 147, 150, 218, 230
Harrell, D. E., Jr., 132, 230
Harriman, N. H., 119, 230
Harrington, D. J., 230
Hayford, Jack, 30
Hays, R. B., 230
Hebert, A. G., 208, 230
Heine, R. E., 102, 230
Hemphill, K., 184, 230
Hermas, 94, 97, 98, 103, 104, 230
Hewett, J. A., 19, 230
Higton, Tony, 40, 230
Hill, Clifford, 26, 230

243

Index of Names

Hirsch, Alan, xi, 35, 36, 58, 88, 140, 176, 181, 200, 201, 221, 228
Hocken, Peter, ix, xiv, 21, 46–48, 134, 193, 230, 231
Hodge, Charles, 148, 224
Hollenweger, W. J., 7, 231
Hopkins, Bob, 42–44, 56, 77, 88, 140, 141, 200, 221, 231
Hopkins, Mary, 77, 231
Horne, B., 231
Horsley, Graham, 46, 231
Hudson, Neil, 38
Humphrey, T., 231
Hunter, Todd, 14, 204, 238
Hutchinson, W. O., 124
Hybels, Bill, 24

Ibbotson, Stephen, 45, 231
Ignatius of Antioch, 94–96
Innokenti of Cherson, 113
Irenaeus of Lyons, 94, 98, 99, 104, 179, 237
Irving, Edward, vii, 6, 111–13, 115, 116, 123, 130, 141, 225, 232, 235
Irvine, John, 34

Jackson, Bill, 27, 28, 125, 149, 190, 232
Jacobs, Cindy, 30
Jakes, T. D., 25
Jeffreys, George, 38
Jerome, 92, 102, 113, 130, 230, 232
Johnson, Bill, 18, 20, 25, 26, 48, 196, 215, 232
Johnson, Todd, 6, 118, 132, 212, 224, 232
Jones, Bob, 27, 215
Jones, Bryn, xiii, 50, 81, 196
Jones, S., 99, 232
Rev Dr Jones, 120
Jongeneel, J. A. B., 230
Joyner, Rick, 21, 26, 30, 58, 59, 184, 215, 232

Kallestad, Walt, 34, 59, 72, 73, 76, 225
Kärkkäinen, V.-M., 180, 232
Kaung, Stephen, 123
Kay, William, viii, ix, 40, 49–51, 57, 124, 196, 216, 223, 232, 239
Kelly, John, 24, 66
Kendall, R. T., 30, 135
Kenyon, E. W., 82, 86, 238
Kilpatrick, John, 215
Kinnaman, G. D., 233
Kinnear, A., 123, 233
Kirby, Gilber, 40, 230
Kissell, Barry, xvi, 56, 133
Kruse, Colin, 10, 94, 176, 233
Küng, Hans, 57, 139, 174, 175, 179, 180, 233
Kuyper, Abraham, 187, 233

Lacunza, Emanuelo, 113
Lake, John G., 119
Lambert, Pere, 113
Lane, T., 233
Leade, Jane, 113
Lederle, H.I., 40, 233
Lee, Witness, 28, 29, 123, 167, 233
Lehanne, Brendan, 103, 233
Liardon, R., 233
Lidner, H., 238
Lie, G., 233
Lightfoot, J. B., 78, 153, 159, 169, 170, 233
Lillie, David, 81, 122,
Lincoln, A. T., 157, 233
Lindsay, Gordon, 82, 86, 87, 119–21, 197, 221, 233
Lings, G., 233
Lloyd-Jones, Martyn, 78, 81
Lombard, John, Jr., 11
Long, Brad, 17, 233
Lowe, V. G., 132, 233
Luther, Martin, 71, 178, 189, 233
Lynch, G., 234

MacArthur, John, 174
MacCulloch, Diarmaid, 102, 234
MacDonald, G., 234
Male, Dave, 42, 217
Mansfield, Stephen, 59, 60, 234
Marfleet, D., 195, 234
Martin, David, 6, 55, 234
Martin, Ralph, 21
Martin, Ralph P., 233, 237
Martin, Thomas, 102
Bishop Mason, 8
Matthew, D., 126, 234, 238
Matthews, Walter, 21
Mazur, E. M., 234
McAlpine, Rob, 59, 64, 65, 127, 234
McBain, Douglas, 44
McCallum, Dennis, 122, 234
McDermott, Scott, 46
McGrath, A., 226, 234, 239
McCarthy, K., 234
McGee, G. B., xii, 234
McKay, John, 94, 100, 103, 105, 110, 133, 234
Melton, G. J., 226
Menzies, William, 135, 161, 234
Meyer, Joyce, 30
Millar, Sandy, 37, 204
Miller, Donald, 23
Miller, L., 54, 234
Mills-Powell, Mark, 43, 224, 231, 233, 234
Mitchell, Roger, 71
Moberly, R. C., 234
Mobsby, I., 227
Moffatt, J., 234
Moody, C., 9
Moody, D. L., 119
Moore, Peter, 225, 234, 234
Moore, S. D., 64, 65, 126, 127, 234
Morton, Tony, 50
Mowat, H., 237
Moynagh, Mike, 42
Muller, D., 234
Mullings, Lynette, 51, 234

Mumford, Bob, 126, 127
Mumford, John, 28, 50, 51
Munroe, Myles, 30
Murray, Andrew, 122
Murray, Frank, 119, 235
Murray, I., 109, 235
Murray-Williams, Stuart, 36, 106–8, 140, 200, 235

Nee, Watchman. 28, 29, 65, 77, 81, 91, 122, 123, 126–28, 130, 131, 159, 160, 168, 218, 233–35
Nelson, Shirley, 119, 122, 235
Newbigin, J. E. L., 235
Newton, Isaac, 113
Nglass, Emmanuel, 41
Nichols, A. H., 235
Noble, John, 156, 157

Oloyede, P. J., 51, 235
Oluyomi, Dipo, 52
Osgood, Hugh, 50
Oss, D. A., 235
Osteen, Joel, 25,
Owen, John, 109, 235

Packer, J. I., 81, 109, 133, 148, 149, 174, 235
Parham, Charles, 6, 7, 123
Parsley, Rod, 30
Partington, John, 39
Paterson, R., 184, 235
Patterson, R. M. R., 112, 235
Pattison, S., 240
Pavia, B. A., xii, 234
Pawson, David, 44, 168, 169, 235
Payne, Dave, 48, 235
Penn-Lewis, J., 122
Percy, M., 191, 202, 203, 235
Peters, John Reverend, 40
Peters, John, 235
Petts, David, 39
Phillips, Ron, 19,

Index of Names

Phypers, David., 40, 106, 225
Pink, A. W., 81,
Plumer, E., 101, 236
Plummer, A., 236
Polycarp, 94, 96–99
Porter, William, 46, 47
Powys Smith, Rob, 37
Prince, Derek, vii, xvi, 5, 58, 59–65, 87, 126, 169, 182, 186, 190, 194, 196, 202, 221, 227, 234, 236
Pytches, David, xvi, 6, 40, 56, 133, 134, 236

Rahner, Karl, 58
Ramsey, Michael, 175, 178, 236
Rees, E., 33, 35, 41, 236
Resane, K. T., 184, 191, 236
Riss, R. M., 82, 125, 236
Robeck, C. M., Jr., 236
Roberts, Evan, 122
Roberts, Oral, 18, 230
Rosochaki, Rudolf, 118
Ross, Chris, 9, 61, 211, 212, 236
Rowell, A., 29, 236
Rowell, John, 23, 24, 236
Rowe, W. A. C., 124
Rufus, 96
Ruthven, Jon, vii, 161–71, 175, 182, 184, 236

Sandford, Frank Weston, 118, 119, 121, 235
Sargeant, Kimon, 132
Saucy, R. L., 237
Schaff, P., 94, 96, 98, 237
Schweizer, Eduard, 177, 237
Schmaus, M., 237
Schmithals, W., 92, 148, 158, 160, 237
Scotland, Nigel, 46, 112, 237
Seymour, William, 6
Schwartz, Friedrich, 118
Schwarz, Christian, 33, 34

Shnackenberg, R., 148, 160, 168, 171, 237
Simmons, Mennonite, 107, 237
Simpson, A. B., 119, 122
Simpson, Charles, 126
Smail, Tom, 44, 135, 175, 231
Smith, Joseph, 116, 117, 122
Spurgeon, Charles, 81
Stackhouse, Ian, 56, 190, 213, 237
Stafford, Tim, 150, 237
Stanton, Noel, 50
Stark, R., 237
Stephanou, Eusebius, 21, 22, 49, 105, 226
Stibbe, Mark, 136, 237
Stone, D., 237
Storms, C. S., 237
Stott, John, viii, 81, 148–51, 155–58, 160, 161, 171, 184, 198, 223, 233, 237
Strader, Stephen, 47
Sullivan, Francis, 92, 95, 179, 237
Sumner, Sarah, 164, 237
Sweet, Ben, 93, 237
Swinton, J., 237
Sykes, S., 237
Symeon the New Theologian, 21, 105, 106, 177, 238
Synan, Vinson, 8, 16, 24, 25, 87, 110, 197, 216, 221, 230, 237, 238

Taylor, Jack, 19
Tertullian, 99, 100, 238
Thecla, 98, 103, 223
Theodoret, 101
Tillin, Tricia, 82, 238
Tomlinson, Dave, xiii
Turner, H. J. M., 105, 238
Turner, Max, 135, 164, 165, 175, 238
Tuttle, Robert, 18
Tyson, Tommy, 18

Index of Names

Urquhart, Colin, xvi, 6, 37, 50, 122, 137, 182, 193, 216, 235, 238

Van Fleteren, Frederick, 101
Verkuyl, J., 137
Victorinus, Marius, 100
Virgo, Terry, vii, xiii, xvi, 40, 50, 58, 77–81, 87, 122, 136, 149, 168, 169, 182, 185, 186, 194, 196, 202, 221, 231, 238
Viola, Frank, 14, 28–30, 123, 182, 185, 186, 218, 236, 238
Volf, Miroslav, 175, 180, 238
Von Eiken, E., 238

Wagner, Peter, vii, xii, xiii, xvi, 6, 9, 11, 15, 21, 23–26, 28, 30, 31, 34, 38, 52, 54, 55, 57, 58, 65–72, 77, 87, 130, 131, 134, 137, 139, 169, 182, 184–94, 196, 201, 238, 239, 202, 211, 215, 216, 221–23, 234
Walker, Andrew, ix, xi, 6, 50, 77, 115, 116, 126–27, 156, 237, 239
Wallis, Arthur, 40, 81, 127, 239
Ward, Pete, 239
Ware, T., 239
Warfield, B. B., 161, 174, 175
Warner, R., 131, 132, 197, 198, 200, 239
Warner, W. E., 239

Warren, R., 240
Watson, David, 40, 240
Weaver, C. Douglas, 110, 111, 240
Weber, Max, 58, 240
Webster, J. H., 240
Weddell, S., 23, 240
Weldon, J., 117, 122, 223
Wesley, John, 178
Whitehead, Charles, 48, 218, 231
White, Rob, 44, 56
Whitthal-Smith, Hannah, 119
Williams, Don, 27, 240
Williams, D. H., 240
Williams, D. P., 124,
Williams, George H., 107, 240
Williams, J. Rodman., 16, 17, 240
Williams, Rowan., 138, 139, 204, 240
Wimber, John., 21, 26-28, 50, 65, 71, 134, 149, 190, 240
Witherington, B., 236
Woodhouse, F. V., 111, 240
Woodward, J., 240
Wright, A., ix, 240
Wright, Nigel, 6, 44, 45, 56, 240
Wright, N. T., 148, 158, 240
Wright, T., ix

Xavier, Francis, 4

Zizioulas, John, 58, 179, 180, 240
Zosimus, 96

Index of Churches and Church Networks

Anglican Church, 3, 41, 45, 59, 111, 149, 175, 204, 217
Anglican Church of Nigeria, 204
Anglican Church in North America (ACNA), 13, 14, 204, 223
Anglican Church in Uganda, 204
Apostolic Church UK, vii, 32, 37, 39, 124, 125, 130, 182, 211, 223
Apostolic Faith Church, 124
Assemblies of God, 8, 87, 161, 221, 224, 228
Assemblies of God Australia, 9, 87, 221, 226, 227
Assemblies of God Canada, 9
Assemblies of God UK, 39, 81, 224
Assemblies of God USA, 8–10, 25, 26, 81, 86, 110, 125
Baptist Church USA, 3, 5, 18, 19, 22, 24
Baptist Church UK, 44–45, 110
Brethren, 28
The Catholic Apostolic Church, 6-7, 15, 32, 111, 112, 114–18, 120–21, 123, 130–31, 136, 182, 226–28, 230
Christian Catholic Church, 120,
Christian Church (Disciples of Christ), 109, 226
Churches in Community, 50
Church of Christ (Mormon), 117

Church of England, xiii, 40, 41, 43, 72, 135–36, 138, 204–7, 217, 219, 224–27, 233–35
Church of God in Christ, 8, 228
Church of God (Cleveland), 8, 10
Church of God of Prophecy, 37, 38
The Church of Jesus Christ of Latter Day Saints, 226
Elim, 6, 37, 38, 50, 87, 197, 221, 228
Episcopalian Church United States of America, 13–14, 22
Free Churches, 28, 175, 200
Ground Level, 50
Ichthus, 50, 54, 194, 196, 218
International Church of the Foursquare Gospel, 8, 11, 236
International Pentecostal Holiness Church, 8, 11, 232, 237
Jesus Fellowship, 50
Kingdom Faith, 6, 50, 54, 196, 216
Lutheran Church, 3, 4, 14, 15, 16, 25
Little Flock, 28, 122, 123, 128
Methodist Church, 3
Methodist Church in Britain, 42, 46,
Methodist Church in USA (United Methodist Church), 17, 18, 26
The New Apostolic Church, 117, 118, 121, 122, 128, 131, 182, 235

Index of Churches and Church Networks

Newfrontiers International, 50, 54, 58, 78, 196, 214, 216
New Testament Church of God, 37, 38
Orthodox Church, 98, 105, 106, 108, 130, 142, 174, 177, 187, 188, 193, 199, 204, 205
Orthodox Church in Britain, 49, 211, 214, 217–18
Orthodox Church in USA, 21, 22
Pentecostal Church of God, 8, 12, 235, 239
Pioneer, 50, 71, 196
Presbyterian Church, 3, 139
Redeemed Christian Church of God, 53, 236
The Re-organized Church of Jesus Christ of Latter-Day Saints, 117
River Fellowship International, 53, 236
Roman Catholic Church, 4, 6, 23, 28, 108, 130, 132, 142, 180, 193, 205, 218
Roman Catholic Church in Britain, 47, 48, 196
Roman Catholic Church USA, 3, 20, 22
Salt and Light, 50
United Pentecostal Church, 8, 12, 229
United Reformed Church in Britain, 18, 42, 45, 217
Vineyard, 14, 23, 26–28, 30, 50, 54, 149, 197, 214, 232
Willow Creek 26, 33, 35

~

Local Churches

All Souls Church, Langham Place, 149, 150,
Bethel Church, 26
Emmanuel Church, Wimbledon, 175
Everlasting Arms Ministry, 51
Glory House, 51
Holy Trinity Brompton (HTB), 78, 215
House of Praise, 51, 53, 231
House on the Rock, 51
Jesus House Church, 53, 232
Kansas City Fellowship (KCF), 26, 27, 229
Kensington Temple, 50
Kingsway International Christian Centre (KICC), 51, 52, 53, 232, 233
New Wine Ministries, 51
Ruach Ministries, 51–53, 236
St Andrews Chorleywood, 215
St Barnabas Church, Kensington, 34, 236
St Helens, Bishopsgate, 175
St. Thomas' Church, Sheffield, 33, 40, 58, 72, 75, 215
Toronto Airport Fellowship Church, 26
Trinity Baptist Church, 51

~

Evangelical or Charismatic Organisations and Ministries

Acts 29, 13–14
Aldersgate Renewal Ministries, 18, 26, 223
Alliance of Renewal Churches, 15, 16, 223
Anglican 1000, 14, 223
Brotherhood of St. Symeon the New Theologian, 123, 225
Catholic Charismatic Renewal, 21, 48, 142

Index of Churches and Church Networks

Catholic Charismatic Renewal USA, 21, 30
Catholic Charismatic Renewal UK, 48
Christian International Ministries Network, 71
Covenant Ministries International, 50
Cornerstone, 50
Derek Prince Ministries, 60, 227
Derek Prince Ministries, UK, 60, 227
European Church Planting Network (ECPN), 72
Evangelical Alliance UK, 136, 150, 228
Fresh Streams (formerly Baptist Mainstream), 44, 228
Group for Evangelism and Renewal (GEAR), 17, 45
Holy Spirit Renewal Ministries, 18, 19, 231
Holy Spirit Teaching Mission, 122, 231
Ignite Revival, 46, 47, 231
International Coalition of Apostles, 65, 66, 215, 216, 231
International House of Prayer, 26, 231
John Stott Ministries, 155, 232
Kansas City Prophets, 71, 137
Kenneth Hagin Ministries, 81, 82, 232
Langham Partnership, 150, 233
Lutheran Renewal, 14, 15, 194, 223, 234
Methodists Evangelicals Together (MET), 46
MorningStar, 26
New Wine network, 40, 44, 58, 133, 134, 215
Presbyterian and Reformed Ministries International (PRMI), 16, 17, 20, 45

3DM, 72, 238
Wagner Leadership, 65, 239

~

Gift Courses

Bodywork, 33, 34, 236
LifeShapes, 33, 34, 40, 59, 72, 75,
Network, 33, 35, 41, 197
S.H.A.P.E., 33-35, 41, 197, 236

~

Media

GOD channel, 50
Leadership Network, 101, 233
New Wine magazine, 122, 126, 127, 231
Premier radio, 46, 50
Renewal magazine, 122

~

Significant Religious Events or Movements

Church Growth Movement, 33, 34, 190
Conservative Evangelicalism, xiii, 33, 78, 148–50, 152, 174, 217
Fresh Expressions, 41, 42, 55, 140, 204, 211, 214, 217, 227, 228, 235
Higher Life Movement, 28, 119, 122
House Church, 28–30, 218
Lakeland Revival, 47, 215
Latter Rain Movement, Canada, vii, 9, 27, 28, 64, 71, 86, 125, 126, 127, 130, 137
Ministries Today Symposium, 32, 234

251

Index of Churches and Church Networks

Mormonism, 71, 109, 116–18, 121, 128, 130–31, 135–36
New Apostolic Reformation (NAR), 10, 13, 15, 16, 18, 20, 23–26, 30, 38, 39, 55, 61, 69, 72, 77, 87, 130, 142, 161, 182–84, 189–91, 211, 221, 222, 227, 236, 239
Oxford Movement, 188
Pentecostal Charismatic Movement, vii, xiii, xv, xvi, 5, 21, 22, 24, 25, 49, 50, 55, 59, 76, 128, 132–37, 141, 142, 148, 200, 212, 214, 220, 233
Radical House Church Movement, xiii, 32, 36, 40, 45, 50, 55, 77, 81, 116, 126, 127, 137, 156, 164, 239
Soul Survivor, 215
Spring Harvest, 50, 78, 136, 196, 215
Stoneleigh Bible weeks, 78
Vatican II, 4, 21, 130, 136, 238
Westminster Assembly, Westminster Confession, 5, 240
World Council of Churches, 138, 240

~

Miscellaneous

Arsenal Books, 6, 57, 224
Diocese of Ely, 138, 227
Ekklesia (think tank), 140, 228
Greek Orthodox Archdiocese of America, 205, 229
Mission-Shaped Church, 40, 41, 58, 77, 140, 205, 207, 215, 217, 227
Natural Church Development, 33, 34
Ridley Hall, Cambridge, 42, 149, 217
Westcott House, Cambridge, 42, 217

Index of Scripture

Isaiah
43:19	xii

Matthew
10:40	93
16:18	163
20:16	30
28:16–20	158

Luke
5:37-8	xii
24:47	158

John
3:34	83
13:16	155
17:23	195
20:21	158

Acts
1:8	158
2:14	163
1:15–22	83
13:2–3	34, 35, 220
14:4	92, 95
15:32	163

Romans
1:5	34, 35
5	108
10:12–15	220
11	xiv
12	33, 58, 108
15:19–20	30
16:7	158

1 Corinthians
2:14	164
3:10	30, 64, 77, 186
4:9	30, 158
4:15–16	52
9:1	95, 167, 168
9:2	158
12	7, 31, 58, 108
12-14	29, 134, 166
12:4–6	68
12:4–11	39
12:7–11	12
12:27–8	12
12:28	39, 77, 84, 87, 120, 130, 164, 165, 167, 171, 183–85, 197, 221
12:28–29	34, 35
12:28—13:13	162
12:31	162
13:8	113
14	108
15	153, 166
15:3–8	151
15:3–9	159
15:7	100, 106, 153
15:7–8	95, 106
15:8	106, 157, 158, 164, 169
15:8–9	167
15:9	100

Index of Scripture

2 Corinthians

5:16	168
8:23	10
11–12	170
11:13	159

Galatians

3:3	164
3:17	166
4:21	166

Ephesians

2:19–20	117, 151
2:20	30, 65, 67, 71, 77, 83, 87, 130, 153, 156–58, 161–67, 182–87, 197, 221, 236
3:5	153, 156, 157, 165, 166, 187
3:5–6	167
4	31, 33, 41, 47, 58, 61, 76, 108, 113
4:7–16	39
4:11	10, 84, 106, 109, 157, 158, 165, 167, 197
4:11–12	12, 34, 35
4:11–13	xii, 11, 12, 20, 27, 29, 30, 33, 41, 54, 60, 73, 77, 81, 82, 86–88, 101, 108, 111, 112, 115, 116, 122, 123, 125, 129, 130, 133, 151, 154, 155, 160, 162, 164, 166, 171, 173–76, 183, 184, 190, 197, 198, 200, 212, 217, 221, 222
4:11–16	117
4:12–13	78
4:13	162

1 Thessalonians

1:1	169
2:6	154, 169

1 Timothy

3:1–8	84, 85

2 Timothy

1	108

Hebrews

1:1–2	153

Revelation

2:2	159
4:9–11	28
18:20	170
21:14	83, 153, 169, 170
22:18–19	153

www.ingramcontent.com/pod-product-compliance
Lightning Source LLC
Chambersburg PA
CBHW050344230426
43663CB00010B/1983